# CRIMINAL LAW

# CRIMINAL LAW

**KENNETH M. WELLS**
Public Defender
Sacramento County, California
Adjunct Professor of Law
McGeorge School of Law
University of the Pacific

**PAUL B. WESTON**
Professor
Department of Criminal Justice
California State University—Sacramento

Goodyear Publishing Company, Inc.
Santa Monica, California 90401

**Library of Congress Cataloging in Publication Data**

Wells, Kenneth M
  Criminal law.

  Includes indexes.
  1. Criminal law—United States.  I. Weston, Paul B., joint
author. II. Title.
KF9219.W38              345'.73              77-17489
ISBN 0-87620-207-5

Y-2075-3

Current Printing (last digit)
10 9 8 7 6 5 4 3 2 1

Printed in the United States of America

Cover and Text Design: Tom Lewis

# CONTENTS

# LIST OF ILLUSTRATIONS

# PREFACE

This is a book about criminal law, about the substantive criminal law that explains the concepts of crimes and establishes the essential elements of specific offenses, from murder to disorderly conduct. It is based on the concepts, statutes, and cases that are the contemporary criminal law in America. It is a book planned to provide readers with knowledge of the multi-jurisdictional criminal law as enforced in state and federal courts and the application of criminal culpability to the administration of criminal justice in America.

Part One, "Introduction," covers the historical development of criminal law, the philosophy of law, and the nature of legal research. It also offers a perspective on the evolution of law.

Part Two, "Concepts of Law," deals with the making of laws and the limitations on lawmaking, criminal responsibility, crime classifications, and jurisdiction. This segment also covers the concepts that are the foundation for statutes defining specific crimes.

Part Three, "Specific Crimes," presents an overview of the major crimes, from those against people to those against public order. These chapters define the essential elements of the major felonies and focus on the statutes and cases that are the primary literature of substantive criminal law. This segment links the development of the concepts of law in Part Two with these definitions of specific crimes, and adds to the discussion of each crime material on prosecution problems and common defenses.

Each chapter is headed by an introductory segment containing the chapter's objectives, legal terms first mentioned in the chapter, and a series of questions to aid study of the chapter's content. Presenting this material at the beginning of a chapter helps the reader in developing an understanding of the material in each chapter. In addition, emphasis has been added by printing in italics the main

thrust or essential ruling of major court decisions quoted and/or discussed in the text, in order to further illuminate the objectives and material in each chapter.

Cases have been edited for clarity and to focus attention upon the primary aspects of the court's opinion. The selected extracts from the court's opinion offer adequate information for an understanding of the facts of the case and the court's decision and reasoning. Unless an understanding of a case required the inclusion of footnotes or citations in the opinions, these references were deleted.

*Kenneth M. Wells*
*Paul B. Weston*

# PART ONE
## INTRODUCTION

# 1

# EVOLUTION OF THE LAW

## OBJECTIVES

*This chapter reveals the growth of law from primitive taboos and religious principles to common law and statutory law; develops the rule of legal precedents from its base in common law to its application in contemporary law; and describes in detail the chief sources of law.*

## LEGAL TERMS*

Stare decisis. *The rule of judicial precedent; the policy of courts to stand by decided cases (precedents).*
Ratio decidendi. *The legal principle upon which a court's decision is based; the determining point in a case.*

## QUESTIONS FOR STUDY

*1. How does the judicial process contribute to the evolution of criminal law?*

*2. In the sequential growth of the criminal law, at what stage or stages are legal transplants likely to occur?*

*3. What is the link-up between the doctrine of* stare decisis *and the* ratio decidendi *of a case?*

*4. Develop the theme that politics and moral standards are often linked to the growth pattern of criminal law.*

*5. Trace the sources of Roman law. Continental law. English law. American law.*

*6. Describe the role of the French Civil Code of Napoleon in the growth of the written law.*

*Legal terms will be listed in the order of appearance in each chapter.

*7. What was the role of Sir Edward Coke in the development of English common law? Of Sir William Blackstone?*

*8. Trace the development of the common law in England to American statutory law.*

*9. What are the similarities and differences between common law and contemporary case law?*

---

**T**he criminal law has moved from yesterday to today by a process of restatement and revision. This principle of growth surmounts any problems caused by change.

Growth through the judicial process is a primary source of evolution in criminal law. Judges must develop and extend the law whenever changing circumstances make development or extension necessary. There are situations where the law is fixed; other areas provide a judicial opportunity for a choice which will establish a new right and a new wrong.[1]

Legislators revise laws by enactment of new or revised prohibitions or by repeal of existing prohibitions or punishments whenever they are found, after a fair use experience, to be inconsistent with the current legislative intent, or when a law has atrophied by disuse. Modern legislatures descend from a system of assemblies of persons who mixed law finding with lawmaking. Lon L. Fuller, in his *The Anatomy of the Law,*[2] notes that these assemblies functioned at a time when there was uncertainty about the division of power among the different agencies of government, and customary law was being reshaped by statutory law. Fuller states that in its origin the English Parliament was primarily an adjudicative (law finding) assembly, and that it only gradually assumed its legislative (lawmaking) role.[3]

The history of legal systems begins with statements of custom and usage and ends with a written code. Primitive law developed within a society as a system of taboos which, when writing developed, were embodied in a code of written laws. Changes are consciously made to improve the law by some modification. The authority for the law or for the enforcement of the law came from religion or the sovereign or a combination of both.

Sir Henry Maine identifies six stages in the evolution of law. These stages are described in the lead chapters of his text, *Ancient Law: The Connection with the Early History of Society and Its Relation to Modern Ideas,* first published in 1861.[4] Maine's analysis does reveal remarkable insight into the process by which law grows. In brief, these stages are:

1. Usage or habit as law (the "way things are" as the basis for settling disputes).

2. Customary law (perception of a need for shared and accepted rules of conduct).

3. Codes (reduction to writing of customary law and publication of such rules).

4. Legal fictions (restatement or revision of laws to achieve change without open declaration of new law: giving new law the apparent form of the old).

5. Equity (law reform guided by a set of legal principles; law guided by natural equity—*naturalis aequitas*).

6. Legislation (law by explicit declarations; enactments by a legislature empowered to impose obligations on members of a community).[5]

Roman law provided a fund of legal knowledge that was influential in the evolution of English and American legal thought. The law of the early Roman Republic was customary. Roman statutes began as written customs: authoritative rulings on disputed points of custom. Emphasis on written law, however, presented a challenge to jurists to clarify situations not covered by that which was written. They took the idea of *regula* from the discipline of grammar, and *definito* from the discipline of rhetoric. The notion of *regula* in juristic terminology is that a relevant rule can govern all factual situations which can be brought under its principle. *Definito*, according to rhetoricians and accepted in juristic terminology, means that a definition should have as its object the identification of the essential elements of the thing defined. *Regula* and *definito* helped Roman jurists to put that which was not written law into a more orderly arrangement and set the stage for future legislative recasting in written form.[6]

## LEGAL TRANSPLANTS

Part of the evolution of law is the moving of a rule of law, or even a system of law, from one country to another. Generally, a people's law is something unique and special, illustrative of the national identity. However, so-called transplants occur when a people move into a new territory and take their law with them, or when a people voluntarily accept a part of the law of another people. The conquests of Alexander of Greece took Grecian law to the far corners of the then known world and the Roman legions, under the Caesars, carried Roman law as far as England to the west and east and south to the lands of Israel and Egypt. Written law has a greater chance of spreading, but the English common law was well received in the far-flung colonies of England and in America, even after the Revolution, despite the fact it was not statutory (code) law but rather lowly case decision (juristic law).[7]

# GROWTH PATTERNS

When the law is viewed as a means of identifying, detecting, and controlling deviant behavior, the growth pattern of the law usually results from one or more of the following:

1. Moral and religious standards.
2. Legal theory.
3. Response to threat.
4. Politics.
5. Legal transplants.
6. Court decisions.

People get indignant about moral deficiencies. The term "permissiveness" indicates outrage at rule breaking. Lawmaking is viewed as a means of forbidding immoral or unhealthy behavior.

Changes in the law emanating from criminal justice professionals, attorneys, or judges, are usually linked with developing statute law as part of a legal system. These changes attempt to improve the rule of law, and to develop coherence and unity.

Threats to the good order and welfare of society are social problems and result in legislation aimed at reducing the reality of these threats. Such lawmaking counters perceived threats by punitive action against the behavior that is viewed as a social problem.

Political uses of the law are many and varied. Legislation fostered by political considerations are statutes that benefit one party or group at the expense of others. Creation of a law is associated with its enforcement, and this joinder can be an advantage to one political or pressure group and a disadvantage to others.

Politics and moral standards are often linked as sources of legislation. Persons in elective public office sometimes try to convince voters of their alignment with and support of certain moral values, and in the name of morality seek political advantage. A casual look at the history of narcotic and drug legislation will show increases and decreases in punishment related to the pressures and politics of the day.

# CHIEF SOURCES OF THE LAW

The chief source of Anglo-American law is English law and Continental or civil law. In turn, the basic sources of both English and Continental law are the three great classical western civilizations: Jewish, Greek, and Roman.

Ancient Hebrews borrowed from the famous Babylonian Code of Hammurabi in preparing their early law. The Greeks of Homer's day were influenced by Minoan, Mycenaean, Mesopotamian, and Egyptian law. Early Roman law reveals the influence of earlier Greek law and the laws of other people within the orbit of the Roman Empire. Each of these legal systems was influenced by primitive customs.[8] (See Figure 1.)

**Figure 1. CHIEF SOURCES OF JEWISH, GREEK, AND ROMAN LAW.**

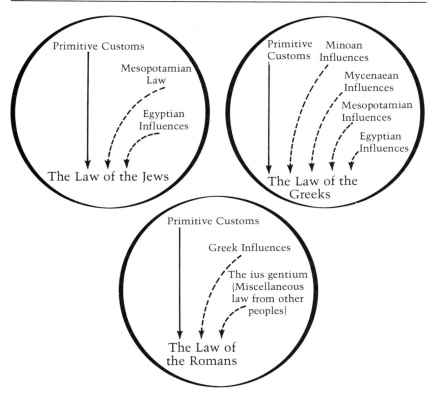

From *The Law*, copyright © 1949, by Rene A. Wormser. Reprinted by permission of Simon & Schuster, Inc.

The feudal law had its basic source in the Roman law and the law of the Germans (whose early origin was the primitive customs of the clan); church or canon law was influenced by three basic sources: the Jewish law, the Greek philosophers (particularly Aristotle), and Roman law; Continental law had its primary source in German law, with the Roman, feudal, and church or canon law as secondary influences.[9] (See Figure 2.)

Celtic law was one of the sources of the English law. Saint Patrick is said to have commissioned a group of scholars to compile Irish law: their work is the *Senchus Mor*. Roman law certainly served as a model for later English law; the Romans ruled England for four centuries, beginning in 55 B.C. German law was another major influence on English law. The Germans followed the Romans as invaders and rulers of England, beginning in A.D. 417, and gave English law its Anglo-Saxon overtones. The Norman conquest of

**Figure 2. CHIEF SOURCES OF FEUDAL, CHURCH (CANON), AND CONTINENTAL (CIVIL) LAW.**

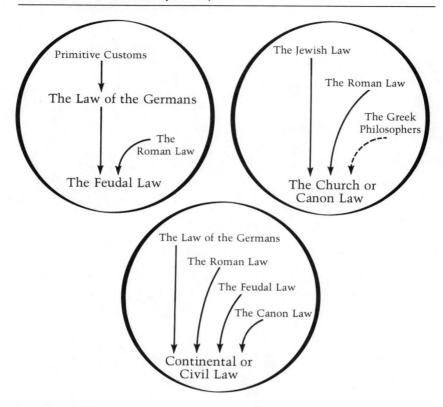

From *The Law*, copyright © 1949, by Rene A. Wormser. Reprinted by permission of Simon & Schuster, Inc.

England brought to English law the influence of feudal, Continental, canon, and Roman law. (See Figure 3.)

English law is the most direct source of American law. The early settlers of this country included many immigrants of European origin; therefore, there are influences from the Continental law. Since many of the colonists were highly religious persons, there is also a definite tracing back to the influence of the Jewish law. (See Figure 3.)

## LEGAL TRADITIONS

The three major contemporary legal traditions are the common law, the Continental or civil law, and socialist law. Whereas the common law is identified with England, the British Commonwealth, and the United States, the Continental law tradition has dominated the legal systems of most Continental European countries. Until the

**Figure 3. CHIEF SOURCES OF ENGLISH AND AMERICAN LAW.**

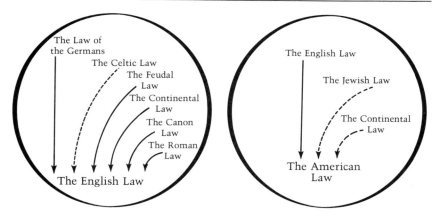

From *The Law*, copyright © 1949, by Rene A. Wormser. Reprinted by permission of Simon & Schuster, Inc.

rise of the socialist-law tradition in Russia's post-revolutionary period (1919), the legal system of the Russian Empire was based on Continental law. The socialist legal tradition is now identified with countries under Soviet influence in Europe and elsewhere; it is a fusion of socialist ideology with the principles of Continental law.

There are many countries whose legal systems are not aligned with any of these three major legal traditions. Scandinavian law is an example of an indigenous legal tradition. In Africa, the Middle East and Asia, the legal systems of many nations are responsive to the legal traditions of Moslem law. India and Japan are countries whose laws are influenced by native and religious traditions.[10]

The major codifications considered landmarks in the growth of written law are within the Continental or civil law tradition. Flavius Anicius Justinianus, known as Justinian, succeeded to the throne of the Roman Empire in A.D. 527 and appointed a commission of jurists to organize the contemporary Roman laws. Their work led to publication of *Corpus Juris Civilis*. The French Civil Code of Napoleon, published in 1804, blended the customary law of France with the Code of Justinian. The spread of the Code Napoleon accounts for the spread of the Continental or civil law tradition.[11]

## THE COMMON LAW

The beginning of the common law is often dated from A.D. 1066, the advent of the Norman conquest of England. All or much of the law was a matter of "ordeal."* It was not until Henry III in A.D.

*A test of truth by fire, water or combat.

1219 that the ordeals by fire and water were forbidden. Trial by battle (combat) was not unusual in Queen Elizabeth's day (sixteenth century) and was not abolished in England until A.D. 1819 by Parliamentary statute.

During the ensuing years the common law has had substantial influence on the laws of many nations. The legal systems in Great Britain, Ireland, America, Australia, and New Zealand are closely identified with the common law.

The English common law originated in the daily life of English society. It served as social rules for a people, a society that was once agricultural but which rapidly developed as urban subsequent to the industrial revolution. As changes occurred in the life-style of the English people, the common law was adapted by judicial interpretation and restatement to reflect the changing social order. It was judge-made law, building upon a set of precepts and principles (mainly religious) in case after case, one or more prior decisions serving as guidelines for subsequent judicial action. It was an upward structuring of the law, as the process of legal change was based on cases in which people took their different fact problems to court. Reports of trials, opinions, decisions, and particular fact patterns totaled a body of law. The common law was usually defined as the body of case decisions prescribing social conduct and justifiable in the royal courts of England.[12]

Contributing to the coherence and unity of the common law was the doctrine of *stare decisis*: using judicial precedents to formulate a basis for present judicial decisions or similar fact patterns.

The *ratio decidendi* of a case is the ground, or principle upon which a case is decided. Precedental force in judicial decision making comes from the discovery of the *ratio decidendi* in a prior judicial decision. The legal principle linked by similarities and parallels in a past case or cases and in the pending case is the basis of *ratio decidendi*.

There is a close relationship between contemporary *case law* and common law. In fact, case law is often termed common law to distinguish it from statutory law. The judicial decisions that comprise case law often interpret and give meaning to the wording of statutory law. These interpretations are not statutory in themselves, but they have impact on the statutory law as precedents for future judicial decisions.

In its earliest development the common law grew from the English system of writs—that is, pleadings for the trial of a dispute. The writ spelled out the nature of the action, and a different writ existed for every kind of dispute. Ranuld de Glanville, Chief Justiciar of England in the thirteenth century, authored one of the most valuable books in the history of English law, *Treatise on the Laws and Customs of England*. It was written primarily to explain the

writ system which had grown to such a degree that it was extremely difficult to select the appropriate writ for a particular cause of action. Glanville's code served as a guide to the proper selection of writs. However, it was a book of precedents of pleadings, not of the decisions of substantive case law.

The medieval courts in England exhibited great respect for the doctrine that like cases should be judged in like fashion. The courts were guided by tradition and custom, with the records of past cases serving as an official memory bank. In the thirteenth century, when Henry III ruled England, Henry de Bracton, in his *Note Book*, collected two thousand cases from the first twenty-four years of Henry's reign.[13] He established a foundation for a legal system built on case law, formulating a doctrine of precedents. Bracton's text proposed to standardize the English law. He set out case law in a form similar to the written law of Rome.

A half-century after Bracton's death in 1268, the *Year-Books* began. They were records of litigation, similar to notes taken by law students in court, and they are identified as the first reporting of law. The *Year-Books* were compiled by unknown and probably only semi-official reporters until 1535, when this reporting unaccountably stopped. They were primarily concerned with procedure (Winfield refers to them as "hints on pleading collected from proceedings in the courts"). Many of the reports, in addition, contained the arguments of the disputants and judicial comment.[14]

The history of law reporting after the close of the *Year-Book* period is one in which reports acquired considerable accuracy and completeness. Coke's *Reports*, from 1572 to 1616, dominated this period. Sir Edward Coke was both reporter and learned commentator. He tried to set forth principles of law in his reports. The influence of Coke's *Reports* was considerable in shaping English common law; they were constantly cited in the courts.[15]

The common law has been termed the unwritten law (*lex non scripta*) by Sir William Blackstone (1723–1780), scholar and jurist, but Blackstone notes that this does not mean merely oral law, or law solely communicated by word of mouth. Blackstone wrote that the totality of common law, its monuments and evidences of its legal provisions, is contained in books of reports and judicial decisions, and in the treatises of learned sages of the profession, preserved and handed down from times of the highest antiquity. They are styled *lex non scripta* because their original institution and authority are not set down in writing as are the acts of Parliament.[16]

The four volumes of Blackstone's *Commentaries on the Laws of England* were first published from 1765 to 1769. Since the first volume appeared in 1765, Blackstone's work has occupied a unique position in the history of English law as the first authoritarian statement of the principles of common law. The acceptance of Black-

stone's *Commentaries* by Americans at the time of the struggle for independence contributed to the transplanting of the English legal tradition to the New World. Blackstone's writings became the "bible" of American lawyers and legal institutions, and the foundation for the development of the Anglo-English legal tradition.[17]

Many of the so-called common-law crimes have been codified in the criminal statutes of the various states. However, problems arise when the statutory law forbids an act, but fails to thoroughly define the act that is forbidden. An early case (1903) in the transition of American law from the common law to statutory law concerns the prosecution of C. J. DeWolfe for exposing the citizens of the village of Bennett to a contagious disease by negligently keeping an infected person in a public place. DeWolfe claimed this was no crime, that "The Code particularly sets forth what acts shall be deemed a nuisance, and provides a penalty therefor, and, failing to specify the acts complained of, no prosecution can be maintained therefor."

On appellate review the court stated:

> The question then to be considered, is whether common-law nuisances which have not been enumerated in the Criminal Code are punishable as crimes. In this state all public offenses are statutory; no act is criminal unless the Legislature has in express terms declared it to be so, and no person can be punished for any act or omission which is not made penal by the plain import of the written law. But, while there are in this state no common-law crimes, the definition of an act which is forbidden by the statute, but not defined by it, may be ascertained by reference to the common law. A statute declaring all common nuisances to be criminal is to be construed as prohibiting every act which was by the common law indictable as a nuisance. Without a clear expression of its purpose to do so, we can not believe that it was the intention of the Legislature to so limit the meaning of the word "nuisance" as to make conduct blameless which has always been considered inherently wrong and deserving of punishment. If the theory upon which the trial court decided this case is correct, a large number of common-law nuisances are not crimes in this state, and many vicious, immoral, and revolting acts may be committed in public with impunity.
>
> If the enumerated acts were the only ones intended to be made criminal, it was quite unnecessary to declare in the first clause that every person who should erect, keep up or continue and maintain any nuisance to the injury of any part of the citizens of this state should be punished. And it is hardly probable that the words "any nuisance" would have been used if the Legislature had in mind only the few nuisances which it was about to enumerate.[18]

Criminal law in America has departed from its English common-law heritage in that federal and state constitutions and penal codes are in writing; but in harmony with its common-law ancestry, American law can be interpreted by judicial decision in individual cases when the written law needs clarification.

## NOTES

1. Benjamin N. Cardozo, *The Growth of the Law* (1924, reprinted, Westport, Conn.: Greenwood Press, 1973).

2. Lon L. Fuller, *The Anatomy of the Law* (New York: Praeger Publishers, Inc., 1968).

3. Fuller, p. 56.

4. Henry Sumner Maine, *Ancient Law: The Connection with the Early History of Society and Its Relation to Modern Ideas* (1861, 1931, reprinted, Gloucester, Mass.: Peter Smith, n.d.).

5. Maine, pp. 1–59; Fuller, pp. 49–57.

6. Peter Stein, *Roman Law and English Jurisprudence Yesterday and Today* (Cambridge: Cambridge University Press, 1969), pp. 15–24.

7. Alan Watson, *Legal Transplants: An Approach to Comparative Law* (Charlottesville: University Press of Virginia, 1974), pp. 21–30, 93–94.

8. Rene A. Wormser, *The Law* (New York: Simon & Schuster, 1949), pp. 1–154.

9. Wormser, pp. 155–233.

10. John Henry Merryman, *The Civil Law Tradition: An Introduction to the Legal Systems of Western Europe and Latin America* (Stanford, Calif.: Stanford University Press, 1969), pp. 1–6.

11. Merryman, pp. 7–14.

12. Arthur R. Hogue, *Origins of the Common Law* (1966, reprinted, Hamden, Conn.: The Shoe String Press, 1974).

13. Hogue, pp. 22–23 and 188–191.

14. Percy H. Winfield, *The Chief Sources of English Legal History* (New York: Burt Franklin & Company, 1972), pp. 158–173.

15. Winfield, pp. 188–189.

16. Gareth Jones, ed., *The Sovereignty of the Law: Selections from Blackstone's Commentaries on the Laws of England* (Toronto: University of Toronto Press, 1973), p. 45.

17. Daniel J. Boorstein, *The Mysterious Science of the Law* (Boston: Beacon Press, 1958), pp. 3–8.

18. *State* v. *DeWolfe*, 93 N.W. 746 (1903, Neb.).

# 2
# PHILOSOPHY OF LAW

## OBJECTIVES
The chapter utilizes the philosophical theories of law to understand the function of law in society; develops the nature of law as a coercive form of social control linked to the moral code of a community; and pinpoints the sanctions inherent in the concept that there is no crime without a penalty.

## LEGAL TERMS
Natural law (jus naturale). The law of God, divine law; as opposed to law as the product of reason or law as established by kings, legislative action, or courts. Also denotes a primitive social environment in which men and women were governed solely by a rational and consistent obedience to the needs, impulses, and drives of their true nature.

Sanction law. A term for the criminal law emphasizing the coercive threat of penalties for criminal behavior.

## QUESTIONS FOR STUDY
1. What is the general objective of a philosophy of law?
2. Outline the Thomistic theory of law.
3. Describe the principle of utility in the positivist philosophy of law.
4. How does legal realism (the realist movement) differ from the positivist legal philosophy? From the Thomas Aquinas theory of law?
5. Is it in the nature of law that its application may depend on contemporary moral and political doctrines, public policy, and other factors? Explain.

6. *Justify the linking of the moral code of a society with criminal law.*

7. *What is the basis for the belief that criminal law is coercive?*

8. *What is the primary objective of the penalties in criminal law?*

9. *Develop the theme that there is no crime without a punishment.*

---

**E**ssentially the philosophy of law is a projection of various philosophical systems, and its primary objective philosophically is to understand the function of law in society. The philosophy of law attempts to develop general ideas in explanation of human experience and seeks to link these ideas with the law and its enforcement. In its broad sense, law is a way of living rather than a series of formulas.

Over the years, the philosophy of law has changed to accommodate the current tide of philosophy itself. From its origins in antiquity, law has been associated with the theory of natural law, maintaining a special connection between law and morals. More recently, the theory of legal positivism presents law as the sovereign's command; the theory of legal realism views law as predictions of what the courts will do; and theorists in the sociology of law hold that rights and obligations in law arise from the relations of man to man: the order of human associations.

## THEORIES

Early philosophical theories of law agreed that law was indispensable, and that it turned men to justice and away from injustice, functioning in the interests of the entire community.

Plato believed law was the product of reason; its major objective was the discovery of reason; and the aim of law was to produce men who were completely good.[1]

Aristotle viewed law as a contract between the state (sovereign) and the individual with an aim of making men good, and he linked *good* with his concept of justice. He defines *universal justice* as complete virtue, saying a man is unjust if he breaks the law of the land or if he takes more than his share of anything.[2]

Cicero perceived a heavenly law of true or right reason, in agreement with nature, diffused throughout society, unchanging and timeless, with a capability of imposing a duty by its commands and/or prohibitions. He also saw, in a secondary role, the idea of natural law. This idea links nature and reason with life according to reason becoming the natural life. He defined *reason* in this relationship as that which teaches and explains what should be done —and what should be left undone. Cicero discussed a third kind of

law, but rejected it as the crowd's idea of law. This is law in written form that commands or prohibits, but which cannot be categorized within or identified with heavenly or natural law.[3]

St. Thomas Aquinas developed his theory of law in the thirteenth century. The Thomistic theory of law was the first systematically complete philosophy of law. It places law on a theological foundation. Through the instruction of God's law and the assistance of His grace, man can be helped to moral behavior.

Thomas Aquinas argued that the legal rule must be understood as subject to a higher law or reason; that human law implements divine law, and the will of God is the last and final ground of all laws. Aquinas defines *law* as the ordering of reason for the common good, promulgated by sovereign authority (one who has to take care of the community). If sovereigns enact laws contrary to reason, their commands cease to be laws and should not be obeyed. Aquinas believed it was the role of the church in society to make certain sovereigns act in accordance with Christian views, obeying the admonitions of the church and its priests.[4]

Thomas Hobbes's legal philosophy is positivist: the only source of law is the sovereign, and laws only achieve validity when a government with the power to command and enforce declares them to be valid. This relates law to power. However, the principle of utility (self-preservation) is inherent in Hobbes's legal philosophy. Men recognize peace and order as useful and for this reason accept law and obey its provisions. Men make a covenant among themselves to establish a climate of peace and order, subjecting themselves to one sovereign who makes laws and administers them.[5]

John Austin defined *a law* as a rule laid down for the guidance of an intelligent being by another intelligent being with power over him. The aggregate of such rules is the positive law—distinguishable from natural law (the law of God) as its origin is political. The positive law is established by monarchs, sovereign bodies, or political superiors. There is a command which obliges a person to obey and follow a prescribed course of conduct.[6]

Justice Oliver Wendell Holmes was an adherent of the realist movement. Legal realism concludes that the law consists of prophecies as to how the courts will act in their use of the public power (force). The laws of any state are composed of rules which the courts (judicial organs of the state) lay down for the determination of legal rights and duties. It is not that the judiciary enacts law, but that they interpret it—serving as discoverers rather than creators. Legal realists view the judiciary as "law-givers," not because they are the persons who write the laws, but because they have absolute authority to interpret them.[7] Holmes believed that court-made law is aligned with the realist postulate that the law is not a body of rules but of facts: "The prophecies of what the courts will do in fact and

nothing more pretentious are what I mean by law."[8]

Roscoe Pound believed that the enactment of laws and their application in courts should take account of social facts. The sociological theory of law holds that law should be studied in relation to society and the function it fulfills in communal existence. The social study of law seeks the social origins of law, its impact on society, the role of law in a community, and what social criteria can be used in testing the validity of law. Sociological jurisprudence is concerned with interpreting and administering law with reference to the needs of society.

Pound wrote of the law as a social institution to satisfy social wants and the end of law as a widening recognition and satisfaction of human wants or claims or desires.[9]

The American philosophy of law stresses relativism. Rigid rules are not to be applied inflexibly without regard to the circumstances of a case. Nothing is more certain in modern society than the principle that there are no absolutes, that a name, a phrase, or a standard has meaning only when associated with the considerations that gave birth to the nomenclature.[10]

The American philosophy of law has a scientific base. Law as a totality is viewed as a field for study equal to the field of any other science. Its rules and principles, and definitions and generalizations, are tools used to communicate the accumulated body of knowledge; and scientific procedures can be used to test the law in action.

## NATURE OF CRIMINAL LAW

Criminal law is derived from basic human rights, from the nature of man and the interactions of social relations. Law prescribes regulative norms for human behavior. Law reflects the interest of society in the security of person and property, serving to order human relations in a manner that will insure a firm and stable social order. Individuals and their behavior in society are required to adjust to laws telling them to do something or to refrain from particular prohibited conduct.

The life of the law is in its application. The necessities of community life at a particular time, prevalent moral and political theories, public policy, and even the prejudices of the judiciary and others have influenced the rules of law.

Criminal law is not rule alone; it is action: the act that transgresses sets all subsequent acts into motion. The circumstances of the act spell out the essential elements of a specific crime. Rules of law detail prohibited conduct, but it is the act of applying these rules to a particular set of circumstances that is the criminal law.

The adjudication of cases in which there is reasonable cause to believe an accused person has violated a specific law or laws is the role of criminal courts. Trial juries and judges make the deci-

sions on guilt versus innocence and related matters in dispute, and impose sanctions when the ultimate verdict is guilty.

In adjudicating cases and in imposing sentences, courts consider one principle above all others: the law of the land is supreme in the land; before the majesty of the law all men stand equal.[11]

Early forms of law were grounded in vengeance—the idea that an intentional wrong had been done and some form of compensation was warranted. Penalties in criminal law started from a moral basis, from the thought that someone was to blame when the criminal law was violated.[12]

Criminal law resembles an order or command backed by threats. It indicates various kinds of conduct that are unlawful and applies a prohibition to a general class of persons who are expected to see that it applies to them and to comply with it. The substance of laws may not be addressed to individuals as an order would be in a face-to-face situation, but the existence of laws is a form of communication, that orders backed by threats will be implemented in the event of disobedience. Laws are valid even if those affected are left to find out for themselves what laws exist and who they affect.[13]

The concept that criminal law is a coercive order emanates from the fact that certain options as to human behavior are restricted or certain behavior is obligatory, and violations can lead a court to apply specific sanctions. The basic threat inherent in any coercive order is the court's reaction to disobedience.

However, because of its nature, the criminal law is habitually obeyed by the majority of persons. It is a major form of social control that communicates generally acceptable standards of conduct. Criminal law is linked to the morality of a given society: the ideals shared by many individuals. The moral code of a community is closely aligned with, though distinguishable from, local criminal law.

Criminal law says to each member of a community, "Thou shalt not." The law of the Western World, as the rule of God, is a heritage of the Old Testament. God in speaking to Moses communicated His laws for His people, and by his obedience to the law the worth of a person could be demonstrated. When man did not justify himself by obedience to the law, justice required appropriate atonement.[14]

The late Justice Oliver Wendell Holmes referred to the law as a body of dogma enclosed within definite lines, and linked it with prophecies of what the courts will do in fact. He suggested looking at the law as a "bad man" would, for a real knowledge of the law. Holmes's reasoning was that while a "good man" finds reasons for law-abiding behavior in his conscience, the "bad man" cares only for the restrictions in law ending in the material consequences for

its violation. The "bad man" cares little for law as a system of reason; or that it is a deduction from the principles of ethics. He does want to know what the courts are likely to do in fact.[15]

# PUNISHMENT

Every legal system employs sanctions to protect public order. The penalty provisions of criminal law provide for sanctions of varying severity. The pattern of sanctions in the penal codes of the United States varies from state to state, but over the span of the last century there has been a general trend to shift emphasis from severe to mild sanctions.[16]

Deterrence of criminal behavior is a primary objective of the penalties in criminal law. Prevention of crime may begin in the social contract inherent in modern society and its emphasis on positive inducements resulting from living in harmony with a community's norms of behavior. The essence of social control is to build up in individuals various internal controls in support of conforming behavior. The true roadblock to criminal behavior, however, is the negative inducement of prompt penalties imposed on violators.

There is no crime without a punishment. If the statute provides only a remedy it is not a crime. To indemnify is not punishment but for the benefit of and at the discretion of the injured party. Punishment is the imposition of suffering for public purposes and there is no direct reference to the interests of the victim. Punishment is imposed at the discretion of those who represent the public rather than at the discretion of the victim. Punishment may be any of the following: death, imprisonment, probation, fine, removal from office, or disqualification to hold and enjoy any office of honor, trust, or profit.

Punishments are generally determined, when there is judicial discretion, by the degree of moral turpitude of the offender; what his or her purpose and motive was; whether, if co-defendants, one was the active rather than the passive partner (relative culpability); the criminal act itself; and the facts surrounding the criminal act.

At one time the imposition of prompt penalties was linked to the severity of penalties (sanctions) as supplementing the deterrence factor of law as a secondary social control. Then it became apparent that maximum penalties did not deter many individuals from committing crimes, but they did interfere with the rehabilitation of convicted offenders.

Criminal law today is a coercive threat—but a threat that exists within a framework of minimum penalties which safeguard convicted offenders from imposed penalties so damaging that released offenders are unable to reenter the community and assume the duties and responsibilities of conforming members of society.

# NOTES

1. Huntington Cairns, *Legal Philosophy, From Plato to Hegel* (Baltimore: The Johns Hopkins University Press, 1949), pp. 29–76.

2. Cairns, pp. 77–126.

3. Cairns, pp. 127–162.

4. Carl Joachim Friedrich, *The Philosophy of Law in Historical Perspective* (Chicago: University of Chicago Press, 1957), pp. 42–48.

5. Friedrich, pp. 84–87.

6. John Austin, "Law as the Sovereign's Command," in *The Nature of Law: Readings in Legal Philosophy*, ed. M. P. Golding (New York: Random House, 1966), pp. 77–98.

7. John Chipman Gray, "The Judge as Law-Giver," in *The Nature of Law*, pp. 187–199.

8. M. R. Cohen, "Nominalism and the Reality of Rules," in *The Nature of Law*, pp. 240–46.

9. Roscoe Pound, *An Introduction to the Philosophy of Law*, rev. ed. (New Haven: Yale University Press, 1952), pp. 25–47.

10. *Dennis* v. *United States*, 341 U.S. 494 (1950).

11. *United States* v. *Pendergast*, 28 F. Supp. 601 (1939).

12. Oliver Wendell Holmes, Jr., *The Common Law* (Boston: Little, Brown and Company, 1948), pp. 5–37.

13. H. L. A. Hart, *The Concept of Law* (London: Oxford University Press, 1961), pp. 20–25.

14. Friedrich, pp. 8–12.

15. Julius J. Marke, ed., *The Holmes Reader* (New York: Oceana Publications, 1955), pp. 62–63.

16. Richard Arens and Harold D. Lasswell, *In Defense of Public Order: The Emerging Field of Sanction Law* (New York: Columbia University Press, 1961), p. 197.

# 3

# LEGAL RESEARCH

## OBJECTIVES
The objectives of Chapter Three are to reveal the access routes to information stored in the records of America's legal system, to describe the digests and summaries that can focus the search for specific laws and court decisions, and to suggest a standard form for "briefing" court decisions.

## LEGAL TERMS
Citation. *References indicating where a case—court decision —can be found. Also original process; a writ of a court.*
Annotated. *In legal texts this term indicates that each seg-*ment of the law contains notes describing and citing appropriate cases.
Prima facie. *On its face; at first examination.*
Headnote. *A note at the beginning of a case report giving relevant information and a summary of the case.*
Corpus Juris. *A body of law. A compilation of criminal law in the United States based on all reported cases. Corpus Juris Secundum is the second series of this compilation.*
Briefing. *In legal research the preparation of a digest or summary of a court's decision and opinion.*

## QUESTIONS FOR STUDY
1. Articles in law reviews and other criminal justice periodicals are sometimes described as "persuasive literature." What is the meaning of this term?
2. What are the two basic problems of legal research?
3. What are the advantages of an annotated criminal (penal) code when researching the provisions of state or federal law?
4. What is the difference in cases reported in U.S. Reports *and* in the Supreme Court Reporter?
5. What is meant by "Shepardizing" a case?

6. *List the necessary elements of a court decision that must be included when "briefing" a case.*

7. *What data should be contained in the "decision" segment of a brief?*

8. *Describe the major route or routes useful in locating a specific case and its related cases.*

9. *Describe the major route or routes useful in researching a particular section of state law. Federal law.*

---

**S**tatute law is recorded when enacted, repealed, or revised; codification in a criminal or penal code is an orderly recording of existing law. References are simple, usually a section number and the title of the code.

Court decisions are recorded in all courts of the United States. Courts of appellate jurisdiction usually file a joint decision and opinion in cases reviewed. This is the holding of the court and the judge's reasons for the decision. It usually includes references (citations) to other cases which were influential in the court's decision and rationale. These decisions are reported in a series of volumes concerned with the court in which the case was decided. Reference is to the volume of this series (by number), the "shorthand" identification of the series, and the page number at which the court's opinion begins.

Professional writings in criminal-justice periodicals form what is best described as persuasive literature about the criminal law and its application in the real world of courts and people. Contemporary literature does not have the "strength" of statute or case law, but it can often serve to tip the scales one way or the other on a legal question. These articles are usually learned writings in which the text is well supported by reference to statutes and cases.

Legal research can only be as effective as the resources of the available library. Most college and university libraries will have its state criminal or penal code (annotated), the United States Code (annotated); one of the series of volumes reporting United States Supreme Court decisions and the *Federal Reporter* series (cases in United States courts other than the Supreme Court); and reports of its state courts. Law school, state or county law libraries, and the libraries of major courts usually shelve the entire *National Reporter* series which contains the decisions and opinions of all state courts. The volumes in this series are identified by regions (groups of states).

Legal research and case study in the field of criminal law usually involves:

1. Locating the applicable statute.
2. Locating the applicable case law.
3. Locating related articles in professional journals.

The legal question forming the motive for research may be simple or complex. The first problem is identifying the subject matter involved and then narrowing the research objective to the appropriate subdivision. The second problem is collecting and arraying all the applicable authorities and applying this data to the legal question.

## SEARCHING FOR STATUTE LAW

State statutes collected in criminal (penal) codes provide the wording of the various provisions of criminal law. From the wording of the statute, the essential elements of a specific crime can be determined. Sometimes, words of the statute are defined in an accompanying "Words and Phrases" or "Definitions" segment. In addition, many of these codes offer an effective date of the basic legislation and its amendments.

Annotated criminal (penal) codes not only contain the state statutes in their official wording, but also offer brief notes and citations on court decisions in which the elements of the crime or statutory words and phrases have been construed by courts.

In *West's Annotated California Codes,*[1] for instance, the section on homicide begins with the statutory definition of murder (Section 187, California Penal Code) and its legislative history, followed by pages of notes describing and citing cases based on the many complexities of murder. Lesser homicides than murder are then listed, and again, each subdivision has numerous cases clarifying the statutory language and/or previous case-decision applications. A sample page from this publication is shown in Figure 4 to illustrate how these annotations clarify the wording or application of a specific statute law.

Federal statutes related to criminal law are codified in Title 18, United States Code. This is now positive law and it is no longer necessary to refer to *Statutes at Large* for the exact text of any enactment. It is the official restatement in convenient form of the general and permanent laws of the United States. It is *prima facie* federal criminal law.

*The United States Code Annotated (USCA), Title 18, Crimes and Criminal Procedures,*[2] has a format similar to annotated state penal codes: provisions are given in their statutory language, and this is followed by notes of cases clarifying various segments of the statutory law or its language.

## CASE REPORTS

*United States Reports*[3] are indicated as the source of a case when the initials "U.S." are in the case citation. These are the official case reports of the United States Supreme Court. Case citations to *United States Reports* give the common or proper name of the case, volume,

### 3. Elements of offense—In general

"Murder" is the unlawful killing of a human being with malice aforethought, malice being implied where no considerable provocation appears or when the circumstances attending the killing show an abandoned and malignant heart. People v. Endner (1946) 165 P.2d 712, 73 C.A.2d 20; People v. Weeks (1930) 286 P. 514, 104 C.A. 708.

Any unlawful killing of a human being with malice aforethought, express or implied, "when no considerable provocation appears," is murder, under the express provisions of this section, and § 188, regardless of the degree. People v. Ford (1914) 143 P. 1075, 25 C.A. 388; People v. Suhr (1914) 143 P. 1088, 25 C.A. 805.

Motel owners, who conspired to set fire to premises to collect insurance, could not be charged with murder for death of accomplice, who died from burns sustained when he negligently set the fire. People v. Jennings (1966) 52 Cal.Rptr. 329, 243 C.A.2d 324.

Except when common-law felony-murder doctrine is applicable, essential element of murder is intent to kill or intent with conscious disregard for life to commit acts likely to kill. People v. Washington (1965) 44 Cal.Rptr. 442, 402 P.2d 130, 62 C.2d 777.

Killing is first degree murder if act of killing is preceded by a concurrence of will, deliberation, and premeditation on plaintiff's part, regardless of how rapidly those thoughts might succeed each other or how quickly they might be followed by act of killing. People v. Jones (1963) 30 Cal.Rptr. 280, 215 C.A.2d 341.

A defendant in order to be guilty of murder in the first degree, must have weighed in his mind and considered the course of action he was taking, and after having considered the reasons for and against such course of action, chose to kill his victim, however, direct evidence of malice or of deliberate and premeditated purpose to kill is not required. People v. Cooley (1963) 27 Cal.Rptr. 543, 211 C.A.2d 173.

In murder prosecution, trial court properly allowed jury to consider returning a verdict of guilty of first-degree murder if and only if there was substantial evidence from which jury reasonably could have inferred all elements of first-degree murder including, in addition to malice, the elements of deliberation and premeditation. People v. Bush (1960) 2 Cal.Rptr. 29, 177 C.A.2d 117.

The distinguishing element between murder and manslaughter is the presence or absence of malice. People v. Lewie (1959) 344 P.2d 861, 174 C.A.2d 281.

Homicide committed with malice is either first or second degree murder. People v. Reid (1946) 167 P.2d 234, 73 C.A.2d 610.

### 4. —Intent to kill, elements of offense

Statutory requirement for first-degree murder that it be found to have been willful, deliberate, and premeditated indicates intention to require substantially more reflection than may be involved in mere formation of specific intent to kill. People v. Risenhoover (1968) 73 Cal.Rptr. 533, 447 P. 2d 925, 70 C.2d 89, certiorari denied, 90 S.Ct. 123, 396 U.S. 857, 24 L.Ed. 108.

Even though the court of appeal must assume that the trier of fact determined the defendant convicted of first-degree murder did have the mental capacity at the time to form intent to kill, such conclusion does not foreclose inquiry as to whether the evidence was sufficient to find defendant guilty of murder of the first degree. People v. Theriot (1967) 60 Cal.Rptr. 279, 252 C.A.2d 222.

Even though facts and circumstances might justify an inference that the defendant possessed and exercised the mental state necessary for first-degree murder, psychiatric evidence showing that he could not engage in the requisite premeditation and deliberation or entertain the specified malice may control disposition of the case. 1d.

Actual intent to kill is not necessary component of second-degree murder, and malice is implied from assault with dangerous weapon, in absence of justifying or mitigating circumstances. Jackson v. Superior Court of City and County of San Francisco (1965) 42 Cal.Rptr. 838, 399 P.2d 374, 62 C.2d 521.

The crime may be murder although the person killed is not the one whom the ac-

**462**

Figure 4. *Sample page,* West's Annotated California Penal Code, *1970 ed. Published by West Publishing Company, St. Paul, Minn.*

and page number. For instance, a well-known case on electronic eavesdropping is termed *United States* v. *United States District Court*, and cited as : 407 U.S. 297 (1972). In volume 407, this case begins at page 297.

Each of these reports is a full text of the Court's majority opinion as well as other opinions, concurring or dissenting, in the case. The report is preceded by a "headnote" giving the full names of the parties involved, the route of the case in reaching the Court, case number, and dates the case was argued and the decision made. This is followed by a summary of the facts of the case and the Court's holding. The holding of the Court is often subdivided to spell out the Court's decision and these segments are referenced to pages of the opinion containing the full text of this portion of the Court's holding. This is followed by brief data on the opinions filed and the legal representation in the case. (See Figure 5.)

West Publishing Company also publishes the full text of United States Supreme Court opinions. Their series is known as the *Supreme Court Reporter*. It is identified in the case citations by the abbreviation "S.Ct." or "S.C.," along with the volume and page number and year: 92 S.Ct. 212 (1972) for the case of *United States* v. *United States District Court*. In this publication the headnote is keyed to West's key number system. This is a topical division into hundreds of topics, each of which is assigned a number. One of the paragraphs in the headnote of the above case is "Criminal Law 394.3." Under this heading is material that can be related to other cases coming under this topic and key number.

A series of volumes known as the *Lawyer's Edition*[4] also offers these reports with headnote references, a summary of the case, and the full text of the opinion(s).

Reports from lesser courts are indexed to volume and pages of various official reports and to West's *National Reporter* system. These reports are:

F. series—United States Circuit Courts of Appeals (—F.—, and —F. 2d—)

F. Supp. series—United States District Courts (F. Supp.)

Ala., Conn., N.H., etc.—State court appellate reports (—Ala. —, —Conn.—, —N.H.—)

**NATIONAL REPORTER:**

*Atlantic*. Maine, Vermont, New Hampshire, Connecticut, New Jersey, Delaware, Pennsylvania, Maryland, and Rhode Island (—A.—; —A. 2d—)

*North Eastern*. Massachusetts, New York, Ohio, Indiana, Illinois (—N.E.—; —N.E. 2d—)

*North Western*. Michigan, Wisconsin, Minnesota, Iowa, North Dakota, South Dakota, Nebraska (—N.W.—; —N.W. 2d—)

# UNITED STATES *v.* UNITED STATES DISTRICT COURT FOR THE EASTERN DISTRICT OF MICHIGAN ET AL. (PLAMONDON ET AL., REAL PARTIES IN INTEREST)

CERTIORARI TO THE UNITED STATES COURT OF APPEALS FOR
THE SIXTH CIRCUIT

No. 70–153.   Argued February 24, 1972—Decided June 19, 1972

The United States charged three defendants with conspiring to destroy, and one of them with destroying, Government property. In response to the defendants' pretrial motion for disclosure of electronic surveillance information, the Government filed an affidavit of the Attorney General stating that he had approved the wiretaps for the purpose of "gather[ing] intelligence information deemed necessary to protect the nation from attempts of domestic organizations to attack and subvert the existing structure of the Government." On the basis of the affidavit and surveillance logs (filed in a sealed exhibit), the Government claimed that the surveillances, though warrantless, were lawful as a reasonable exercise of presidential power to protect the national security. The District Court, holding the surveillances violative of the Fourth Amendment, issued an order for disclosure of the overheard conversations, which the Court of Appeals upheld. Title III of the Omnibus Crime Control and Safe Streets Act, which authorizes court-approved electronic surveillance for specified crimes, contains a provision in 18 U. S. C. § 2511 (3) that nothing in that law limits the President's constitutional power to protect against the overthrow of the Government or against "any other clear and present danger to the structure or existence of the Government." The Government relies on § 2511 (3) in support of its contention that "in excepting national security surveillances from the Act's warrant requirement, Congress recognized the President's authority to conduct such surveillances without prior judicial approval." *Held:*

   1. Section 2511 (3) is merely a disclaimer of congressional intent to define presidential powers in matters affecting national security, and is not a grant of authority to conduct warrantless national security surveillances. Pp. 301–308.

**Figure 5.** *An opinion of the U.S. Supreme Court as it appears in t*

2. The Fourth Amendment (which shields private speech from unreasonable surveillance) requires prior judicial approval for the type of domestic security surveillance involved in this case. Pp. 314–321; 323–324.

(a) The Government's duty to safeguard domestic security must be weighed against the potential danger that unreasonable surveillances pose to individual privacy and free expression. Pp. 314–315.

(b) The freedoms of the Fourth Amendment cannot properly be guaranteed if domestic security surveillances are conducted solely within the discretion of the Executive Branch without the detached judgment of a neutral magistrate. Pp. 316–318.

(c) Resort to appropriate warrant procedure would not frustrate the legitimate purposes of domestic security searches. Pp. 318–321.

444 F. 2d 651, affirmed.

POWELL, J., delivered the opinion of the Court, in which DOUGLAS, BRENNAN, MARSHALL, STEWART, and BLACKMUN, JJ., joined. DOUGLAS, J., filed a concurring opinion, *post,* p. 324. BURGER, C. J., concurred in the result. WHITE, J., filed an opinion concurring in the judgment, *post,* p. 335. REHNQUIST, J., took no part in the consideration or decision of the case.

*Assistant Attorney General Mardian* argued the cause for the United States. With him on the briefs were *Solicitor General Griswold* and *Robert L. Keuch.*

*William T. Gossett* argued the cause for respondents the United States District Court for the Eastern District of Michigan et al. With him on the brief was *Abraham D. Sofaer. Arthur Kinoy* argued the cause for respondents Sinclair et al. With him on the brief were *William J. Bender* and *William Kunstler.*

Briefs of *amici curiae* urging affirmance were filed by *Stepehn I. Schlossberg* for the International Union, United Automobile, Aerospace, and Agricultural Implement Workers of America (UAW), and by *Benjamın Dreyfus* for the Black Panther Party et al.

*South Eastern.* Georgia, North Carolina, South Carolina, Virginia, West Virginia (—S.E.—; —S.E. 2d—)
*South Western.* Missouri, Kentucky, Tennessee, Arkansas and Texas (—S.W.—; —S.W. 2d—)
*Southern.* Alabama, Florida, Louisiana, Mississippi (—So.—; —So. 2d—)
*Pacific.* Alaska, Arizona, California, Colorado, Hawaii, Idaho, Kansas, Montana, Nevada, New Mexico, Oklahoma, Oregon, Utah, Washington, Wyoming (—P.—; —P. 2d—)

# DIGESTS AND SUMMARIES

A useful digest in searching for applicable cases, or state and federal statutes is *Shepard's Acts and Cases by Popular Names*.[5] This compilation of popular names by which federal and state acts (legislation) and cases have been referred to or cited gives the references necessary to locate the legislation or court decision. For instance, the Dyer Act is identified as concerned with stolen automobiles and its location given as Sections 2311 to 2313 of Title 18, U.S. Code; the *Miranda* case (*Miranda* v. *Arizona*) is referenced to *United States Reports*, the Lawyer's edition of these reports (L.Ed.), and West's *Supreme Court Reporter*: 384 U.S. 436, 16 L.Ed. 2d 694, and 86 S.C. 1602.

*Corpus Juris Secundum*[6] is an encyclopedic compilation of the criminal law based on all reported cases. Each segment of the criminal law (such as homicide, murder, etc.) is defined as it was in common law and/or as it has been defined by statutes. Cases applicable to each element of the definition or its language are then footnoted, with brief explanatory notes serving as annotations to groups of cases. (See sample page, Figure 6.)

The *Criminal Law Digest*[7] combines in one volume digests of the leading court decisions concerned with criminal law. Each edition is cumulative, the 1970 volume going back to 1965, the date the *Criminal Law Bulletin*[8] was established. The *Digest* contains notes in paragraph form of case reports previously published in the monthly *Bulletin*. Each paragraph notes briefly the court's holding on the legal issue in the case, and is referenced by case citation and to the volume and page number of the *Criminal Law Bulletin* (CLB) in which it was originally reported. Also noted are articles published in the CLB and concerned with the same subject matter. For instance, page 65 of the 1970 *Digest*, under the subject "Stop and Frisk," notes two articles, then lists *Terry* v. *Ohio* and other stop and frisk cases. (See Figure 7.) Subsequent editions are planned to bring the case material up to date. For instance, the *Criminal Law Digest—1975 Supplement*[9] is a classified digest of legal decisions and articles published in the *Criminal Law Bulletin* from January 1970 through November 1974 inclusive, and includes other signif-

## II. MURDER

## A. IN GENERAL

### § 13.  Definition

Murder consists in the unlawful killing of a human being with malice aforethought. Murder, as defined at common law and by

statutes declaratory thereof, consists in the unlawful killing of a human being with malice aforethought.[25] The statutes in some jurisdictions simply prescribe the punishment for murder without

35. U.S.–U. S. v. Martin, D.C.Or., 17 F. 150, 9 Sawy. 90.
Ariz.–Lasater v. State, 81 P.2d 83, 52 Ariz. 366–Williams v. Territory, 114 P. 556, 13 Ariz. 306.
Cal.–People v. Lee Look, 70 P. 660, 137 Cal. 590–People v. Evans, 56 P. 1024, 124 Cal. 206–People v. Schmidt, 63 Cal. 28–People v. Cronin, 34 Cal. 191–People v. Murray, 10 Cal. 309–People v. Weeks. 286 P. 514, 104 Cal.App. 708–People v. Anderson, 208 P. 204, 57 Cal.App. 721–People v. Huntington, 97 P. 760, 762, 8 Cal.App. 612–People v. Frank, 83 P. 578, 2 Cal.App. 283.
Colo.–Murphy v. People, 13 P. 528, 9 Colo. 435.
Conn.–State v. Jacowitz, 20 A.2d 470, 128 Conn. 40.
Del.–State v. Donovan, 8 A.2d 876, 1 Terry 257.
Idaho.–State v. Phinney, 89 P. 634, 13 Idaho 307, 12 L.R.A.,N.S., 935, 12 Ann. Cas. 1079–People v. O'Callaghan, 9 P. 414, 2 Idaho 143.
Ill.–People v. Lewis, 31 N.E.2d 795, 375 Ill. 330, certiorari denied Lewis v. People of State of Illinois, 62 S.Ct. 58, 314 U.S. 628, 86 L.Ed. 504–People v. Goldvarg, 178 N.E. 892, 346 Ill. 398.
Iowa–State v. Leib, 201 N.W. 29, 198 Iowa 1315.
Me.–State v. Sprague, 199 A. 705, 135 Me. 470–State v. Neal, 37 Me. 468.
Mich.–People v. Austin, 192 N.W. 590, 221 Mich. 635.
Mont.–State v. Chavez, 281 P. 352, 354, 85 Mont. 544—State v. Gondeiro, 268 P.507, 82 Mont. 530–State v. Nielson, 100 P. 229, 38 Mont. 451–State v. McGowan, 93 P. 552, 36 Mont. 422–State v. Hliboka, 78 P. 965, 31 Mont. 455, 3 Ann.Cas. 934–State v. Sloan, 56 P. 364, 22 Mont. 293–Territory v. Manton, 14 P. 637, 7 Mont. 162.
Neb.–Marion v. State, 20 N.W. 289, 16 Neb. 349.

Nev.–State v. Thompson, 12 Nev. 140.
N.M.–State v. Roy, 60 P.2d 646, 655, 40 N.M. 397, citing Corpus Juris.
N.C.–State v. Banks, 57 S.E. 174, 176, 143 N.C. 652.
Pa.–Commonwealth v. McLaughlin, 142 A. 213, 293 Pa. 218–Commonwealth v. Grimm, 5 Pa.Dist. & Co. 287.
S.C.–State v. Bowers, 43 S.E. 656, 65 S.C. 207, 95 Am.S.R. 795.
Utah.–State v. McDonald, 46 P. 872, 14 Utah 173.
Wis.–State v. Scherr, 9 N.W.2d 117, 243 Wis. 65.
29 C.J. p 1083 note 39.
Homicide as including murder see supra § 1.
Murder exists if accused killed deceased unlawfully and maliciously and without justification.–Hill v. State, 138 S.E. 229, 164 Ga. 298.

**Other definitions**
(1) At common law, murder was, and still is, defined to be when a person of sound memory and discretion unlawfully kills a human being, with malice aforethought, either express or implied.–State v. Harrigan, 31 A. 1052, 9 Houst., Del., 69.
(2) Murder is the killing of any reasonable creature in being, with malice aforethought, express or implied.
Del.–State v. Foreman, 41 A. 141, 1 Marv. 517.
Va.–Whiteford v. Commonwealth, 6 Rand. 721, 723, 27 VA. 721, 723, 18 Am.D. 771.
(3) "Murder" is the intentional killing of a human being.–Doggett v. State, 93 S.W.2d 399, 130 Tex.Cr. 208.
(4) Other definitions.
Ark.–Dillard v. State, 46 S.W. 533, 535, 65 Ark. 404.
Del.–State v. People, Del., 33 A. 257, 9 Houst. 488–State v. Walker, Del., 33 A. 227, 9 Houst. 464.
Hawaii.–Republic of Hawaii v. Tsunikichi, 11 Hawaii 341.

**857**

**Figure 6.** *Data illustrative of pages of* Corpus Juris Secundum, *edited by Donald J. Kiser. Published by The American Law Book Company, 1944, amended to 1975.*

he is deemed to have waived his right to object. Echols v. State, 201 So.2d 89, 3 CLB 584.

**Florida** Defendant's invitation to enter premises held to be a consent to a search of his premises. Garcia v. Florida, 186 So.2d 556, 2 CLB No. 7, p. 52.

**Illinois** Police need not advise defendant in custody that he has a right not to consent to the search of his apartment. Trial court's finding that defendant consented to search would not be overturned "unless it is clearly unreasonable." People v. Ledferd, 232 N.E.2d 684, 4 CLB 140.

**Iowa** Tape recording of defendant's second bribe attempt made while officer was, by consent, on defendant's premises was not product of an illegal search and seizure. State v. Taylor, 144 N.W.2d 289, 2 CLB No. 9, p. 58.

**Minnesota** Court finds appellant consented to the taking of a sample of his blood while lying in an oxygen tent under sedation the day after he was operated on for a stab would in the chest. State v. Campbell, 161 N.W.2d 47, 4 CLB 546.

**Rhode Island** Failure of the police to advise the defendant of his right to refuse the consent to their search of his automobile does not vitiate his consent to search. Rhode Island Supreme Court refuses to extend *Miranda* v. *Arizona* to such a situation, noting that the United States Court of Appeals for the First Circuit has ruled similarly in *Gorman* v. *United States* (380 F.2d 158). State v. Leavitt, 237 A.2d 309, 4 CLB 193.

## §12.00.  Stop and frisk

"In-Field Interrogation: Stop, Question, Detention and Frisk" by Richard H. Kuh, 3 CLB 597.

"The Constitutional Arguments Against 'Stop and Frisk'" by Kalman Finkel and Gretchen White Oberman, 3 CLB 441.

**United States Supreme Court** Supreme Court upholds stop and frisk where officer had reasonable grounds to believe: (a) that defendant was armed and dangerous; (b) that it was necessary to take swift action for self-protection; and (c) scope of search was limited to patting outer garments. Terry v. Ohio, 392 U.S. 1, 4 CLB 301.

**United States Supreme Court** Where officer suspected narcotics activity but had insufficient reason to suspect that defen-

**Figure 7.** *Sample page from* Criminal Law Digest *(Hanover Lamont Corporation, Boston, Mass., 1970) showing section number, topical heading, and digest notes of articles and cases.*

icant cases on criminal law. In this volume, Section 12.00, Stop and Frisk, contains a reference to a 1973 article on "Airport Frisks," the 1972 case of *Adams* v. *Williams*, and sixteen other federal and state court decisions.

The *Criminal Law Reporter* is published by the Bureau of National Affairs, Inc., Washington, D.C.; weekly issues contain a summary and analysis of current developments (Section #1); and court decisions and proceedings, legislative action, reports, and proposals (Section #2). Another text section (#3) is published as warranted and contains the text of all United States Supreme Court cases and significant legislation, reports, and proposals. A timely alphabetical index by subject matter and an alphabetical table of cases (both referenced to page numbers in Section 3 at which the case law, etc., begins) aid researchers.

## LOCATING CASE LAW

Cases are located by the volume, series, and page number indicated in the citation. Subject matter location of cases is difficult without these citations. However, digests and summaries are helpful when the citation is not known.

To "Shepardize" a case means to look up other related cases by using *Shepard's Citations*.[10] The use of a citator such as Shepard's enables the researcher to gather from a single known case all the case citations related to issues of the known case. In addition, *Shepard's Citations* are footnoted with various symbols indicating the relationship of the cases cited to the basic case. For instance, on the sample page shown in Figure 8, the case summarized in Figure 9 (*Adams* v. *Williams*, 407 U.S. 143) is first located by volume (407 of *United States Reports*) and page number (143). The listing given indicates: *Adams* v. *Williams* has superseded ("s") the court opinion in several cases; there are two subsequent cases in which the doctrine of *Adams* v. *Williams* is explained ("e"); and one in which it is followed ("f")—cited as the controlling case.

## BRIEFING CASES

"Briefing" a case is to prepare a *digest* or *summary* of the court's opinion. The full opinion must be read for comprehensive understanding of the case and to discover key phraseology such as: "the question(s) in this case," "we hold," and "our reason(s)."

Any brief or summary of a court's decision as expressed in the reported opinion is generally along the lines of:
1. Common (proper) name and citation.
2. Facts of the case.
3. Issue (question).
4. Decision (holding) or conclusion (holding and reasoning).

**UNITED STATES SUPREME COURT REPORTS** **Vol. 407**

Ny
335S2d360
Pa
295A2d323
296A2d31
58ABA1063

**-742-**
(32LE453)
(92SC1941)
s404US937
s325FS352
s323ICC48
s335ICC264
345FS765

**-759-**
(32LE466)
(92SC1808)
s400US1019
s404US820
s431F2d394
s442F2d530
s270FS1004
e461F2d$^{1}$1261

**-797-**
(32LE499)
(92SC1899)
s442F2d1163
462F2d$^{1}$1264
465F2d$^{1}$882

347FS$^{1}$1091

**-813-**
(32LE511)
(92SC1931)
US reh den
in406US978
s70C2d369
Calif
s74CaR882
s450P2d258
408US$^{1}$314
16MdA229
Md
295A2d821

**Vol. 407**

**-1-**
(32LE513)
(92SC1907)
s428F2d888
s446F2d907
s464F2d1395
s296FS733
465F2d$^{1}$1078
f466F2d$^{1}$234
e347FS$^{1}$54

**-25-**
(32LE530)
(92SC2006)
s401US908
Fla
s236So2d442
407US$^{1}$141
j407US$^{1}$381
f407US918
463F2d$^{1}$65
463F2d423
f463F2d$^{1}$681
463F2d714
f483F2d$^{1}$715
f465F2d$^{1}$120
465F2d$^{1}$933
465F2d$^{1}$959
468F2d394
346FS$^{1}$301
346FS1396
347FS$^{1}$294
347FS$^{1}$1079
348FS$^{1}$759
f348FS$^{1}$1075
e348FS$^{1}$1320
349FS$^{1}$997
349FS1098
f350FS$^{1}$480
350FS$^{1}$937
28CA3d290
126GaA835

7I1A145
387Mch700
213Va432
130Vt534
56Wis2d288
Calif
104CaR545
105CaR274
Fla
269So2d421
Ga
192SF429
Idaho
501P2d283
Ill
287NE176
288NE396
288NE398
Ky
487SW297
Mich
199NW178
Minn
201NW386
Mo
487SW587
Ohio
289NE407
Tex
486SW331
486SW374
488SW101

Vt
296A2d255
Va
192SE780
Wis
201NW780
58ABA1177

**-67-**
(32LE556)
(92SC1983)
s401US906
s402US994
s317FS954
s326FS127
408US$^{1}$481
f462F2d$^{1}$1056
462F2d$^{1}$1391
j462F2d$^{1}$1395
463F2d1209
d466F2d$^{1}$616
j466F2d689
j466F2d$^{1}$670
f467F2d$^{1}$202
f468F2d$^{1}$847
344FS$^{1}$824
344FS$^{1}$1138
345FS$^{1}$599
f346FS$^{1}$6
346FS$^{1}$123
346FS$^{1}$317
f346FS$^{1}$765

346FS$^{1}$1011
f346FS$^{1}$1063
f347FS$^{1}$80
347FS$^{1}$294
347FS387
347FS$^{2}$388
347FS$^{1}$404
f348FS$^{1}$673
d348FS$^{1}$1020
348FS$^{1}$1336
349FS206
f349FS$^{1}$744
349FS$^{1}$864
349FS$^{1}$1166
350FS$^{1}$187
e350FS$^{1}$242
350FS$^{1}$405
350FS$^{1}$447
350FS737
350FS$^{1}$1014
d350FS$^{1}$1312
39Ap2d277
40Ap2d73
40Ap2d86
27CA3d36
28CA3d875
8C3d667
127GaA281
42McA117
388Mch347
70Msc2d637
70Msc2d836

119Su417
121Su13
121Su266
7WAp200
7WAp220
7WAp679
55Wis2d547
Alk
502P2d149
502P2d156
Ariz
502P2d1329
Calif
103CaR571
105CaR401
105CaR679
Del
297A2d422
Fla
266So2d660
Ga
193SE208
Iowa
200NW536
200NW537
La
269So2d190
Mass
285NE417
Mich
200NW695
201NW380

NJ
291A2d861
295A2d408
296A2d564
NY
333S2d955
334S2d686
335S2d506
337S2d692
337S2d708
339S2d80
339S2d409
Ohio
287NE846
Ore
503P2d482
RI
298A2d523
Wash
498P2d887
499P2d94
501P2d1245
Wis
102NW17

**-104-**
(32LE584)
(92SC1953)
s404US1014

Continued
359

**Figure 8.** *Sample page 359, volume 407*—Shepard's United States Citations, Cases, *1971–73 Supplement, published by Shepard's Citations, Inc., Colorado Springs, Colorado, 80901. Bold-faced print indicates volume and page numbers of* United States Reports *at which the Court's opinion begins. Figures in columns show case citations of related cases; symbols indicate relationship to basic case.*

A well-known case on search and seizure would be briefed as follows:

**CHIMEL v. CALIFORNIA, 395 U.S. 752 (1969).**

*Facts*: Santa Ana (California) police officers, armed with an arrest warrant but not a search warrant, were admitted to petitioner's home by his wife, where they awaited petitioner's arrival. When he entered he was served with the warrant. Although he denied the officer's request to "look around," they conducted a search of the entire house "on the basis of the lawful arrest." At petitioner's trial on burglary charges, items taken from his home were admitted over objection that they had been unconstitutionally seized. His conviction was affirmed by the California appellate courts, which held, despite their acceptance of petitioner's contention that the arrest warrant was invalid, that since the arresting officers had procured the warrant "in good faith," and since in any event they had had sufficient information to constitute probable cause for the arrest, the arrest was lawful. The courts also held that the search was justified as incident to a valid arrest.

*Issue*: What is the permissible scope under the Fourth Amendment of a search incident to a lawful arrest?

*Decision*: The scope of the search was "unreasonable" under the Fourth and Fourteenth Amendments, and the petitioner's conviction cannot stand (reversed).

*Reason*: Application of sound Fourth Amendment principles to the facts of this case produces a clear result. The search here went far beyond the petitioner's person and the area from within which he either might have obtained a weapon or destroyed something that could have been used as evidence against him. There was no constitutional justification, in the absence of a search warrant, for extending the search beyond that area.

The *Decisions of the United States Supreme Court—Term*[11] is a series of annual volumes in which the decisions of the United States Supreme Court are summarized. While it is of recent origin, it is a source of contemporary decisions in short form and extremely helpful to researchers who must brief these cases. The styles of these summaries are shown in Figure 9.

FREDERICK E. ADAMS, Warden, Petitioner,

v

ROBERT WILLIAMS

407 US 143, 32 L Ed 2d 612, 92 S Ct 1921

Argued April 10, 1972.   Decided

June 12, 1972.

**Decision:** Police officer held to have acted reasonably, on basis of informer's tip, in making forcible stop, reaching into automobile, and seizing loaded rovolver from occupant's waistband.

## SUMMARY

At about 2:15 a.m., while a police officer was alone on patrol car duty in a high crime area, a person known to him came to his patrol car and informed him that an individual seated in a nearby car was carrying narcotics and had a gun at his waist. After calling for assistance on his police radio, the officer approached the nearby car to investigate the informer's report. The officer tapped on the car window and asked the respondent, who was the occupant of the car, to open the door, but the respondent rolled down the window instead. The officer reached into the car and removed from the respondent's waistband a loaded revolver which had not been visible from outside the car. The officer arrested the respondent for unlawful possession of the revolver, and in a search conducted after other officers arrived, substantial quantities of heroin were found on the respondent's person, and a machete and a second revolver were found hidden in the car. The items found on the respondent's person and in the car were admitted in evidence at the respondent's trial in a Connecticut state court, and the respondent was convicted of illegal possession of weapons as well as possession of heroin. After the Connecticut Supreme Court affirmed his conviction and the United States Supreme Court denied certiorari, he instituted habeas corpus proceedings in the United States District Court for the District of Connecticut. The District Court denied relief and the United States Court of Appeals for the Second Circuit initially affirmed, but the Court of Appeals later reversed, on rehearing en banc, and held that since the officer had neither probable cause to arrest the respondent nor any other sufficient cause for reaching into his waistband, the evidence seized was improperly admitted at the respondent's trial, and the respondent's conviction had to be set aside (441 F2d 394).

On certiorari, the United States Supreme Court reversed. In an opinion by **Rehnquist, J.,** expressing the views of six members of

**Figure 9.** *Sample case summary from* Decisions of the United States Suprem

indicia of reliability to justify the officer's forcible stop of the the court, it was held (1) that the informer's tip carried enough respondent, (2) that the officer's action in reaching to the spot where the gun was thought to be hidden constituted a limited intrusion designed to insure his safety, and was reasonable, and (3) that probable cause existed to arrest the respondent for unlawful possession of the weapon, and the search of his person and of the car incident to that arrest was lawful.

**Douglas, J.,** joined by **Marshall, J.,** dissenting, expressed the view that the court's decision involved a serious intrusion on Fourth Amendment safeguards.

**Brennan, J.,** dissented on the grounds that the state had not made a showing of sufficient cause to justify the officer's forcible stop, especially since (1) the informer was unnamed, (2) he was not shown to have been reliable with respect to guns or narcotics, and (3) he gave no information which demonstrated personal knowledge or which could not readily have been manufactured by the officer after the event.

**Marshall, J.,** joined by **Douglas, J.,** dissented on the grounds (1) that the officer was not justified in encountering the respondent, (2) that it was illegal to frisk the respondent, since there was no reason for the officer to infer that the respondent was dangerous, and (3) that since Connecticut law did not make it illegal for private citizens to carry guns, the officer did not, after seizing the gun, have probable cause to arrest the respondent.

## COUNSEL

Donald A. Browne argued the cause and filed briefs for petitioner.

Edward F. Hennessey argued the cause and filed a brief for respondent.

Briefs of amici curiae urging reversal were filed by Solicitor General Erwin N. Griswold, Assistant Attorney General Petersen, and Beatrice Rosenberg for the United States; by Frank S. Hogan, pro se, Michael R. Juviler, and Herman Kaufman for the District Attorney of New York County; and by Frank G. Carrington, Jr., Alan S. Ganz, Wayne W. Schmidt, and Glen R. Murphy for Americans for Effective Law Enforcement, Inc., et al.

Burt Neuborne and Melvin L. Wulf filed a brief for the American Civil Liberties Union as amicus curiae.

Court, 1971–72 *(Rochester, N.Y.: Lawyer's Cooperative Publishing Co., 1972).*

# NOTES

1. *West's Annotated California Codes*, Penal Code (St. Paul, Minn.: West Publishing Co., 1970).

2. *United States Code Annotated (USCA), Title 18, Crimes and Criminal Procedures* (St. Paul, Minn.: West Publishing Co.; and Mineola, New York: Edward Thompson Company, 1969).

3. U.S. Supreme Court, *United States Reports* (Washington, D.C.: Government Printing Office).

4. *United States Supreme Court Reports, Lawyer's Edition, 2d Series* (Rochester, N.Y.: The Lawyer's Co-operative Publishing Co.; and San Francisco, Calif.: Bancroft-Whitney Co.).

5. *Shepard's Acts and Cases by Popular Names* (Colorado Springs, Colo: Shepard's Citations, Inc., 1968).

6. Donald J. Kiser, ed., *Corpus Juris Secundum* (Brooklyn, N.Y.: The American Law Book Co., 1974, amended to 1975).

7. Boston, Mass: Hanover Lamont Corp.

8. A monthly publication of Warren, Gorham, and Lamont, Inc., Boston, Mass.

9. *Criminal Law Digest—1975 Supplement* (Boston, Mass: Warren, Gorham, and Lamont, 1975).

10. *Shepard's United States Citations* (Colorado Springs, Colo.: Shepard's Citations, Inc.).

11. *The Decisions of the United States Supreme Court: 1963–64, 1964–65, 1965–66, 1966–67, 1967–68, 1968–69, 1969–70, 1970–71, 1971–72, 1972–73*, 10 vols. (Rochester, N.Y.: The Lawyer's Co-operative Publishing Co.). *The Decisions of the United States Supreme Court: 1973–74, 1974–75* (Rochester, N.Y.: The Lawyer's Co-operative Publishing Co.).

# PART TWO
## CONCEPTS OF LAW

# 4

# THE LAWMAKERS

## OBJECTIVES

*This chapter focuses on legislative assemblies as having the power to make and change laws, and the judiciary as possessing the power to review an enacted law for its constitutionality and, when necessary, interpret the meaning of statutory law. The chapter also presents public opinion as a factor influencing legislative decision making and having impact on judicial decisions.*

## LEGAL TERMS

Bills of attainder. *Special acts of the legislature imposing penalties without trial.*

Pro tempore. *Temporary; provisionally.*

Habeas corpus. *A writ having the function of releasing unlawfully imprisoned persons.*

Habeas corpus ad subjiciendum. *A writ directing a person detaining another to produce the body of the prisoner before the issuing court on a date specified.*

Habeas corpus ad testificandum. *A similar writ declaring "You have the body to testify"; and directing the person having custody of the prisoner to bring him or her before the issuing court on a date specified.*

Ex post facto. *After the fact; opposed to ab initio, from the beginning.*

Ex nunc. *From now; after.*

## QUESTIONS FOR STUDY

*1. How is statutory law influenced by judicial review and public opinion?*

*2. Develop the theme of the separation of powers in government.*

*3. Why is it necessary that the United States Constitution be considered the supreme law? State constitutions, the supreme law of the state, subject only to the United States Constitution?*

*4. Define a bicameral legislative assembly. Unicameral.*

5. Is the power of inquiry, along with process to enforce it, an appropriate auxiliary of a legislative assembly?

6. What is the distinction between a legislative act and a judicial pronouncement?

7. Describe the circumstances under which a statutory law may be ex post facto within the scope of the constitutional prohibition.

8. Is a law postdating a crime, but mollifying rather than aggravating its punishment, an ex post facto law within the constitutional prohibition?

9. What is the scope of judicial review of statutory law?

10. Is the impact of public opinion on legislators discoverable? How?

---

Only the government can make law and within the government only the legislature can make law.

The doctrine of the separation of powers into executive, legislative, and judicial branches is of comparatively recent origin. In medieval Europe and England, law came from the king as the sole appropriate source of sovereign control. In modern democratic societies, the legislative assembly is the proper source of law. In totalitarian nations, the dictator or ruler assumes the kingly role despite the fact that a legislative assembly may appear to be the source of sovereign control.

The foundation of American law was the English common law, but the colonists became embittered by confiscations, bills of attainder, and guilt by association during their struggle for independence. After the Revolutionary War the distrust of anything English led to a form of government in which the legislative branch was empowered to enact law in place of the common-law system of court-made law or law by royal decree.

The democratic system of lawmaking is attained when there is no law but the written law and recorded judicial interpretations; when executive authority is divorced from both legislative and judicial authority; and when the norms of the legislators are in harmony with the value judgments and general interests of a community.

Enacted law, as opposed to customary law, is the product of legislative thought and will. However, once a law is enacted, it begins to live a life of its own, a life quite independent of its source and generally in harmony with popular consciousness. Its growth or diminishment is influenced by both judicial interpretation and public opinion.[1]

## CONSTITUTIONS

Inherent in the federal government—that is, in the United States —is a constitutional division of governmental power. The powers

granted to the central government are enumerated, with residual powers granted to the individual state government or the people.

The Constitution establishes three great coordinate departments of the national government—the legislative, the executive, and the judicial—and distributes among them the powers conferred to that government by the people. Each department is dealt with in a separate article; the legislative in the first, the executive in the second, and the judicial in the third. The Constitution was framed on the fundamental theory that a larger measure of liberty and justice would be assured by vesting the three great powers—the legislative, the executive, and the judicial—in separate departments, each relatively independent of the others; and it was recognized that without this independence—if it was not made both real and enduring—the separation would fail in its purpose. All agreed that restraints and checks must be imposed to secure the requisite measure of independence; otherwise the legislative department, inherently the strongest, might encroach on or even come to dominate the others, and the judicial, naturally the weakest, might be dwarfed or swayed by the other two, especially by the legislative.[2]

The history of the years 1933 to 1974, however, has shown a dominant and stronger executive in the federal government. The executive branch has encroached upon or dominated the judicial and legislative branches. The executive power during the years of Presidents Franklin D. Roosevelt, John F. Kennedy, and Lyndon B. Johnson took on new dimensions: seemingly unlimited exercise of power by the Federal Bureau of Investigation (FBI) and the Central Intelligence Agency (CIA), and the assumption of the war-making authority by the President. In 1974 and 1975, the legislature rediscovered its power in concluding the presidency of Richard M. Nixon. There is no doubt that the Nixon impeachment hearings and the public investigations into the past exercise of power by the FBI and the CIA indicate the reassertion of power by the legislature.

A constitution sets forth the principles upon which the government is founded. It not only establishes the divisions of government but also distributes among those various branches the powers given to the government by the conferring authority. A constitution often contains a listing of the basic rights or powers retained by its citizens.[3]

The essence of any federal system of government is that its constitution must constitute a supreme law, superior to subsequent or prior statutory law enacted by the central government legislature or the legislatures of the various subdivisions (e.g., the states). This is achieved by granting the power to invalidate legislative acts contrary to the supreme constitution to a national supreme court (United States), a constitutional council (France), or a referendum of the electorate (Switzerland).[4]

Constitutions are planned by their authors to form a fundamental law for governing a community. To guard against errors and omissions, and to adjust one or more provisions of the constitution to new generations of citizens, arrangements are made to amend the constitution. Constitutions, at the time of formulation, could not be expected to contain the provisions necessary to cope with social and economic changes of future centuries.

Despite the fact that the American Constitution is not easily amended, the demand for constitutional protection for citizens' rights led to almost immediate amendment. This demand was formulated into a Bill of Rights: ten constitutional amendments reciting basic human rights. The original document provided only for the grants of and limitations on the exercise of federal governmental power.

From 1791, the date of these ten amendments, there have been sixteen others, one of which repealed an earlier amendment.[5] In the post-Civil War period, the Thirteenth (1865), Fourteenth (1868), and Fifteenth (1870) Amendments prohibited slavery, established the doctrines of equal rights and due process of law enforceable against state-made law and state exercise of power, and gave all adult male citizens the voting privilege. More recently, in 1964, the Twenty-fourth Amendment reaffirmed this elective franchise by a provision that no citizen is to be denied the right to vote by reason of failure to pay any poll tax, or other tax.

In the United States the power of amending the Constitution is based in the citizens as voters. The amending process allows for popular will to formulate itself with due deliberation, and the process of ratification provides a supplementary means for the expression of the feelings and beliefs of the whole electorate. Both processes guard against hasty and ill-considered actions by a numerical majority. There is a need for a continuing majority opinion to achieve change in the basic Constitution.[6]

Each of the states has its own constitution. They are modeled, to some extent, on the federal Constitution. States with constitutions predating the federal Constitution revised the state document to align it with the federal Constitution; new states organized their constitutions to fulfill the conditions of being a part of the federal union. These state constitutions establish the framework for government within the states' boundaries. There are traces of Roman law in several state constitutions. Louisiana was a Latinized state (French and Spanish influences) as were New Mexico, Arizona, and California (Spanish influence). State constitutions also provided for a deliberate amending process to change the basic constitution.

The provisions of a state constitution are the supreme law of the state, subject only to the provisions of the federal constitution.

# LEGISLATURES

The sovereignty of the people in a democratic community calls for either direct lawmaking action by a majority or other percentage of the electorate or delegated lawmaking action by elected representatives of the electorate. In government by elected representatives, the legislative assemblies are given the power to legislate and to make and change laws. The concept of legislative power includes the power to investigate and gather information necessary to the lawmaking role.

American legislatures, both federal and state, are products of the English Parliament; of the need for a representative assembly with power opposed to royal or executive power.

All modern nations organized under a federal constitution have bicameral or unicameral representative assemblies. Bicameralism is a dual-assembly form of representation: one assembly based on population—that is, on voters as numerical entities; the other assembly, on a geographic or regional basis. Unicameralism is a single representative assembly elected by popular vote. The Congress of the United States is a bicameral assembly made up of the House of Representatives and the Senate: "All legislative Powers herein granted shall be vested in a Congress of the United States, which shall consist of a Senate and House of Representatives."[7]

All of the states except Nebraska also have bicameral legislative assemblies.[8] However, as contrasted to the federal Congress, both assemblies of the bicameral state are now based upon population representation rather than geographical representation.[9]

Legislatures possess the power to organize themselves. In America, the Constitution authorizes the House of Representatives to choose its Speaker, and for the Senate to elect a president *pro tempore** and other officers to determine procedural rules and to compel attendance of members.

A position in the leadership of the United States Congress is generally won on the basis of seniority and competence. Chairmen of various committees and minority and majority leaders (each representing one of the traditional two parties in American politics) make up the leadership group.

Committees consider all legislation and related matters in Congress. Neither assembly (House or Senate) will act on a matter until it has been considered in a committee. Committee hearings, open to the public, are the first forum for discussion and for compromise, a necessary component of this process.

---

*The Constitution designates the Vice-President of the United States as President of the Senate. He presides without a vote unless the vote of the Senate would otherwise be tied. The president *pro tempore* serves only when the Vice-President is absent or when he is exercising the power of the President of the United States.

When a matter is considered by either the House of Representatives or the Senate, a majority constitutes a quorum to do business. To become law a proposed law (bill) must be passed by both the House of Representatives and the Senate. Bills that have passed the House and the Senate become law only after being presented to the President of the United States for his signature of approval. If he does not approve a bill by signing it, the bill is vetoed and must be returned to the assembly in which it originated (House or Senate) along with presidential objections. If two-thirds of the originating assembly agree to pass the bill upon reconsideration, it is sent to the other assembly, where it is also reconsidered. If also approved by a two-thirds vote in that assembly, the bill becomes law. The two-thirds majority of both assemblies of Congress overrides a presidential veto.[10]

The legislative power to investigate is a power to probe and pry into every circumstance relevant to the lawmaking responsibility.

The United States Supreme Court, in *McGrain* v. *Daugherty*,[11] upheld this investigative power as an auxiliary power necessary and appropriate to the express powers granted the two assemblies of Congress. In this case a reluctant witness was taken into custody under authority of a warrant of attachment issued by the Senate. The witness successfully petitioned for his release on a writ of *habeas corpus* in a federal court under jurisdiction of the place of arrest and the case came to the Supreme Court on a direct appeal by the government. The following selected extracts from this case reveal the scope of the legislative power to investigate:

> The principal questions involved are of unusual importance and delicacy. They are (a) whether the Senate—or the House of Representatives, both being on the same plane in this regard— has power, through its own process, to compel a private individual to appear before it or one of its committees and give testimony needed to enable it efficiently to exercise a legislative function belonging to it under the Constitution, and (b) whether it sufficiently appears that the process was being employed in this instance to obtain testimony for that purpose.
>
> The Constitution provides for a Congress consisting of a Senate and House of Representatives and invests it with "all legislative powers" granted to the United States, and with power "to make all laws which shall be necessary and proper" for carrying into execution these powers and "all other powers" vested by the Constitution in the United States or in any department or officer thereof. (Art. I, Secs. 1, 8.) Other provisions show that, while bills can become laws only after being considered and passed by both houses of Congress, each house is to be distinct

from the other, to have its own officers and rules, and to exercise its legislative function independently. (Art. I, Secs 2, 3, 5, 7.) But there is no provision expressly investing either house with power to make investigations and exact testimony to the end that it may exercise its legislative function advisedly and effectively. So the question arises whether this power is so far incidental to the legislative function as to be implied.

In actual legislative practice power to secure needed information by such means has long been treated as an attribute of the power to legislate. It was so regarded in the British Parliament and in the Colonial legislatures before the American Revolution; and a like view has prevailed and been carried into effect in both houses of Congress and in most of the state legislatures.

We now shall notice some significant congressional enactments. May 3, 1798, c. 36, 1 Stat. 554, Congress provided that oaths or affirmations might be administered to witnesses by the President of the Senate, the Speaker of the House of Representatives, the chairman of a committee of the whole, or the chairman of a select committee, "in any case under their examination." February 8, 1817, c. 10, 3 Stat. 345, it enlarged that provision so as to include the chairman of a standing committee. January 24, 1857, c. 19, 11 Stat. 155, it passed "An Act more effectually to enforce the attendance of witnesses on the summons of either house of Congress, and to compel them to discover testimony." This act provided, first, that any person summoned as a witness to give testimony or produce papers in any matter under inquiry before either house of Congress, or any committee of either house, who should wilfully make default, or, if appearing, should refuse to answer any question pertinent to the inquiry, would, in addition to the pains and penalties then existing, be deemed guilty of a misdemeanor and be subject to indictment and punishment as there prescribed; and secondly, that no person should be excused from giving evidence in such an inquiry on the ground that it might tend to incriminate or disgrace him, nor be held to answer criminally, or be subjected to any penalty or forfeiture, for any fact or act as to which he was required to testify, excepting that he might be subjected to prosecution for perjury committed while so testifying. January 24, 1862, c. 11, 12 Stat. 333, Congress modified the immunity provision in particulars not material here. These enactments are now embodied in sections 101-104 and 859 of Revised Statutes. They show very plainly that Congress intended thereby (a) to recognize the power of either house to institute inquiries and exact evidence touching subjects within its jurisdiction and on which it was disposed to act; (b) to recognize that such inquiries may be conducted through committees; (c) to subject defaulting and contumacious witnesses to in-

dictment and punishment in the courts, and thereby to enable either house to exert the power of inquiry "more effectually"; and (d) to open the way for obtaining evidence in such an inquiry, which otherwise could not be obtained, by exempting witnesses required to give evidence therein from criminal and penal prosecutions in respect of matters disclosed by their evidence.

We are of the opinion that the power of inquiry—with process to enforce it—is an essential and appropriate auxiliary to the legislative function. It was so regarded and employed in American legislatures before the Constitution was framed and ratified. Both houses of Congress took this view of it early in their history—the House of Representatives with the approving votes of Mr. Madison and other members whose service in the convention which framed the Constitution gives special significance to their action—and both houses have employed the power accordingly up to the present time. The acts of 1798 and 1857, judged by their comprehensive terms, were intended to recognize the existence of this power in both houses and to enable them to employ it "more effectually" than before. So, when their practice in the matter is appraised according to the circumstance in which it was begun and to those in which it has been continued, it falls nothing short of a practical construction, long continued, of the constitutional provisions respecting their powers, and therefore should be taken as fixing the meaning of those provisions, if otherwise doubtful.

We come now to the question whether it sufficiently appears that the purpose for which the witness's testimony was sought was to obtain information in aid of the legislative function. The court below answered the question in the negative.

We are of the opinion that the court's ruling on this question was wrong, and that it sufficiently appears, when the proceedings are rightly interpreted, that the object of the investigation and of the effort to secure the witness's testimony was to obtain information for legislative purposes.

The only legitimate object the Senate could have in ordering the investigation was to aid it in legislating; and we think the subject-matter was such that the presumption should be indulged that this was the real object.[12]

## LEGISLATION

The term "legislation" means the deliberate creation of legal precepts by a legislative branch of government which has been established for this purpose and to give articulate expression to such creative activity in a formal legal document—thus distinguishing legislative law (statute law) from the customary law (common law) which manifests its existence through actual observance by members of a community, supported by judicial decisions.

The expression of a legal rule or principle by a judge does not have the same authoritative formulation as legislation. The main function of the judiciary and the courts is to decide disputes under existing laws. When the law to be applied in a specific case is complete or unambiguous a judge need not augment or supplement the existing law. The creation of "new law" by judicial edict is only warranted when the existing law and its sources give him no guidance in the circumstances of a particular case. For this reason, the term "judicial legislation" should be avoided or at least used with extreme care.[13]

Justice Oliver Wendell Holmes made the distinction between a legislative act and a judicial pronouncement in his opinion in *Prentis* v. *Atlantic Coast Line Co.*[14] The distinction is that a judiciary inquiry investigates, declares, and enforces liabilities as they stand on present or past facts and under existing laws, while legislation looks to the future and changes conditions, making new rules to be thereafter applied.

## BAN ON *EX POST FACTO* LAWS

Roman law contained a strong presumption against retrospective legislation: *ex post facto* laws. The eminent English jurists—Bracton, Coke, and Blackstone—supported this legal principle until it was recognized by statute in England. In the United States, *ex post facto* statutes in criminal law are forbidden by the United States Constitution.[15]

Law is generally enacted to solve various problems of social control that have surfaced in the life of a community. After enactment, a specific law is applied by courts to situations and disputes that postdate the legislation. These enactments take effect *ex nunc*: after promulgation of legislation.

An *ex post facto* law is defined as a law that:

1. Makes an action punishable as a crime when such action was not a crime at the time of occurrence.
2. Aggravates a crime or makes it greater than it was when committed (that is, makes a former misdemeanor a felony).
3. Changes the punishment and inflicts a greater penalty than that previously assigned to a crime committed prior to the enactment.
4. Alters the legal rules of evidence, and receives less or different testimony than the law required at the time of the commission of the offense, in order to convict the offender.

In addition, the following fall within the general definition of *ex post facto* laws:

1. A law which, while only assuming to regulate civil rights and remedies, in effect imposes a penalty for an action which when committed was lawful, or deprives a person of a right.

2. A law which deprives persons accused of crime of some lawful protection to which they have become entitled, such as the protection of a former conviction or acquittal, or of a proclamation of amnesty.

3. Every law which, in relation to the offense or its consequences, alters the situation of a person to his disadvantage.[16]

In any inquiry as to whether new legislation is *ex post facto*, each case depends on its own particularized circumstances. If the circumstances are simple, as when legislation punishes for past conduct, the issue can be readily resolved. However, when the legislation may alter the position of a person as to crime or criminal prosecution, the issue may be more difficult: the retroactive application of a law changing the mode of a criminal trial was held to be unconstitutional in *Thompson* v. *Utah*.[17] Thompson and one Jack Moore were charged with grand larceny and found guilty by a jury of twelve persons in 1895 when Utah was a territory. Defendant Thompson appealed and a new trial was granted, but Thompson was not again tried until after the admission of Utah into the Union as a state. Thompson was found guilty at his second trial by a jury of eight persons. He appealed on the grounds (among others) that at the time of the commission of the offense a lawful jury was composed of twelve persons, not eight. Thompson's second conviction was affirmed in the state court.

Selected extracts from the court's comment concerning *ex post facto* laws follow:

> It is not necessary to review the numerous cases in which the courts have determined whether particular statutes come within the constitutional prohibition of *ex post facto* laws. It is sufficient now to say that a statute belongs to that class which by its necessary operation and in its relation to the offence, or its consequences, alters the situation of the accused to his disadvantage.
>
> Of course, a statute is not of that class unless it materially impairs the right of the accused to have the question of his guilt determined according to the law as it was when the offence was committed. And, therefore, it is well settled that the accused is not entitled of right to be tried in the exact mode, in all respects, that may be prescribed for the trial of criminal cases at the time of the commission of the offence charged against him. But it was held in *Hopt* v. *Utah*, 110 U.S. 574, 590, that a statute that takes from the accused a substantial right given to him by the law in force at the time to which his guilt relates would be *ex post facto* in its nature and operation, and that legislation of that kind cannot be sustained simply because, in a general sense, it may be said to regulate procedure. The difficulty is not so much as to the

soundness of the general rule that an accused has no vested right in particular modes of procedure, as in determining whether particular statutes by their operation take from an accused any right that was regarded, at the time of the adoption of the Constitution, as vital for the protection of life and liberty, and which he enjoyed at the time of the commission of the offence charged against him.

In our opinion, the provision in the constitution of Utah providing for the trial in courts of general jurisdiction of criminal cases, not capital, by a jury composed of eight persons, is *ex post facto* in its application to felonies committed before the Territory became a State, because, in respect of such crimes, the Constitution of the United States gave the accused, at the time of the commission of his offence, the right to be tried by a jury of twelve persons, and made it impossible to deprive him of his liberty except by the unanimous verdict of such a jury.[18]

## JUDICIAL REVIEW

Since the essence of any constitution in a federal system is that this document serve as a supreme law of the land, contradictory legislative acts by the federal or state legislatures must be invalidated. The United States Constitution, in Article III, Section 1, assigns the judicial power to "one Supreme Court, and in such inferior courts as the Congress from time to time ordain and establish"; and Section 2, following, states that: "The judicial power shall extend to all cases, in law and equity, arising under this Constitution."

In 1803, the United States Supreme Court asserted its claim of judicial review as ultimate arbiter of the limitations on both federal and state legislatures as to the constitutionality of legislation. The case was *Marbury* v. *Madison*,[19] and it was the first Supreme Court decision holding an Act of Congress unconstitutional.

The concluding paragraph of this opinion stated:

> The particular phraseology of the Constitution of the United States confirms and strengthens the principle, supposed to be essential to all written constitutions, that a law repugnant to the Constitution is void; and that courts, as well as other departments, are bound by that instrument.[20]

Interpretations of constitutions may be historical or contemporaneous. Uncertainties regarding the constitution should be resolved (1) by recourse to the prevalent understanding of the questioned segment at the time of its origin or adoption, or (2) on the basis of knowledge, needs, and experience existing in the community at the time the interpretation is made. Contemporaneous interpretation cannot extend to changes which would subvert the spirit of a constitution and transform its provisions into opposites, despite the exigencies of contemporary community life.[21]

In 1950, the United States Supreme Court was confronted with the question of whether a federal law (Smith Act) violated the First Amendment's safeguard of free speech. The Smith Act made it a crime for any person to advocate the overthrow of the government by force or violence. In his concurring opinion in this case, Justice Felix Frankfurter summed up the role of the Court in judicial review of constitutional questions:

> Free-speech cases are not an exception to the principle that we are not legislators, that direct policy-making is not our province. How best to reconcile competing interests is the business of legislatures, and the balance they strike is a judgment not to be displaced by ours, but to be respected unless outside the pale of fair judgment.[22]

A similar balancing between historic and contemporaneous doctrines of interpretation is operable in the area of statutory language, the meaning of legislation. When a legislative act is clear and is susceptible of but one construction, the words of the legislation should be given their plain meaning. However, legislative intent may be a factor overriding the plain-meaning doctrine. Courts probe the purpose of the legislation, going beyond its statutory language, to discover and identify the intent of the lawmakers at the time the legislation was enacted. Interpretation based on the plain meaning of the language used is often at conflict with the purpose-oriented rule, but when the plain-meaning interpretation is in variance with the policy of the legislature, recourse must be to the legislature's intent, and this is discoverable in legislative records of the debate on the legislation, in committee hearings, or when the bill was assessed on its merits by the full assembly of legislators.

The Supreme Court, in *United States* v. *American Trucking Associations*,[23] offers this doctrine* on statutory interpretation:

> In the interpretation of statutes, the function of the courts is easily stated. It is to construe the language so as to give effect to the intent of Congress. There is no invariable rule for the discovery of that intention. To take a few words from their context and with them thus isolated to attempt to determine their meaning, certainly would not contribute greatly to the discovery of the purpose of the draftsmen of a statute, particularly in a law drawn to meet many needs of a major occupation.
>
> There is, of course, no more persuasive evidence of the purpose of a statute than the words by which the legislature undertook to give expression to its wishes. Often these words are sufficient in and of themselves to determine the purpose of the legislation. In such cases we have followed their plain meaning.

*Extracts only; footnotes and citations are deleted.

When that meaning has led to absurd or futile results, however, this Court has looked beyond the words to the purpose of the act. Frequently, however, even when the plain meaning did not produce absurd results but merely an unreasonable one plainly at variance with the policy of the legislation as a whole this Court has followed that purpose, rather than the literal words. When aid to construction of the meaning of words, as used in the statute, is available, there certainly can be no "rule of law" which forbids its use, however clear the words may appear on superficial examination. The interpretation of the meaning of statutes, as applied to justiciable controversies, is exclusively a judicial function. This duty requires one body of public servants, the judges, to construe the meaning of what another body, the legislators, has said. Obviously there is danger that the court's conclusion as to legislative purpose will be unconsciously influenced by the enacting body. A lively appreciation of the danger is the best assurance of escape from its threat but hardly justifies an acceptance of a literal interpretation dogma which withholds from the courts available information for reaching a correct conclusion. Emphasis should be laid, too, upon the necessity for appraisal of the purposes as a whole of Congress in analyzing the meaning of clauses or sections of general acts. A few words of general connotation appearing in the text of statutes should not be given a wide meaning, contrary to a settled policy, excepting as a different purpose is plainly shown.[24]

## PUBLIC OPINION

*Popular will* insofar as lawmaking is concerned is the general public opinion at the time legislation is considered. Examination of so-called preparatory materials involved with legislation can reveal the range of public opinion at the time. These are committee minutes and reports, debate at the time legislation is proposed to the full legislative membership, and proposed amendments and their fate before enactment.

*Popular will* insofar as judicial review is concerned is a question of the impact of public opinion on the judiciary. Inherent in the doctrine of contemporaneous interpretation of constitutional questions and in the purpose-oriented interpretation of statutes is a reaction to the current ebb and flow of public opinion. While such reaction is not as discoverable as the reaction of legislators, it can be discerned in many decisions.

## NOTES

1. Carleton Kemp Allen, *Law in the Making*, 7th ed. (London: Oxford University Press, 1964), p. 427.
2. *Evans* v. *Gore*, 253 U.S. 245 (1920).

3. Edgar Bodenheimer, *Jurisprudence: The Philosophy and Method of the Law*, rev. ed. (Cambridge, Mass.: Harvard University Press, 1974), p. 404.

4. Thomas R. Adam, *Elements of Government: An Introduction to Political Science* (New York: Random House, 1960), p. 30.

5. The Twenty-first Amendment repealed the Eighteenth Amendment (intoxicating liquor).

6. "The Congress, whenever two thirds of both Houses shall deem it necessary, shall propose Amendments to this Constitution, or, on the Application of the Legislatures of two thirds of the several States, shall call a Convention for proposing Amendments, which, in either Case, shall be valid to all Intents and Purposes, as part of this Constitution, when ratified by the Legislatures of three fourths of the several States, or by Conventions in three fourths thereof, as the one or the other Mode of Ratification may be proposed by the Congress. . . ." (Article V.).

7. U.S. Const., Art. I, Sec. 1.

8. Adam, pp. 108–112.

9. *Reynolds* v. *Sims*, 377 U.S. 533 (1964).

10. U.S. Const., Art. I, Sec. 7.

11. 273 U.S. 135 (1927).

12. *McGrain* v. *Daugherty*, 273 U.S. 135 (1927).

13. Bodenheimer, pp. 326–30.

14. 211 U.S. 210 (1908).

15. "No Bill of Attainder or ex post facto Law shall be passed." (Article I, Section 9, Clause 3). "No State Shall . . . pass any . . . ex post facto Law. . . ." (Article I, Section 10, Clause 1).

16. *State* v. *Rowe*, 181 A. 706 (1935, N.J.).

17. 170 U.S. 343 (1898).

18. *Thompson* v. *Utah*, 170 U.S. 343 (1898).

19. 5 U.S. 137 (1 Cranch) (1803).

20. *Marbury* v. *Madison*, 5 U.S. 137 (1 Cranch) (1803).

21. Bodenheimer, pp. 404–09.

22. *Dennis* v. *United States*, 341 U.S. 494 (1950).

23. 310 U.S. 534 (1939).

24. *United States* v. *American Trucking Associations*, 310 U.S. 534 (1939).

# 5

# LIMITATIONS ON LAWMAKING

## OBJECTIVES
*Chapter Five shows the obligation of lawmakers to exercise the government's police power only in the public interest: to promote safety, health, and general welfare. The chapter pinpoints the concepts of public harm, fair notice, preemption, and opposition to excessive penalties in the lawmaking process.*

## LEGAL TERMS
Obscene. *An act or thing is obscene when it is offensive to modesty or decency; when it corrupts, depraves, or debauches the morals of individuals; and when it tends to stir sex impulses or lower the standard of right and wrong in regard to sexual relations. Pornography relates to obscene material. Legally (*Roth v. U.S. 354 U.S. 476*) the material is obscene if to the average individual applying contemporary community standards the material (taken as a whole) appeals to prurient interest, if it is utterly without redeeming social importance, if it goes substantially beyond customary limits of candor in description or representation, and if it is characterized by patent offensiveness.*

Tort. *A private or civil wrong or injury; a wrong independent of any contract. In general, a violation of some duty imposed by law or otherwise, but not arising from an agreement between parties.*

Sodomy. *Long termed the crime against nature. Unnatural sexual relations as between persons of the same sex, or with beasts, or between persons of different sex but in an unnatural manner.*

Certiorari. *A judicial process calling upon an inferior court to send up a case or proceeding for review.*

## QUESTIONS FOR STUDY

*1. What is the link between crimes without victims and the "overreach" of the criminal law?*

*2. What is the extent of the public-harm justification for legislation prohibiting certain kinds of behavior?*

*3. Discuss the theme that certain acts by married persons done with mutual consent cannot be prohibited by statutory law.*

*4. What is the* Roth *rule for determining obscenity?*

*5. Why has narcotic addiction been considered a status or condition rather than a crime?*

*6. What is the primary reason for the doctrine of fair notice in statutory law?*

*7. Does a federal law bar state enactment of legislation in the same area? Do state laws bar enactment of local laws at municipal or county levels?*

*8. Does the constitutional prohibition against cruel and unusual punishment forbid judicial as well as legislative imposition of such punishments?*

---

There is a long history of sin as criminal law, but the overcriminalization of immoral acts has resulted in a legislative backlash in which many of the laws concerned with immoral conduct were repealed or revised. The laws against prostitution, gambling, and drug abuse, the traditional crimes without victims,[1] have been liberalized, and there is recognition among lawmakers that religious and moral codes should not be models for penal codes.[2]

Laws should give potential violators fair notice. Those that are void for vagueness upon judicial review do not forewarn potential violators. Part of this fair notice is that laws are "visible" in criminal or penal codes, and not buried in the mass of case law, as is the common law. In addition, when a state has pre-empted a field of law, lesser governmental units such as municipalities must avoid enactment of conflicting legislation; the scope of criminal law is limited to public wrongs, not private wrongs (torts), and both public and judicial opinion are opposed to excessive penalties in criminal law.

## PUBLIC HARM

Regulation by legislative enactment of individual conduct is founded on the exercise of the government's police power in the general public interest. The use of this power is linked to the maintenance of public safety, health, morals, and general welfare.

In 1859, John Stuart Mill published his essay *On Liberty*. Mill's philosophy in this area was that the police power should only

be exercised in preventing harm to others, that an adult person's own welfare, physical or moral, is not sufficient ground to justifiy repressive legislation:

That the only purpose for which power can be rightfully exercised over any member of a civilized community, against his will, is to prevent harm to others. His own good, either physical or moral, is not a sufficient warrant. He cannot rightfully be compelled to do or forbear because it will be better for him to do so, because it will make him happier, because, in the opinion of others, to do so would be wise, or even right. These are good reasons for remonstrating with him, or reasoning with him, or persuading him, or entreating him, but not for compelling him, or visiting him with any evil in case he do otherwise. To justify that, the conduct from which it is desired to deter him must be calculated to produce evil to some one else. The only part of the conduct of any one, for which he is amenable to society, is that which concerns others. In the part which merely concerns himself, his independence is, of right, absolute. Over himself, over his own body and mind, the individual is sovereign.

It is, perhaps, hardly necessary to say that this doctrine is meant to apply only to human beings in the maturity of their faculties. We are not speaking of children, or of young persons below the age which the law may fix as that of manhood or womanhood. Those who are still in a state to require being taken care of by others, must be protected against their own actions as well as against external injury.[3]

John Stuart Mill's philosophy has been the subject of extensive debate, but it has enjoyed an enduring vitality not only in its impact upon legislators but also in its acceptance by the judiciary. The United States Supreme Court's general alignment with Mill's beliefs on the scope of the state power to regulate individual conduct is illustrated by the case of *Griswold* v. *Connecticut*.[4]

The appellants in this case, the Executive Director of the Planned Parenthood League of Connecticut, and its medical director, a licensed physician, were convicted as accessories for giving married persons information and medical advice on how to prevent conception and, following examination, prescribing a contraceptive device or material for the wife's use. A Connecticut statute makes it a crime for any person to use any drug or article to prevent conception. Appellants claimed the accessory statute as applied violated the Fourteenth Amendment. An intermediate appellate court and the state's highest court affirmed the judgment.

The Court's holding in *Griswold*, which follows in part,* was

*Extracts only; footnotes and citations are deleted.

that a Connecticut statute forbidding use of contraceptives violates the right of marital privacy which is within the scope of specific guarantees of the Bill of Rights:

We do not sit as a super-legislature to determine the wisdom, need, and propriety of laws that touch economic problems, business affairs, or social conditions. This law, however, operates directly on an intimate relation of husband and wife and their physician's role in one aspect of that relation.

The Fourth and Fifth Amendments were described in *Boyd* v. *United States*, 116 U.S. 616, as protection against all governmental invasions "of the sanctity of a man's home and the privacies of life." We recently referred in *Mapp* v. *Ohio*, 367 U.S. 643, to the Fourth Amendment as creating a "right to privacy, no less important than any other right carefully and particularly reserved to the people." The right of privacy which presses for recognition here is a legitimate one.

The present case, then, concerns a relationship lying within the zone of privacy created by several fundamental constitutional guarantees. And it concerns a law, which, in forbidding the *use* of contraceptives rather than regulating their manufacture or sale, seeks to achieve its goals by means having a maximum destructive impact upon that relationship. Such a law cannot stand in light of the familiar principle, so often applied by the Court, that a governmental purpose to control or prevent activities constitutionally subject to state regulation may not be achieved by means which sweep unnecessarily broadly and thereby invade the area of protected freedoms. Would we allow the police to search the sacred precincts of marital bedrooms for telltale signs of the use of contraceptives? The very idea is repulsive to the notions of privacy surrounding the marriage relationship.

We deal with a right of privacy older than the Bill of Rights —older than our political parties, older than our school system. Marriage is a coming together for better or worse, hopefully enduring, and intimate to the degree of being sacred. It is an association that promotes a way of life, not causes; a harmony in living, not political faiths; a bilateral loyalty, not commercial or social projects. Yet it is an association for as noble a purpose as any involved in our prior decisions.[5]

## OVERCRIMINALIZATION OF STATUTE LAW

When the criminal law invades private morality it exceeds its proper limits and has proven to be, in this instance, an inefficient instrument for imposing the legislative view on others. Most of the legislation concerning abortion, drunkenness, drug abuse, gambling, prostitution, sex deviancy, and pornography and obscenity is mis-

guided if the criminal law is viewed as a means of modifying human behavior in these areas. This "overreach" of criminal law prohibits the supply of goods and services demanded by many individuals; and it is certainly an attempt to enforce laws which do not command the respect or compliance of the general public. While it is true that no criminal law ever fully achieves its stated objectives, some laws are less enforceable than others. In addition, the attempt to use the criminal law as a questionable moral code encourages disrespect for other laws, and has led to huge profits for those who provide the illegal goods or services. There are multiple opportunities for bribing and corrupting public officials and police personnel.[6]

There has been decriminalization in several of the following areas: abortion, gambling, prostitution, and sex deviancy. Public intoxication is now viewed as a condition or status requiring treatment rather than imprisonment, and the laws which prohibit pornography and obscenity have been modified by judicial review.

This ongoing revision of existing law illustrates legislative response to the concept that "crimes without victims" involve attempts to legislate morality for its own sake, and perhaps a growing realization that legislators should scan existing and proposed laws for criteria related to victimization (i.e., is there, in the particular circumstances, any real victimization?).[7]

In *Stanley* v. *Georgia*,[8] the United States Supreme Court reduced the impact of Georgia's anti-obscenity law. In *Stanley*, police officers, under authority of a warrant to search appellant's home for evidence of his alleged bookmaking activities, found some films in his bedroom. The films were projected and deemed to be obscene. Appellant was arrested for their possession. He was thereafter indicted, tried, and *convicted* for knowingly having possession of obscene matter in violation of a Georgia law. The Georgia Supreme Court affirmed, holding it "not essential to an indictment charging one with possession of obscene matter that it be alleged that such possession was 'with intent to sell, expose, or circulate the same.'" Appellant contended that the Georgia obscenity statute is unconstitutional insofar as it punishes mere private possession of obscene matter. Georgia, relying on *Roth* v. *United States*,[9] argued the statute's validity on the ground that obscenity is not within the area of constitutionally protected speech or press.

The Court's holding in *Stanley* was that the First Amendment, applicable to the states by the Fourteenth Amendment, prohibits making mere private possession of obscene material a crime:

> It is true that in *Roth* this Court rejected the necessity of proving that exposure to obscene material would create a clear and present danger of antisocial conduct or would probably induce its recipients to such conduct. 354 U.S. 476, at 486–487. But

that case dealt with public distribution of obscene materials and such distribution is subject to different objections. For example, there is always the danger that obscene material might fall into the hands of children, or that it might intrude upon the sensibilities or privacy of the general public. No such dangers are present in this case.

We are faced with the argument that prohibition of possession of obscene materials is a necessary incident to statutory schemes prohibiting distribution. That argument is based on alleged difficulties of proving an intent to distribute or in producing evidence of actual distribution. We are not convinced that such difficulties exist, but even if they did we do not think that they would justify infringement of the individual's right to read or observe what he pleases. Because that right is so fundamental to our scheme of individual liberty, its restriction may not be justified by the need to ease the administration of otherwise valid criminal laws.

We hold that the First and Fourteenth Amendments prohibit making mere private possession of obscene material a crime. *Roth* and the cases following that decision are not impaired by today's holding. As we have said, the States retain broad power to regulate obscenity; that power simply does not extend to mere possession by the individual in the privacy of his own home.[10]

The same right to privacy is opposed to the overreach of the criminal law in a case involving sodomy. This is *Cotner* v. *Henry*.[11] Cotner was convicted under Indiana's sodomy statute; while imprisoned under a two-to-fourteen-year sentence, he sought federal *habeas corpus* relief. The U.S. Court of Appeals, Seventh Circuit, made this comment:*

Cotner attacks the Indiana Sodomy Statute on the grounds that it violates Article I, Sec. 12 of the Indiana Constitution, and the Fourteenth Amendment of the United States Constitution, because it is vague and because, as applied, it violates his right of privacy under the Supreme Court decision in *Griswold* v. *State of Connecticut*, 381 U.S. 479 (1965). In *Griswold* the Supreme Court recognized a constitutional right to marital privacy and held that the right is violated by the imposition of criminal sanctions for the use of birth control devices by married couples. The import of the Griswold decision is that private, consensual, marital relations are protected from regulation by the state through the use of a criminal penalty. No appellate court in Indiana has had the opportunity to interpret the Indiana Sodomy Statute in light of its potential application to the privacy of married couples. Under *Griswold* Indiana courts could not interpret the statute constitutionally as making private consensual physical relations

*Extracts only; footnotes and citations are deleted.

between married persons a crime absent a clear showing that the state had an interest in preventing such relations, which outweighed the constitutional right to marital privacy. The Indiana courts might, however, construe the statute as being inapplicable to married couples or as outlawing such physical relations between married couples only when accomplished by force. Under the latter interpretation, the protection of the *Griswold* rule would not be available to Cotner if there was a showing that Cotner employed force.

Cotner was charged by his wife, in an affidavit, with the commission of an act of sodomy. The affidavit contained no charge that he used force. He was prosecuted under a statute which prohibits sodomy but which does not explicitly mention force and which no Indiana court has construed as requiring force when applied to married couples in the privacy of the bedroom. The circumstances revealed by the present record show that Cotner was not given adequate notice of any allegation, or any need of an allegation, of force, or of a defense of consent. The charge was merely read to him.

He was allowed to waive his right to counsel and to plead guilty without being informed that there was a substantial question later revealed by *Griswold*, whether certain acts by married persons with mutual consent can constitutionally be prohibited by the state.

Because of these circumstances, Cotner's conviction must be vacated as based on a plea of guilty which was not made with a full understanding of the charge against him.

The decision of the district court is *reversed* and the cause is remanded with instructions to grant the writ and order that Cotner be released from custody unless the state proceeds with prosecution of its charge within a reasonable time. This procedure could, if prosecution, conviction, and appeal followed, give the Indiana courts an opportunity to resolve the substantial constitutional questions which may be involved in Cotner's case.[12]

## REJECTION OF STATUS CRIMES

The zenith of the overreach of criminal law is the so-called status offenses: crimes for "being." The essential elements of the offenses are not acts done with the requisite intent, but rather a condition: of being a vagrant, drug addict, habitual drunkard, sex offender, or criminal.

At one time this type of legislation was viewed as preventing crime, zeroing in on people as a class, more or less. Judicial decisions have diminished this vague open-end class and there is now a general requirement for evidence of specific acts in vagrancy cases. The crime of being a drug addict was denounced as part of criminal law in *Robinson* v. *California*.[13] Habitual drunkenness is now viewed

primarily as an illness, with arrests for public intoxication more for the protection of the arrestee than the protection of the public. Being a habitual offender of any kind and thus violating a specific law calling for restriction of an offender's liberty or registration of some kind has also been criticized as verging on cruel and unusual punishment.

The core area of the rejection of status legislation is thoroughly explored in the United States Supreme Court's majority opinion in *Robinson*. A California statute made it a misdemeanor punishable by imprisonment for any person to be addicted to the use of narcotics, and, in sustaining petitioner's conviction thereunder, the California courts construed the statute as making the "status" of narcotic addiction a criminal offense for which the offender may be prosecuted at any time before he reforms, even though he has never used or possessed any narcotics within the state and has not been guilty of any antisocial behavior there.

The Court's decision* in *Robinson* held that a state law so construed and applied inflicts a cruel and unusual punishment in violation of the Eighth and Fourteenth Amendments:

> The appellant was convicted after a jury trial in the Municipal Court of Los Angeles. The evidence against him was given by two Los Angeles police officers. Officer Brown testified that he had had occasion to examine the appellant's arms one evening on a street in Los Angeles some four months before the trial. The officer testified that at that time he had observed "scar tissue and discoloration on the inside" of the appellant's right arm, and "what appeared to be numerous needle marks and a scab which was approximately three inches below the crook of the elbow" on the appellant's left arm. The officer also testified that the appellant under questioning had admitted to the occasional use of narcotics.
>
> Officer Landquist testified that he had examined the appellant the following morning in the Central Jail of Los Angeles. The officer stated that at that time he had observed discolorations and scabs on the appellant's arms.
>
> In their brief in this Court counsel for the State have emphasized that it is "the proof of addiction by circumstantial evidence . . . by the tell-tale track of needle marks and scabs over the veins of his arms, that remains the gist of the section."
>
> This statute, therefore, is not one which punishes a person for the use of narcotics, for their purchase, sale, or possession, or for antisocial or disorderly behavior resulting from their administration. It is not a law which even purports to provide or require medical treatment. Rather, we deal with a statute which makes the "status" of narcotics addiction a criminal offense, for which the offender may be prosecuted "at any time before he reforms."

*Extracts only; footnotes and citations are deleted.

California has said that a person can be continuously guilty of this offense, whether or not he has ever used or possessed any narcotics within the State, and whether or not he has been guilty of any antisocial behavior there.

It is unlikely that any State at this moment in history would attempt to make it a criminal offense for a person to be mentally ill, or a leper, or to be afflicted with a venereal disease. A State might determine that the general health and welfare require that the victims of these and other human afflictions be dealt with by compulsory treatment, involving quarantine, confinement, or sequestration. But, in the light of contemporary human knowledge, a law which made a criminal offense of such a disease would doubtless be universally thought to be an infliction of cruel and unusual punishment in violation of the Eighth and Fourteenth Amendments.

We cannot but consider the statute before us as of the same category. In this Court counsel for the State recognized that narcotic addiction is an illness. (In its brief the appellee stated: "Of course it is generally conceded that a narcotic addict, particularly one addicted to the use of heroin, is in a state of mental and physical illness. So is an alcoholic." Thirty-seven years ago this Court recognized that persons addicted to narcotics "are diseased and proper subjects for medical treatment." *Linder* v. *United States*, 268 U.S. 5, 18 (1925). Indeed, it is apparently an illness which can be contracted innocently or involuntarily. (Not only may addiction innocently result from the use of medically prescribed narcotics, but a person may even be a narcotics addict from the moment of his birth.)

*We hold that a state law which imprisons a person thus afflicted as a criminal, even though he has never touched any narcotic drug within the State or been guilty of any irregular behavior there, inflicts a cruel and unusual punishment in violation of the Fourteenth Amendment.* [Emphasis added.] To be sure, imprisonment for ninety days is not, in the abstract, a punishment which is either cruel or unusual. But the question cannot be considered in the abstract. Even one day in prison would be a cruel and unusual punishment for the "crime" of having a common cold.[14]

## FAIR NOTICE

The constitutional requirement of definitiveness is violated by a criminal statute that fails to give a person of ordinary intelligence fair notice that his or her contemplated conduct is forbidden by statute. In other words, no person should be held criminally responsible for conduct which he could not reasonably understand to be proscribed.[15]

Fair notice requires that a statute have an apparently clear

meaning. When there is a new and unusual interpretation of the meaning of a statute, there must be an accompanying notice of this new construction of a specific law.

The case of *Bouie* v. *Columbia*[16] is illustrative. Bouie was one of several black sit-in demonstrators during the struggle for civil rights for all citizens. Bouie and his associates entered a drug store in Columbia, South Carolina, and took seats in the restaurant section without any notice from the proprietor that blacks would not be served. Upon such notice, Bouie and his friends refused to leave, as requested, and they were arrested and convicted under state law for criminal trespass. Their convictions were affirmed by the South Carolina Supreme Court, but *the U.S. Supreme Court held that any retroactive application of judicial construction of a statute was violative of the due process clause of the Fourteenth Amendment, as citizens are not afforded fair warning that the conduct now specified as unlawful was prohibited.*

The case of *Papachristou* v. *Jacksonville*[17] involved eight defendants who were convicted in a Florida municipal court of violating a Jacksonville (Florida) vagrancy ordinance. The majority opinion states:*

> Those generally implicated by the imprecise terms of the ordinance—poor people, nonconformists, dissenters, idlers—may be required to comport themselves according to the life-style deemed appropriate by the Jacksonville police and the courts. Where, as here, there are no standards governing the exercise of the discretion granted by the ordinance, the scheme permits and encourages an arbitrary and discriminatory enforcement of law. It furnishes a convenient tool for harsh and discriminatory enforcement by local prosecuting officials, against particular groups deemed to merit their displeasure. It results in a regime in which the poor and the unpopular are permitted to stand on a public sidewalk only at the whim of any police officer.
>
> A presumption that people who might walk or loaf or loiter or stroll or frequent houses where liquor is sold, or who are supported by their wives, or who look suspicious to the police are to become future criminals is too precarious for a rule of law. The implicit presumption in these generalized vagrancy standards— that crime is being nipped in the bud—is too extravagant to deserve extended treatment. Of course, they are nets making easy the roundup of so-called undesirables. But the rule of law implies equality and justice in its application. Vagrancy laws of the Jacksonville type teach that the scales of justice are so tipped that even-handed administration of the law is not possible. The rule of law, evenly applied to minorities as well as majorities, to the poor as well as the rich, is the great mucilage that holds society together.[18]

*Extracts only; footnotes and citations are deleted.

# PRE-EMPTION

In some areas, federal legislation can make clear it intends no regulation except its own. The test of the applicability of state laws is whether the matter on which the state asserts the right to act is in any way regulated by a federal act. If it is, the federal scheme prevails though it is a more modest, less pervasive regulatory plan than that of the state. The question in each case is what the purpose of Congress was. There is an assumption that the historic police powers of the states were not to be superseded by any federal act unless that was the clear and manifest purpose of Congress. Such a purpose may be evidenced in several ways. The scheme of federal regulation may be so pervasive as to make reasonable the inference that Congress left no room for the states to supplement it. Or, the act of Congress may touch a field in which the federal interest is so dominant that the federal system will be assumed to preclude enforcement of state laws on the same subject. Likewise, the object sought to be obtained by the federal law and the character of obligations imposed by it may reveal the same purpose. Or, the state policy may produce a result inconsistent with the objective of the federal statute.[19]

State law takes precedence over county or municipal local laws when both state and local lawmaking bodies enact legislation in the same area. Generally, this rule of pre-emption makes state law supreme when the area involved is one in which the state, by legislation, occupies the entire area; the local law is in conflict with existing state law; or the area has developed a state-wide application and can no longer be considered an area for local laws.

# OPPOSITION TO EXCESSIVE PENALTIES

In eighteenth-century England the death penalty was imposed for many crimes, even petty theft and pickpocketing. When public opinion is opposed to the penalty provisions of a law, the members of the trial jury react and roadblock the penalty, either by a verdict of not guilty despite adequate evidence of guilt, or a verdict of guilt to a lesser degree of the crime charged—when this is possible. When public opinion is not opposed, but the good order of the community may be in issue, judicial options are likely to reflect opposition to excessive penalties.

The case of *Furman* v. *Georgia*[20] is illustrative of judicial opposition to such penalties. In *Furman* three cases were consolidated for review by the United States Supreme Court (*Furman* v. *Georgia*, *Jackson* v. *Georgia*, and *Branch* v. *Texas*). In these three cases the death penalty was imposed, one of them for murder and two for rape. In each the determination of whether the penalty should be death or a lighter punishment was left by the state to the discretion of the judge or of the jury. In each of the three cases the trial was by a jury. Their route to the United States Supreme Court was pe-

titions for *certiorari*, which were granted but limited to the question of whether the imposition and execution of the death penalty constitute "cruel and unusual punishment" within the meaning of the Eighth Amendment as applied to the states by the Fourteenth.

*It was the Court's holding that imposition and carrying out of the death penalty in these cases would be cruel and unusual punishment in violation of the Eighth and Fourteenth Amendments.* The Court noted that the requirement of due process which bans cruel and unusual punishment is now settled; and it is also settled that the proscription of cruel and unusual punishments forbids the judicial imposition of them as well as their imposition by the legislature.

The history of the Eighth Amendment's ban against cruel and unusual punishment goes back to the cruel-and-unusual-punishments clause of the English Bill of Rights of 1689. Justice Marshall's concurring opinion* in *Furman* quoted a legal historian who noted:

"This . . . was, first, an objection to the imposition of punishments that were unauthorized by statute and outside the jurisdiction of the sentencing court, and second, a reiteration of the English policy against disproportionate penalties."

Whether the English Bill of Rights' prohibition against cruel and unusual punishments is properly read as a response to excessive or illegal punishments, as a reaction to barbaric and objectionable modes of punishment, or as both, there is no doubt whatever that in borrowing the language and in including it in the Eighth Amendment, our Founding Fathers intended to outlaw torture and other cruel punishments.

The precise language used in the Eighth Amendment first appeared in America on June 12, 1776, in Virginia's "Declaration of Rights," Section 9 of which read: "That excessive bail ought not to be required, nor excessive fines imposed, nor cruel and unusual punishments inflicted." This language was drawn verbatim from the English Bill of Rights of 1689. Other States adopted similar clauses, and there is evidence in the debates of the various state conventions that were called upon to ratify the Constitution of great concern for the omission of any prohibition against torture or other cruel punishments.[21]

*Weems* v. *United States*[22] is a landmark case because it represents the first time that the Court invalidated a penalty prescribed by a legislature for a particular offense. The Court made it plain beyond any reasonable doubt that excessive punishments were as objectionable as those that were inherently cruel. Weems, an officer of the Bureau of Coast Guard and Transportation of the United States Government of the Philippine Islands, was convicted of fal-

*Extracts only; footnotes and citations are deleted.

sifying a "public and official document." He was sentenced to fifteen years' incarceration at hard labor with chains on his ankles, to an unusual loss of his civil rights, and to perpetual surveillance. Called upon to determine whether this was a cruel and unusual punishment, the Court found that it was. (The prohibition against cruel and unusual punishments relevant to *Weems* was that found in the Philippine Bill of Rights. It was, however, borrowed from the Eighth Amendment to the United States Constitution and had the same meaning.) The Court emphasized that the Constitution was not an ephemeral enactment, or one designed to meet passing occasions. Recognizing that time works changes and brings into existence new conditions and purposes, the Court commented that in the application of a constitution our contemplation cannot be only of what has been but of what may be. In striking down the penalty imposed on Weems, the Court examined the punishment in relation to the offense, compared the punishment to those inflicted for other crimes and to those imposed in other jurisdictions, and concluded that the punishment was excessive.

# NOTES

1. Edwin M. Schur, *Crimes Without Victims* (Englewood Cliffs, N.J.: Prentice-Hall, Inc., 1970).
2. Norval Morris and Gordon Hawkins, *The Honest Politician's Guide to Crime Control* (Chicago: University of Chicago Press, 1970), p. 2.
3. Robert Maynard Hutchins, ed., Great Books of the Western World (Chicago, London, Toronto: Encyclopedia Britannica, Inc., 1952), vol. 43, *American State Papers, the Federalist*, J. S. Mill, pp. 271–72. *See also* "Limiting the State's Police Power: Judicial Reaction to John Stuart Mill," 37 *University of Chicago Law Review*, no. 3 (1969–70), pp. 605–27.
4. 381 U.S. 479 (1965).
5. *Griswold* v. *Connecticut*, 381 U.S. 479 (1965).
6. Morris and Hawkins, pp. 2–28.
7. Schur, p. 169.
8. 394 U.S. 557 (1969).
9. 354 U.S. 476 (1957).
10. *Stanley* v. *Georgia*, 394 U.S. 557 (1969).
11. 394 F. 2d 873 (1968).
12. *Cotner* v. *Henry*, 394 F. 2d 873 (1968).
13. 370 U.S. 660 (1962).
14. *Robinson* v. *California*, 370 U.S. 660 (1962).
15. *United States* v. *Harriss*, 347 U.S. 612 (1954).
16. 378 U.S. 347 (1964).
17. 405 U.S. 156 (1972).
18. *Papachristou* v. *Jacksonville*, 405 U.S. 156 (1972).
19. *Rice* v. *Santa Fe Elevator Corp.*, 331 U.S. 218 (1947).
20. 408 U.S. 238 (1972).
21. *Furman* v. *Georgia*, 408 U.S. 238 (1972); Justice Marshall concurring.
22. 217 U.S. 349 (1910).

# 6
# PARTIES TO CRIME

## OBJECTIVES
*This chapter will reveal the thrust of statutory law to overcome the common-law distinction between parties to criminal offenses and to designate all persons concerned in the commission of a crime as principals; and to limit the definition of* accessory *to the post-crime period: accessory after the fact of the crime.*

## LEGAL TERMS
Misprision. *A term denoting contempt against the government; maladministration of* high public office; failure in the duty of a citizen to prevent and/or report crime to the proper authorities. Misprision of felony *is the offense of concealing a felony committed by another.*
Lewd. *Obscene, lustful, indecent, lecherous; usually linked with* lascivious *as in* lewd and lascivious conduct: gross indecency, gross and wanton indecency in sexual relations, and open and illicit sexual intercourse.
Con. *Used to modify* game *or* games, *this term is an abbreviation for* confidence, *as in the term* confidence game.

## QUESTIONS FOR STUDY
*1. Describe the problems of prosecuting criminal offenses under the common-law classification of parties to crime.*

*2. Simply stated, who are principals to a crime?*

*3. Does contemporary statutory law require appearance at the crime scene to qualify as a principal to a crime?*

*4. What is the extent of the liability of a person acting in concert with another to commit a crime?*

*5. Develop the theme that one who aids and abets another in the commission of a crime is a principal.*

*6. What is the basic difference between being a principal to a crime and being a post-crime accessory?*

7. *Under federal law what is the difference between the crime of being an accessory after the fact and misprision of felony?*

8. *What areas of the public interest are served by criminally punishing such post-crime assistance to criminals as harboring felons and compounding a crime?*

---

**C**lassification of, and distinction between, the parties to felonies (except treason) was extensive under the common law. Principals in the first degree were the actual perpetrators of a crime, the "actors" who caused the crime; a principal in the second degree was an accomplice actually present who aided in its commission with the same criminal intent; an accessory before the fact was one who aided and abetted, but who was not present at the crime scene at the time of the crime's occurrence; and an accessory after the fact was the person who helped the offender escape from justice in some affirmative fashion. In treason cases, the common law merged the four categories common to felonies and all were considered principals. These classifications were also true of offenses less than felonies (our present misdemeanors).

This classification of parties to a felony under the common law led to many problems in prosecuting offenders. Indictments had to allege the correct role of the person charged, and the conviction of the accessory depended upon a conviction of the perpetrator/principal in the crime. Legislatures have changed the criminal liability laws to a simple categorization of "principal": the recognition of crime as a joint action of crime partners acting in concert.

The category of accessory after the fact has not been amended to any great extent by contemporary statutes. In some jurisdictions it is linked to misprision of felony, a more serious dependent crime linked to an affirmative act obstructing justice or concealing a crime; or a compounding of a felony for money or other pecuniary benefit.

## PRINCIPALS TO CRIME

Contemporary statutes usually define a principal to a crime as any person who directly commits an offense, aids, and abets its commission, or someone who, though not present, has advised and encouraged its commission.

Accomplices are those persons who are principals to a crime when more than a single principal is involved.

Title 18, U.S. Code, Section 2, defines a principal to a crime:

> (a) Whoever commits an offense against the United States or aids, abets, counsels, commands, induces or procures its commission, is punishable as a principal.

(b) Whoever willfully causes an act to be done which if directly performed by him or another would be an offense against the United States, is punishable as a principal.

In *Maupin v. United States*,[1] the United States Court of Appeals (Tenth Circuit) *affirmed* the judgment of lower courts despite an appeal alleging Maupin was not a principal but only aided and abetted the crime for which he was convicted. *Sentence on a federal charge of bank robbery, the court held, was not void, though evidence showed that petitioner was an aider and abettor to such crime, as an aider and abettor is a principal under statute* (Title 18, U.S. Code, Section 2).

James C. Oldham and Ivan Leeper, Jr., were jointly charged with burglariously entering a motel and robbing and kidnapping three individuals in the state of Idaho. They appealed their conviction and sentence for burglary, robbery, and kidnapping. One of their claims was that the weapon used in the robbery was admitted in evidence against Oldham, but not Leeper. Therefore, Leeper claimed he was less than a principal in the robbery. The court commented:

Appellants maintain that the court erred in failing to grant them separate trials upon the charges brought against them. They reason that Leeper was prejudiced by the joint trial because the twenty-two-caliber automatic was admitted in evidence as to appellant Oldham but excluded as to Leeper. According to appellants' theory, were separate trials to have been granted, the charge of robbery might have been defeated as against Leeper because its instrumentality, the pistol, had been excluded as to him. The granting of separate trials is discretionary with the court, and in the absence of showing an abuse of such discretion it will not be disturbed on appeal.

The distinction between an accessory before the fact and a principal, and between principals in the first and second degree, in felony cases, has been abrogated in Idaho. The evidence from the transcript indicates that both participants were *acting in concert* during the entire course of the robbery. Therefore, under the circumstances, the exclusion of the pistol as to appellant Leeper would make little difference as to the charge of robbery brought jointly against appellants especially when appellants *acted in concert*. [Emphasis added.][2]

## TRANSFERRED LIABILITY OF PRINCIPALS

The liability of a defendant in state law violations depends upon the specific wording of a state's penal code. There is liability for a person acting in concert with another even though the other involved in the crime has not been charged with or prosecuted for the offense; has been acquitted of the offense; has been convicted of another

offense, lacked the culpable mental state required for the offense, was immune or otherwise exempt from prosecution for the offense; or if the offense could only have been directly committed by a member of a particular class of persons to which the defendant does not belong.

The mastermind of a robbery can be found guilty of robbery even though the gunman has not been prosecuted or convicted. In fact, many jurisdictions allow prosecution of a person as an aider and abettor even though the person could not do an act necessary to commission of the offense. For example, a female cannot commit rape, but if she aids and abets a male person in the act, she will not be excluded from liability as a principal because of her sex.

Mrs. Ethyl Smith was prosecuted on charges of rape and lewd and lascivious conduct allegedly committed against her thirteen-year-old daughter. Mrs. Smith appealed her conviction of the crime of rape. The facts reveal that Mrs. Smith and James R. Jenkins were charged in four counts of an indictment with lewd and lascivious conduct and rape alleged to have been committed against the person of Carol Jean Love, Mrs. Smith's daughter, on or about August 16 and August 17, 1961. Nine other counts were charged against Jenkins alone. Jenkins had had sexual intercourse with Carol many times commencing when Carol was nine years old, but did so in somewhat clandestine fashion. Mrs. Smith suspected what was happening, but proof of direct knowledge on her part prior to August 16, 1961, could only rest on circumstantial inferences. No criminal charges are made against her as to any event occurring prior to that date. On August 16, 1961, Jenkins, Carol, and appellant went to Tijuana, in Baja California, Mexico, and visited a marriage broker. The marriage broker was the secretary of a lawyer, but had no authority to perform a marriage ceremony. Carol's age was misrepresented to him to be fifteen years. Acts of sexual intercourse took place between Carol and Jenkins on August 16 and 17, 1961. Defendants Smith and Jenkins did not contend that any applicable exception to the minimum-age requirement existed.

The appellate court *affirmed* the trial court's conviction of Mrs. Smith of the crime of rape. The opinion of the court gave this rationale for its decision:

> Appellant's defense is based principally on her assertion of a good faith belief in the validity of the purported marriage of August 16, 1961, at Tijuana. She testified in substance that the intercourse of Jenkins and Carol prior to August 1961 was concealed from her; that they told her they were going to marry; that she tried to prevent it; that they said they would marry without her consent; that because of this she went to Mexico with them, consented to but did not affirmatively participate in the falsifi-

cation of her daughter's age; and she believed they were legally married.

Appellant admits that conviction as a principal is proper on the theory of aiding and abetting, even though she could not herself have directly committed the act. But, she contends, in the role of aider and abettor, proof of guilty knowledge and specific intent is required under the circumstances here present.

The fact that she willfully falsified or knowingly permitted Carol's age to be falsified, coupled with her laxity in Carol's supervision after she at least suspected Jenkin's sexual connections with Carol, may have caused the jury to place no faith in her testimony. It was not required to believe her. Under the circumstances, they could reasonably have been convinced that the whole marriage plan was sham. A sham marriage is no defense to rape. There is no reason to distinguish in the case of a minor. *Willful participation by appellant, with knowledge that there was, in truth, no marriage, would under the other circumstances here present, be sufficient to support the verdict and judgment.* [Emphasis added.]

Appellant next contends that acquittal of Jenkins on the charge of rape automatically bars conviction of appellant because Jenkins was the male participant and appellant only the aider and abettor. Under some circumstances the rule urged by appellant would be applicable, but not under those here present. No rule can be applied blindly. Each must fit the facts. In the case here at bar the jury found Jenkins guilty as charged in several of the indictments relating to lewd and lascivious conduct (a greater inclusive offense), and appellant was found guilty as charged in two counts of rape.[3]

## ACTING IN CONCERT

There is an equality of guilt whenever individuals act in concert to perpetrate a crime. In *State* v. *Owen*, the reviewing court ruled *against an attempt of one of the participants in a crime to claim "accessory" rather than "principal" status.* William L. Owen and Kenneth R. Hastings, each armed with a gun and intent on robbery, entered a grocery store. The grocer resisted Owen's threats and display of a gun and Owen shot and killed him. There is a conflict as to which robber left the store first or whether they exited together; they fled immediately following the shooting. Owen and Hastings were found guilty of first-degree murder. They appealed. Hastings filed a supplementary brief claiming his exit was before the shooting and he thus was only an accessory. The court noted:

These assignments of error are based upon the contention that, since he did not do the actual killing, the essentials of mal-

ice, premeditation and deliberation on his part was that imposed by law because of his participation in the attempt to commit robbery; and that, since the evidence shows that he had withdrawn and left the premises prior to the shooting, he could not be charged and convicted upon evidence which otherwise would be sufficient against an accessory. Section 19–1430, Idaho Code, provides:

"The distinction between an accessory before the fact and a principal and between principals in the first and second degree, in cases of felony, is abrogated; and all persons concerned in the commission of a felony, whether they directly commit the act constituting the offense, or aid and abet in its commission, though not present, shall hereafter be prosecuted, tried, and punished as principals, and no other facts need be alleged in any indictment against such an accessory than are required in an indictment against his principal."

Under this section Hastings was properly charged, tried and convicted as a principal. There is a dispute in the evidence as to whether he had left the premises before the fatal shot was fired or at about the same time. This was a question for the jury. But, assuming that he was a few paces ahead of Owen in flight, would that fact relieve him? *We think not. He was equal in guilt with Owen.* [Emphasis added.][4]

The case of *State* v. *So*, an involved fraud, illustrates the joint action by participants in a crime acting in concert. Mr. So appealed his larceny conviction and complained, in part, that he was not a "real" principal. The facts in the *So* case are the traditional unfolding of a "con" game in which Mr. So, Mr. Montana, and a person only identified as "the Filipino," or Johnny, jointly defrauded Mr. Okamura. Mr. So, a cook by occupation, left Denver, together with Mr. Montana and the Filipino, en route to Pocatello. Mr. So testified that he was employed by Mr. Montana to make the trip. Leaving Denver on April 3, 1949, they drove directly to Pocatello and registered at the Benson Hotel on the evening of April 4. On April 5, Mr. Montana, who had a slight acquaintance with the victim (Mr. Okamura), contacted him by telephone and renewed the acquaintance. Meetings were arranged with him as part of the build-up and come-along for what happened thereafter. Eventually Mr. Montana asked Mr. Okamura if he would claim ownership of, and deliver a package to be brought in by a sea captain, or his emissary from Europe, represented to contain valuable articles, supposedly jewelry. These articles were to be delivered and sold by Mr. Okamura to a money baron from San Francisco. Following numerous talks Mr. Okamura consented. Mr. Montana thereafter advised Mr. Okamura in substance that the would-be purchaser of the articles had arrived,

and was staying at the Bannock Hotel, and arranged a meeting between Mr. Okamura and the said person.

On April 11, Mr. Montana and Mr. Okamura, in Okamura's car, parked across the street from the Bannock Hotel. A guest of the hotel came out and got in the car; it was Mr. So, who was then identified to Mr. Okamura as the money baron, being introduced to Okamura as Tom Wong. The three parties then drove down the street, parked the car, and Mr. So, alias Tom Wong, inquired about the stuff, and said, "Did you get your stuff—did you get your business done with?" Mr. Montana said he did not have the stuff, but could get it in a short while, and Mr. So said, "Hurry and get it, as I am anxious to leave town. I want to get out." Mr. Montana exhibited a small package, advising Mr. So, alias Tom Wong, that he had fifty more just like it, to which Mr. So, after examining, or pretending to examine, the package replied, "That is fine stuff," and further said, "I am anxious to leave town. I want to get out . . . I brought plenty of money along with me to make the deal, and I want to get it over with quick." Mr. So then took an envelope from his pocket, showed some money and said, "I have fifty thousand dollars here. Take me back to the Bannock Hotel until you get the stuff, then come back and pick me up."

Mr. So was driven back to the hotel and Okamura and Mr. Montana drove to the depot. Mr. Montana introduced Mr. Okamura to the Filipino, who had suddenly appeared as Johnny. Whether Johnny was the emissary of the mysterious sea captain was undetermined. At any rate, he acted as the contact man. The Filipino and Mr. Montana then talked together. Thereupon, Mr. Montana advised Mr. Okamura he did not think he could make the deal, i.e., the purchase, as he did not have enough money; that he was short of cash. The Filipino, being advised by Mr. Montana of the situation, left to interview the mysterious captain, or his emissary, as to the terms of the transaction, and the Filipino later returned and advised Mr. Montana that the captain wanted to get to Seattle to dispose of the package, and any deal made would have to be done quickly. Mr. Montana then requested Mr. Okamura to advance him $6,000 to make the deal, i.e., purchase the supposed jewelry from the sea captain. The contraband, or whatever it was, would then be sold to Mr. So, and Mr. Okamura would get his money back. Mr. Montana advised Mr. Okamura he would make it right with him. Mr. Okamura then raised $5,000 to help make the purchase from the mythical sea captain.

The next morning, April 12, Mr. Okamura and Mr. Montana went again to the depot, and the same parties were present at the meeting as the day before. The Filipino then had, or pretended to have, another alleged talk with the never seen, mysterious captain, or his emissary, and advised Mr. Okamura and Mr. Montana that

the deal could be closed for $14,000, the balance of $1,000 to be paid later. A package was then produced by the Filipino, and he and Mr. Montana put it in one of the depot lockers. Mr. Montana then paid, or pretended to pay the Filipino $9,000, as representative of the said sea captain, and Mr. Okamura advanced $5,000 to the Filipino for the same purpose.

At this point, the Filipino, after receiving Mr. Okamura's money, disappeared as mysteriously as he had originally appeared, and as far as the transcript shows, departed for parts unknown, and has not been seen or heard from since.

Mr. Montana and Mr. Okamura then went to the Bannock Hotel about noon, April 12, to sell the package to the money baron (Mr. So) for the price fixed. Mr. So, however, had checked out (April 12, 1949) leaving a note that he had gone to Salt Lake City and would be back that night. Hence he could not be located at that time. Mr. Montana then gave Mr. Okamura the key to the locker in the depot in which the package of supposed valuables had been deposited, for the purpose of allaying his misgivings and satisfying him that he was fully protected. Together they then went to a place in Pocatello to play pool. During a temporary absence of Mr. Oka-mura, Mr. Montana, like the seldom seen Filipino, disappeared as quickly as Mr. Okamura's money, leaving no forwarding address. Testimony as to the flight of these crime partners indicated that Mr. Montana and Mr. So, immediately following the victimization of Mr. Okamura, left Pocatello together in Mr. So's car.

The court's opinion contained, in the following selected parts, these conclusions:

> The common law distinction between classes of parties to criminal offenses is abolished. All persons concerned in the commission of a crime are principals, and one who aids and abets another in the commission of a crime is a principal.
>
> No reference to accused as an accessory is necessary. Nor is it necessary that facts be set out showing whether the accused was an accessory or a principal.
>
> An accessory to a crime, or a participant therein may be charged as a principal, and the information need not allege facts different from those required to be alleged against the principal.
>
> In the conspiracy depicted in this case Mr. Montana posed and represented himself as the alleged purchaser or would-be pur-chaser of contrabands, or other valuable articles, brought in, or to be brought in, from Europe, by the mythical sea captain, or his emissary; the Filipino posed as a representative or emissary of said sea captain; Mr. So as the tycoon and big money man from San Francisco, and as the intended purchaser from Mr. Montana and Mr. Okamura, of the contraband articles. The transaction

having been completed and the money secured, Mr. Okamura was left holding the bag—in this case the box—which was represented to contain jewelry or other valuables.

*That the appellant* [Mr. So], *Montana and the Filipino* [Johnny] *acted in concert and that there was a preconceived plan or design, was fully established.* [Emphasis added.][5]

# ACCESSORY AFTER THE FACT

The concept of being a post-crime accessory is still viable in criminal law. After the fact of a crime, one having knowledge that the principal has committed, been charged with, or convicted of the felony and who conceals or aids him with the intent that such principal to a felony may avoid or escape from arrest, trial, conviction, or punishment is an accessory to the felony of the principal. Most jurisdictions provide for a lesser punishment for this dependent crime. Jurisdictions are divided in their requirements that the principal crime must be a felony, or may be any offense.

Federal law is illustrative of the role of accessory after the fact to any offense and the diminishing of penalty for such behavior. The federal crime of misprision of felony broadens the scope of dependent crimes. The text of these two provisions of federal law are:

### ACCESSORY AFTER THE FACT

Whoever, knowing that an offense against the United States has been committed, receives, relieves, comforts, or assists the offender in order to hinder or prevent his apprehension, trial or punishment, is an accessory after the fact.

Except as otherwise provided by any Act of Congress, an accessory after the fact shall be imprisoned not more than one-half the maximum term of imprisonment or fined not more than one-half the maximum fine prescribed for the punishment of the principal, or both; or if the principal is punishable by death, the accessory shall be imprisoned not more than ten years. (Title 18, U.S. Code, Section 3.)

### MISPRISION OF FELONY

Whoever, having knowledge of the actual commission of a felony cognizable by a court of the United States, conceals and does not as soon as possible make known the same to some judge or other person in civil or military authority under the United States, shall be fined not more than $500 or imprisoned not more than three years, or both. (Title 18, U.S. Code, Section 4.)

William S. Neal was indicted, tried and convicted upon both counts of an indictment containing two counts, and he appealed. The first count of the indictment charged defendant with being an accessory after the fact to a felony committed by John L. Neal and

the second count charged misprision of the same felony committed by John L. Neal. The defendant and John L. Neal are brothers. At all times material to this case they lived in Minneapolis, Minnesota. The defendant was married and operated an undertaking establishment. His brother John was a bachelor and lived in defendant's home. John had been employed as a clerk or messenger in the office of the treasurer of the Soo Line Railroad at Minneapolis for thirty-two years prior to December 28, 1937. In February, 1938, John was indicted in the United States District Court of Minnesota and charged in ten counts with stealing and carrying away various sums of money from the First National Bank and Trust Company of Minneapolis. He pleaded guilty on five counts and was sentenced to fifteen years in a penitentiary.

The indictment upon which the defendant was tried referred to John L. Neal as principal, or the one who committed the primary felony, and the defendant was charged with the dependent offenses of accessory after the fact and misprision of felony.

In the first count the crime of which the defendant was accused is that he, knowing that the principal had committed and completed the felony above described, became an accessory after the fact thereto in that he aided and assisted the principal in secreting the fruits and proceeds of the felony by clandestinely placing $5,903 of the stolen money in a golf bag in his living quarters, thus suppressing important evidence to the end that the principal might escape punishment.

In the second count it was alleged that the defendant committed the crime of misprision of felony in that with full knowledge of the felony committed by John L. Neal he concealed and failed to disclose and make known such felony as soon as might be possible to some one of the judges of the United States District Court of Minnesota or to the Attorney General of the United States or to the United States Attorney or to other persons in civil authority.

It was further charged that the defendant took two affirmative steps to conceal the crime committed by his brother John: first, he concealed $5,903 of the stolen money in a golf bag at his living quarters; and, second, he altered and expunged from the account books of the Neal Funeral Home operated by him entries showing the investment therein by John L. Neal of the stolen monies.

The Court's opinion reveals the rationale for *reversing* the lower court's decision:

> The serious question under count one of the indictment is whether there is substantial evidence to support the charge that the defendant aided and assisted the principal to escape punishment by suppressing evidence against him by concealing the $5,903 found in the old iron box in a golf bag. The charge in the

indictment is that the defendant concealed $5,903 which consti-
tuted a large part of the fruits and proceeds of the offense of the
principal and was important evidence against him. The proof does
not show when the $5,903 was placed in the old iron box by John.
John's salary was only $140 a month. Over a period of seven years
he stole approximately $118,000. During 1937 he stole $53,000
of this sum, and after August 24th of that year he had taken approximately $18,000 of the amount. The money stolen prior to
August 24, 1937, did not constitute a federal offense, and the
stealing of money prior to that date (effective date of statute making such theft a federal offense) is not charged to be a crime in
the indictment. The defendant's testimony is that when he opened
the iron box on December 28, 1937, the paper money contained
in it appeared to be old and was covered with a thick layer of dust.

The first alleged act, that the defendant concealed $5,903 of
the money stolen by John L. Neal between August 24 and December 28, 1937, is not, as shown above, supported by the
evidence.

Neither is the second alleged affirmative act of the defendant to conceal the crime of John L. Neal supported by substantial
evidence. That charge is that the defendant expunged from the
books of the funeral home the entries showing John L. Neal's in-
vestment of the stolen moneys in that business. There are only
two entries in the books showing investments of John L. Neal in
the funeral business after August 24, 1937. One of these shows
that on October 15, 1937, he "advanced" $125 and the other that
on October 19th he "advanced" the further sum of $100. There
is no evidence whatever connecting these sums with the money
unlawfully taken and carried away from the bank; and the amount
is not sufficient to raise a presumption of fact that they were not
honest savings from his salary.

The basis in the evidence upon which the charge is founded
is that the defendant did on December 29, 1937, instruct the
bookkeeper to delete John L. Neal's name from the entries in the
books. His name or his initials appeared in connection with certain entries on about 30 different sheets of the books. The bookkeeper took these sheets home with him and copied them sub-
stituting for the name or initials of John L. Neal other explanations
such as "administration fees" or "W. Squire Neal." He returned
them to the office of the funeral home on December 31, 1937. He
then took the original sheets home with him without the defendant's knowledge and made a second copy for himself. The orig-
inals were returned to the office on February 17, 1938, and placed
in the books, where they remained and were produced at the trial
unaltered. The defendant did not direct that the original sheets
be destroyed.

The government argues that for a few days after December 27, 1937, the defendant aided in concealing John L. Neal, and that he is therefore guilty of misprision of felony. The evidence shows that he did know where John was in hiding and may have advised with him about escaping, but failure to inform the officers is not sufficient alone to constitute a crime under the statute.[6]

In the 1930s John Dillinger terrorized the banks of the Midwest. His trail of robbery and murder made him the most wanted and publicized criminal of his day. Dillinger decided on surgery to change his appearance and to alter his fingerprints. He persuaded a Mr. Piquett to perform the surgery and Piquett was prosecuted and convicted as an accessory after the fact.[7]

A person who harbors, conceals, or assists in concealing a known felon or a person wanted for a felony, with knowledge he is, or is wanted by police as, a felon, with the intent that such principal escape or avoid arrest, trial, conviction, or punishment is an accessory after the fact.

A crime, felony, or misdemeanor can be compounded; that is, the party injured receives a bribe or restitution or reparation for loss of injury; or a party who has knowledge of a crime receives a bribe to refrain from reporting the crime. The agreement necessary to this crime is that the pecuniary benefit is given and accepted with the understanding that the act(s) done to conceal the crime is intended to cheat the law of the person of the offender and/or the fruits of the crime.

# NOTES

1. 232 F. 2d 838 (1956).
2. *State* v. *Oldham*, 438 P. 2d 275 (1968, Idaho).
3. *People* v. *Smith*, 204 Cal. App. 2d 797 (1962, Calif.).
4. *State* v. *Owen*, 253 P. 2d 203 (1953, Idaho).
5. *State* v. *So*, 231 P. 2d 734 (1951, Idaho).
6. *Neal* v. *United States*, 102 F. 2d 643 (1939).
7. *Piquett* v. *United States*, 81 F. 2d 75 (1936).

# 7

# CRIMINAL RESPONSIBILITY

## OBJECTIVES

Chapter Seven shows by exclusion the persons who are responsible for criminal behavior by describing the conditions of infancy and insanity that relieve the very young and the legally insane of criminal responsibility; by outlining the circumstances justifying otherwise criminal conduct; and by linking the concept of **mens rea** or guilty mind to criminal responsibility. In addition, the common defenses that may excuse criminal behavior are described and discussed.

## LEGAL TERMS

Majority. *In relation to age this term means full age, the legal age at which an individual may manage his or her own affairs and enjoy civic rights.*

Mens rea. *Guilty mind; criminal intent; wrongful design or purpose.*

Peace officer. *This term may have different definitions in state statutes. Usually it includes municipal and other local police, and deputy sheriffs: the "sworn" personnel of public police agencies (employees of public police agencies who have taken an oath of office).*

Duress. *Compulsion or constraint by which a person is illegally forced to do or forbear from some act.*

En banc. *In full court, or with full judicial authority.*

## QUESTIONS FOR STUDY

1. What is the justification for relieving the very young of criminal responsibility? The legally insane?

2. Describe the M'Naghten test of right versus wrong in determining legal insanity. The Durham or "product" test.

3. Distinguish mental illness from legal insanity.

4. What is the concept of mens rea? Outline its importance in determining criminal responsibility.

5. When is a person justified in otherwise criminal conduct?

6. What prison conditions justify the escape of an imprisoned felon?

7. What is the scope of the defense of self-defense?

8. When is withdrawal a defense? A claim of diminished capacity? A claim of consent?

9. Outline the circumstances justifying a defense of entrapment. What is the "but for" rule in entrapment cases?

10. When is ignorance or mistake operable as a defense to excuse criminal behavior?

---

**U**nless an individual is an infant or an insane person, he or she is responsible for any criminal conduct. However, there is excuse from criminal liability when conduct is in response to authority, emergency, duress, or necessity. Self-defense is a classic exoneration, and other defenses may also limit criminal responsibility.

## INFANCY

Society recognizes extreme immaturity as criminal incapacity. When the physical age of a child is under the age of seven, the child has no criminal responsibility; between the age of seven and fourteen there is a presumption of criminal capacity; and from fourteen to the age of majority—usually twenty-one—there is criminal responsibility. However, state laws usually diminish this responsibility by requiring that juveniles (to age sixteen or eighteen, depending on state law) be charged with "juvenile delinquency" when they commit acts that would be criminal if committed by an adult. In some jurisdictions, murder and other serious crimes may be prosecuted as either a felony or the noncrime of juvenile delinquency.

## INSANITY (MENTAL DISEASE OR DEFECT)

Deficiency of intellect is a form of insanity. While terminology differs in various jurisdictions, the idiot, imbecile, and moron may not have a criminal capacity. Various tests may be used to determine the mental "age" of an individual suspected of being mentally deficient; a score or 50 or less on standard intelligence quotient tests indicates a deficiency of intellect.

The classic right vs. wrong (M'Naghten[1]) test for an individual's claim of insanity calls for a lack of mental capacity to know what he or she was doing at the time of the crime, or inability in-

tellectually to distinguish between right and wrong at such time. It is a *no mind* test.

The accused is obligated to introduce proof if he would overcome the presumption of sanity. Knowledge of right and wrong is the test of criminal responsibility in a majority of American jurisdictions. The science of psychiatry has made tremendous strides since that test was laid down in *M'Naghten's* Case, but the progress of science has not reached a point where its learning requires the states to eliminate the right and wrong test from their criminal law. Moreover, choice of a test of legal sanity involves not only scientific knowledge but questions of basic policy as to the extent to which that knowledge should determine criminal responsibility.[2]

Although most states adhere to the *M'Naghten* doctrine many have modified that doctrine to reflect a growing knowledge in the field of psychiatry. *The terms of the original* M'Naghten *rule were: "To establish a defense on the ground of insanity, it must be clearly proved that, at the time of committing the act, the party accused was laboring under such a defect of reason, from disease of the mind, as not to know the nature and quality of the act he was doing; or if he did know it, that he did not know he was doing what was wrong."* [Emphasis added.][3]

In liberalizing the California *M'Naghten* rule the California Supreme Court in *People* v. *Wolff* said:

> The California courts have not been unresponsive to proposals liberalizing the original language of the M'Naghten rule. In evolving our own rule to meet statutory requirements, to apply humane concepts, and at the same time to protect society, we have reformulated the test with a variety of specifications to achieve this end.[4]

Those specifications are spelled out in the recommended jury instructions on insanity.[5] In summary:

1. **THE DEFENSE OF INSANITY.** Legal insanity means a diseased or deranged condition of the mind which makes a person incapable of knowing or understanding the nature and quality of his act, or makes a person incapable of knowing or understanding that his act was wrong. The defendant has the burden of proving his legal insanity by a preponderance of evidence: such evidence as, when weighed with that opposed to it, has more convincing force and great probability of truth.

2. **MENTAL ILLNESS DISTINGUISHED FROM LEGAL INSANITY.** A person may be mentally ill or abnormal and yet not legally insane. Mental illness or abnormality are not necessarily legal insanity. To be a defense to crime, mental illness or abnormality must make a person incapable of knowing or un-

derstanding the nature and quality of his act, or make him incapable of knowing or understanding that his act was wrong.

3. **INSANITY RESULTING FROM INTOXICATION: DRUGS OR NARCOTICS.** A person whose brain is diseased or damaged because of the use of intoxicating liquor or drugs so that he is incapable of knowing or understanding the nature and quality of his act, or make him incapable of knowing or understanding that his act was wrong, is legally insane.

4. **TEMPORARY INSANITY.** Legal insanity of a short duration (temporary), existing at the time of the commission of the offense charged, is as fully recognized as a defense of legal insanity of a longer duration.

5. **INSANITY: LUCID INTERVALS.** A defendant may be legally insane at times and legally sane at others, but he has the burden of proof by a preponderance of evidence that he was legally insane at the time of the commission of the offense.

6. **INSANITY: IRRESISTIBLE IMPULSE.** A person acts at his peril if he knows and understands the nature and quality of his act and that it is wrong, and it is not a defense that he committed the act under an uncontrollable or irresistible impulse.

The basic modification is a requirement of "understanding" as opposed to a knowledge which can be verbalized but not understood by the defendant. Additional modification with the onset of drug use and abuse problems is seen in the decision of *People* v. *Kelly*:[6] temporary psychosis for several weeks from drug use and abuse is a proper insanity defense, even though the psychosis is not permanent; it is sufficient if the insanity is of a "settled nature" resulting from long and continued intoxication.

There are additional sanity tests which have been given judicial and statutory attention. The most liberal of the tests is referred to as the "product" test and originally surfaced in a New Hampshire case in 1870,[7] but came to life in the Federal District Court of the District of Columbia in 1954 with a defendant named Durham. The Federal Court of Appeals defined the test for insanity *in that Federal District* as:

> *The rule we now hold* must be applied on the retrial of this case and in future cases is not unlike that followed by the New Hampshire court since 1870, *State* v. *Pike*, 40 N.H. 399 (1870). It *is simply that an accused is not criminally responsible if his unlawful act was the product of mental disease or mental defect.* [Emphasis added.]

We use "disease" in the sense of a condition which is considered capable of either improving or deteriorating. We use "defect" in the sense of a condition which is not considered capable of either improving or deteriorating and which may be either con-

genital, or the result of injury, or the residual effect of a physical or mental disease.

Whenever there is "some evidence" that the accused suffered from a diseased or defective mental condition at the time the unlawful act was committed, the trial court must provide the jury with guides for determining whether the accused can be held criminally responsible. We do not, and indeed could not, formulate an instruction which would be either appropriate or binding in all cases. But under the rule now announced, any instruction should in some way convey to the jury the sense and substance of the following: If you the jury believe beyond a reasonable doubt that the accused was not suffering from a diseased or defective mental condition at the time he committed the criminal act charged, you may find him guilty. If you believe he was suffering from a diseased or defective mental condition when he committed the act, but believe beyond a resonable doubt that the act was not the product of such mental abnormality, you may find him guilty. Unless you believe beyond a reasonable doubt either that he was not suffering from a diseased or defective mental condition, or that the act was not the product of such abnormality, you must find the accused not guilty by reason of insanity. Thus your task would not be completed upon finding, if you did find, that the accused suffered from a mental disease or defect. He would still be responsible for his unlawful act if there was no causal connection between such mental abnormality and the act.[8]

The original test was modified in *McDonald* v. *United States*,[9] to require that the jury be told a "mental disease or defect includes any abnormal condition of the mind which substantially affects mental or emotional processes and substantially impairs behavior controls."

The modified test was questioned again in 1967,[10] and finally discarded in the 1972 case of *United States* v. *Brawner*. The court in *Brawner* finally dealt with the disturbing realization that the doctors were making the policy decisions of who should be responsible for crime instead of the legislature or the jury. The problems with the *Durham* test as articulated in *Brawner* were:

We view it more modestly, as the court's effort, designed in the immemorial manner of the case method that has built the common law, to alleviate two serious problems with the previous rule (*M'Naghten*).

The first of these was a problem of language which raised an important symbolic issue in the law. We felt that the language of the old right-wrong/irresistible impulse rule for insanity was antiquated, no longer reflected the community's judgment as to who ought to be held criminally liable for socially destructive

acts. We considered the rule as restated to have more fruitful, accurate and considered reflection of the sensibilities of the community as revised and expanded in the light of continued study of abnormal human behavior.

The second vexing problem that *Durham* was designed to reach related to the concern of the psychiatrists called as expert witnesses for their special knowledge of the problem of insanity, who often and typically felt that they were obliged to reach outside of their professional expertise when they were asked, under the traditional insanity rule established in 1843 by *M'Naghten's Case*, whether the defendant knew right from wrong. They further felt that the narrowness of the traditional test, which framed the issue of responsibility solely in terms of cognitive impairment, made it impossible to convey to the judge and jury the full range of information material to an assessment of defendant's responsibility.

A principal reason for our decision to depart from the *Durham* rule is the undesirable characteristic, surviving even the *McDonald* modification, of undue dominance by the experts giving testimony.

There is, indeed, irony in a situation under which the *Durham* rule, which was adopted in large part to permit experts to testify in their own terms concerning matters within their domain which the jury should know, resulting in testimony by the experts in terms not their own to reflect unexpressed judgments in a domain that is properly not theirs but the jury's. The irony is heightened when the jurymen, instructed under the esoteric "product" standard, are influenced significantly by "product" testimony of expert witnesses really reflecting ethical and legal judgments rather than a conclusion within the witnesses' particular expertise.[11]

The *Brawner* doctrine discards the "product" test and adopts for *that federal district* the provisions of the American Law Institute's Model Penal Code segment on the defense of insanity as modified by *McDonald* v. *United States*.[12] This "ALI-McDonald" rule as described in *Brawner* is:

The court sets forth a new standard for the insanity defense:

1. The court adopts as the criterion of insanity, for all trials beginning after today, the rule stated in Section 4.01(1) of the Model Penal Code of the American Law Institute. That rule, which has been adopted in essence by the other Federal circuit courts of appeals, states: "A person is not responsible for criminal conduct if at the time of such conduct as a result of mental disease or defect he lacks substantial capacity to appreciate the

wrongfulness of his conduct or to conform his conduct to the requirements of the law." The rule of *Durham* v. *United States*, 214 F. 2d 862 (1954), which excused an unlawful act if it was the product of a mental disease or defect, will no longer be in effect.

2. The court retains the definition of mental disease or defect adopted in *McDonald* v. *United States*, 312 F. 2d 847 (en banc, 1962): "A mental disease or defect includes any abnormal condition of the mind which substantially affects mental or emotional processes and substantially affects behavior controls."

Though it provides a general uniformity, the ALI rule leaves room for variations. Thus, we have added an adjustment in the *McDonald* definition of mental disease, which we think fully compatible with both the spirit and text of the ALI rule. In the interest of good administration, we now undertake to set forth, with such precision as the subject will permit, other elements of the ALI rule as adopted by this court.

The two main components of the rule define (1) mental disease, (2) the consequences thereof that exculpate from responsibility:

1. *Intermesh of components*. The first component of our rule, derived from *McDonald*, defines mental disease or defect as an abnormal condition of the mind, and a condition which substantially (a) affects mental or emotional processes and (b) impairs behavioral controls. The second component, derived from the Model Penal Code, tells which defendant with a mental disease lacks criminal responsibility for particular conduct: it is the defendant who, as a result of this mental condition, at the time of such conduct, either (i) lacks substantial capacity to appreciate that his conduct is wrongful, or (ii) lacks substantial capacity to conform his conduct to the law. The first component establishes eligibility for an instruction concerning the defense for a defendant who presents evidence that his abnormal condition of the mind has substantially impaired behavioral controls. The second component completes the instruction and defines the ultimate issue, of exculpation, in terms of whether his behavioral controls were not only substantially impaired but impaired to such an extent that he lacked substantial capacity to conform his conduct to the law. Defendant is also exculpated if he lacks substantial capacity to appreciate the conduct is wrongful.

2. *The "result" of the mental disease*. The rule contains a requirement of causality, as is clear from the term "result." Exculpation is established not by mental disease alone but only if "as a result" defendant lacks the substantial capacity required for responsibility. Presumably the mental disease of a kleptomaniac does not entail as a "result" a lack of capacity to conform to the law prohibiting rape.

3. *At the time of the conduct.* Under the ALI rule the issue is not whether defendant is so disoriented or void of controls that he is never able to conform to external demands, but whether he had that capacity at the time of the conduct. The question is not properly put in terms of whether he would have capacity to conform in some untypical restraining situation—as with an attendant or policeman at his elbow. The issue is whether he was able to conform in the unstructured condition of life in an open society, and whether the result of his abnormal mental condition was a lack of substantial internal controls.[13]

In 1961 the Federal Circuit Court in the Third Circuit decided the case of *United States* v. *Currens*. The decision gave impetus to an until then little-used concept of "substantial capacity" quite different from either the *M'Naghten* rule or the doctrine of *Durham*. Defendant Currens was convicted by a jury of a violation of the National Motor Vehicle Theft Act (Title 18, U.S. Code, Section 2312). He appealed, citing the question of his criminal responsibility. *The court's ruling* \* on this substantial capacity concept is stated as follows:

> The evidence introduced on the issue of Currens' criminal responsibility consists of substantially more than his history of recurrent criminal behavior. A reasonable jury could infer that Currens is mentally incapable of ordered social living; that he is subject to hysterical episodes; that under stress he has many symptoms of the incapacitating disease of schizophrenia; and that he is generally subject to depression, fright, and losses of contact with reality. On the basis of such evidence we believe that a jury reasonably could find that he did not possess the necessary guilty mind when he committed the crime of which he is accused.
>
> The court below, relying on the decision of the Supreme Court of the United States in *Davis* v. *United States,* 160 U.S. 469 (1895), on the second *Davis* decision, *Davis* v. *United States,* 165 U.S. 373 (1897), and apparently on *Matheson* v. *United States,* 227 U.S. 540 (1913), charged the jury as to Currens' criminal responsibility in terms of the M'Naghten Rules but added glosses of temporary insanity and irresistible impulse. The backbone of the charge given by the court below was the knowledge of right and wrong by the accused, the so-called "right-and-wrong" test of M'Naghten.
>
> We think that there are cogent reasons why the M'Naghten Rules should not be followed or applied today in the courts of the United States. The vast absurdity of the application of the

\*Extracts only; footnotes and citations are deleted.

M'Naghten Rules in order to determine the sanity or insanity, the mental health or lack of it, of the defendant by securing the answer to a single question: Did the defendant know the difference between right and wrong, appears clearly when one surveys the array of symptomatology which the skilled psychiatrist employs in determining the mental condition of an individual. This is not the place to set this out in detail but the extent of its substance is suggested by psychiatric textbooks. All in all the M'Naghten rules do indeed, as has been asserted so often, put the testifying psychiatrist in a strait-jacket.

To achieve the necessary foundation to resolve the vital issue of criminal responsibility it is necessary that the entire picture of the defendant be presented to the court and to the jury insofar as the rules of evidence will allow. The defendant's entire relevant symptomatology must be brought before the court and fully explained. Such a course assigns to the medical expert, the psychiatrist, his proper duty in the criminal proceedings.

The jury must be further provided with a standard or formula by means of which it can translate that mental condition into an answer to the ultimate question of whether the defendant possessed the necessary guilty mind to commit the crime charged. Our second objective is, therefore, to verbalize the relationship between mental disease and the concept of "guilty mind" in a way that will be both meaningful to a jury charged with the duty of determining the issue of criminal responsibility and consistent with the basic aims, purposes and assumptions of the criminal law.

The concept of *mens rea*, guilty mind, is based on the assumption that a person has a capacity to control his behavior and to choose between alternative courses of conduct. This assumption, though not unquestioned by theologians, philosophers and scientists, is necessary to the maintenance and administration of social controls. It is only through this assumption that society has found it possible to impose duties and create liabilities designed to safeguard persons and property. Thus, the sanctions of the criminal law are meted out in accordance with the actor's capacity to conform his conduct to society's standards, through the capacity for choice control which he possessed with respect to his act.

It follows, we believe, that where there is reasonable doubt as to whether a particular person possesses capacity of choice and control, i.e., capacity to conform his conduct to society's standards, there is a reasonable doubt as to whether he possessed the necessary guilty mind.

*We are of the opinion that the following formula most nearly fulfills the objectives just discussed: The jury must be*

*satisfied that at the time of committing the prohibitive act the defendant, as a result of mental disease or defect, lacked substantial capacity to conform his conduct to the requirements of the law which he is alleged to have violated.* [Emphasis added.]

The following would be an acceptable charge to a trial jury on the issue of the criminal responsibility of Currens (assuming the burden of proof that Currens had the necessary criminal intent had shifted to the United States): "If you the jury believe beyond a reasonable doubt that the defendant, Currens, was not suffering from a disease of the mind at the time he committed the criminal act charged, you may find him guilty. If you believe that he was suffering from a disease of the mind, but believe beyond a reasonable doubt that at the time he committed the criminal conduct with which he is charged he possessed substantial capacity to conform his conduct to the requirements of the law which he is alleged to have violated you may find him guilty. Unless you believe beyond a reasonable doubt that Currens was not suffering from a disease of the mind or that despite that disease he possessed substantial capacity to conform his conduct to the requirements of the law which he is alleged to have violated you must find him not guilty by reason of insanity. Thus, your task would not be completed upon finding, if you did find, that the accused suffered from a disease of the mind. He would still be responsible for his unlawful act if you found beyond a reasonable doubt that at the time he committed that act, the disease had not so weakened his capacity to conform his conduct to the requirements of the law which he is alleged to have violated that he lacked substantial capacity to conform his conduct to the requirements of that law. These questions must be determined by you from the facts which you find to be fairly deducible from the evidence in this case."[14]

## JUSTIFICATION: AUTHORITY, EMERGENCY, DURESS, NECESSITY

A person is justified in conduct which would otherwise be criminal when such conduct is authorized or required by law, or when there is a pressing emergency and such conduct is necessary to avoid imminent public disaster or serious bodily injury to a person or serious damage to property.

The use of force by a peace officer in making an arrest; maintaining custody of a prisoner, preventing escape, and recapturing escapees; or in controlling riots, is therefore justified. Usually this justification extends to persons the officer has called upon to assist him or her.

When immediately necessary, the use of force is usually authorized to break into a house to save a person's life, to seize and

maintain custody over a person with a deadly contagious disease to prevent uncontrolled contact with others, and to control any life or property-endangering situation.

The justification of duress (coercion) or necessity also require similar pressing emergencies to warrant consideration as defense. The defense of necessity requires otherwise unavoidable and irreparable consequences. The person claiming this justification must have a reasonable belief in the harm threatened and an actual belief as to its immediacy; and the act done because of the duress or necessity must be no more than absolutely necessary.

The American Law Institute deals with the defense of duress in the Model Penal Code.[15] This provision stresses that it is an affirmative defense that the accused person engaged in the conduct charged because he was coerced by the use of, or a threat to use, unlawful force against his person or the person of another.

The defense is available if a person of reasonable firmness in his situation would have been unable to resist, but is unavailable if the actor recklessly places himself in a situation in which it is probable that he would be subjected to duress, or if he is negligent in placing himself in such a situation.

The problem of necessity was tragically shown in 1884 when the yacht *Mignonette* wrecked and four of the crew escaped in an open boat: Dudley, the master; Stephen, the mate; Brooks, an able seaman; and Parker, a cabin boy. They had no food or water in the boat. After eighteen days during which the only food they had had was one small turtle and the water they caught in their oilskin capes, the petitioners suggested to Brooks that someone should be sacrificed to save the rest. Brooks refused to agree and the boy, to whom they were understood to refer, was not consulted. On the twentieth day Dudley, with the consent of Stephens but not of Brooks, killed the boy. The three fed upon the boy for four days when they were picked up. It was found that if the men had not fed upon the body of the boy they would probably not have survived, to be so picked up, and rescued; that the boy, being in a much weaker condition, was likely to have died before them; that there appeared to the petitioners every probability that unless they then or very soon fed upon the boy or one of themselves they would die of starvation, and that there was no appreciable chance of saving life except by killing someone for the others to eat; and that, assuming any necessity to kill any one, there was no greater necessity for killing the boy than any of the other three men. The question before the English Court was whether Dudley and Stephens were guilty of murder:

> First it is said that it follows from various definitions of
> murder in books of authority, which definitions imply, if they do

not state, the doctrine, that in order to save your own life you may lawfully take away the life of another, when that other is neither attempting nor threatening yours, nor is guilty of any illegal act whatever towards you or any one else. But if these definitions be looked at they will not be found to sustain this contention. Is there, then, any authority for the proposition which has been presented to us? Decided cases there are none.

The American case cited by my brother Stephen in his Digest, from Wharton on Homicide, in which it was decided, correctly indeed, that sailors had no right to throw passengers overboard to save themselves, but on the somewhat strange ground that the proper mode of determining who was to be sacrificed was to vote upon the subject by ballot, can hardly, as my brother Stephen says, be an authority satisfactory to a court in this country. The observations of Lord Mansfield in the case of R.V. Stratton and Others, 21 How.St.Tr. (1779), striking and excellent as they are, were delivered in a political trial, where the question was whether a political necessity had arisen for deposing a governor of Madras.

Now it is admitted that the deliberate killing of this unoffending and unresisting boy was clearly murder, unless the killing can be justified by some well-recognized excuse admitted by law. It is further admitted that there was in this case no such excuse, unless the killing was justified by what has been called "necessity." But the temptation to the act which existed here was not what the law has ever called necessity. Nor is this to be regretted. Though law and morality are not the same, and many things may be immoral which are not necessarily illegal, yet the absolute divorce of law from morality would be of fatal consequence; and such divorce would follow if the temptation to murder in this case were to be held by law an absolute defence of it. It is not so. To preserve one's life is, generally speaking, a duty, but it may be the plainest and the highest duty to sacrifice it. It is not correct, therefore, to say that there is any absolute or unqualified necessity to preserve one's life. It is not needful to point out the awful danger of admitting the principle which has been contended for. Who is to be the judge of this sort of necessity? By what measure is the comparative value of lives to be measured? Is it to be strength, or intellect, or what? In this case the weakest, the youngest, the most unresisting was chosen. Was it more necessary to kill him than one of the grown men? The answer must be 'No.' It is not suggested that in this particular case the deeds were devilish; but it is quite plain that such a principle once admitted might be made the legal cloak for unbridled passion and atrocious crime.

There is no safe path for judges to tread but to ascertain the

law to the best of their ability and declare it according to their judgment; and, if in any case the law appears to be too severe on individuals, to leave it to the Sovereign to exercise the prerogative of mercy which the constitution has entrusted to the hands fittest to dispense it. It must not be supposed that in refusing to admit temptation to be an excuse for crime it is forgotten how terrible the temptation was; how awful the suffering; how hard in such trials to keep the judgment straight and the conduct pure. We are often compelled to set up standards we cannot reach ourselves, and to lay down rules which we could not ourselves satisfy. But a man has no right to declare temptation to be an excuse, though he might himself have yielded to it, nor allow compassion for the criminal to change or weaken in any manner the legal definition of the crime. *It is therefore our duty to declare the prisoners' act was wilful murder, and that the facts stated in the verdict are no legal justification.* [Emphasis added.][16]

A different type of problem presents itself when the setting for the charge is a prison and the charge is escape. The question presented is whether there is ever "justification" for escape and, if so, under what conditions. In 1974 an appellate court took up the problem. Two inmates (Ms. Lovercamp and Ms. Wynashe) of the California Rehabilitation Center departed from that institution and were promptly captured in a hayfield a few yards away. At trial, they made the following offer of proof:

They had been in the institution about two and a half months and during that time had been threatened continuously by a group of lesbian inmates who told them they were to perform lesbian acts or fight.[The exact expression was "fuck or fight."] They complained to the authorities [several times] but nothing was done about their complaints and on the day of the escape, 10 or 15 of these lesbian inmates approached them and again offered defendants the alternative of fighting or performing lesbian acts ["fuck or fight"]. [This time there was a fight, the results of which were not outlined in the offer of proof. After the fight, Ms. Lovercamp and Ms. Wynashe were told by this group of lesbians that they "would see the group again." At this point, both defendant and Ms. Wynashe feared for their lives. Ms. Wynashe was additionally motivated by a protective attitude toward defendant Lovercamp who had the intelligence of a twelve-year-old. It was represented that a psychiatrist would testify as to defendant's mental capacity.[O]n the basis of what had occurred, the threats made, and the fact that officials had not done anything for their protection, Ms. Lovercamp and Ms. Wynashe felt they had no choice but to leave the institution in order to save themselves.[17]

The trial court rejected the offer of proof. The defendants then offered no evidence. The case was submitted to the jury and the jury found both defendants guilty.

On appellate review of this conviction, the court met the problem of "necessity" head on:

> In I Hale P.G. 611 (1736), it was written that if a prison caught fire and prisoner departed to save his life, the necessity to save his life "excuseth the felony." So, too, we may assume that a prisoner with his back to the wall, facing a gang of fellow inmates approaching him with drawn knives, who are making it very clear that they intend to kill him, might be expected to go over the wall rather than remain and be a martyr to the principle of prison discipline.
>
> However, the doctrine of necessity to "excuseth the felony" carried with it the seeds of mischief. It takes little imagination to conjure stories which could be used to indicate that to the subjective belief of the prisoner conditions in prison are such that escape becomes a necessity. Inevitably, severe limitations were affixed to this defense and the general rule evolved that intolerable living conditions in prison afforded no justification for escape. A reading of the cases invoking this rule presents a harsh commentary on prison life in these United States of America, revealing (with proper consideration of the sources of the complaints), prison life which is harsh, brutal, filthy, unwholesome and inhumane. A sampling of the authorities indicate that the defense of necessity has been rejected in cases involving unsanitary conditions in jail—a filthy, unwholesome and loathsome place, full of vermin and uncleanliness; fear of being shot; unmerited punishment at the hands of the custodian; or escape from solitary confinement when the cell was infested with bugs, worms and vermin and when the toilet was flushed the contents ran out on the floor; extremely bad food, guard brutality, inadequate medical treatment and inadequate recreational and educational programs.

We find the following:

> (1) The prisoners [Lovercamp and Wynashe] were faced with a specific threat of forcible sexual attack in the immediate future. While we must confess a certain naivete as to just what kind of erotica is involved in the gang rape of the victim by a group of lesbians and a total ignorance of just who is forced to do what to whom, we deem it a reasonable assumption that it entails as much physical and psychological insult to and degradation of a fellow human being as does forcible sodomy.
>
> (2) There existed a history of futile complaints to the authorities which made the results of any belated complaint illusory.

(3) Between the time of the fight and the time the ladies went over the wall, there obviously existed no time for resort to the courts by the filing of a petition for an extraordinary writ. (Neither is it realistic that we expect the ladies to await effective "penological reform.")

(4) No force was involved in the escape.

(5) Because the defendants were apprehended so promptly and in such close proximity to the institution, we do not know whether they intended to immediately report to the proper authorities at the first available opportunity. Obviously, even though the defendant may have the mentality of a 12-year-old, on retrial it must be anticipated that she will so testify. Whether that testimony is believable under the facts and circumstances of this case, will be a question of fact addressed to the jury.

Whether any of the conditions requisite to this defense exist is a question of fact to be decided by the trier of fact after taking into consideration all the surrounding circumstances. The offer of proof in the instant case was sufficient to require the submission of this defense to the jury in an appropriate manner. The trial court erred in not submitting this matter to the jury.

In summary, simply alleging an escape to avoid homosexual attack will not suffice to prevent a conviction. This defense is one with severe limitations and it must be established by competent evidence in a trial where the testimony of witnesses is subject to scrutiny by the trier of fact. The credibility to be accorded to such a proposed defense lies solely within the function of the trier of fact and is to be determined by the facts and circumstances of each case as they arise.

We do not conceive that we have created a new defense to an escape charge. We merely recognize, as did an English Court 238 years ago, that some conditions "excuseth the felony."

*We, therefore, conclude that the defense of necessity to an escape charge is a viable defense.* [Emphasis added.] However, before *Lovercamp* becomes a household word in prison circles and we are exposed to the spectacle of hordes of prisoners leaping over the walls screaming "rape," we hasten to add that the defense of necessity to an escape charge is extremely limited in its application. This is because of the rule that upon attaining a position of safety from the immediate threat, the prisoner must promptly report to the proper authorities.[18]

A further claim of necessity arises in the military when the defense is obedience to orders. In the war crime trials after World War II this defense was raised but rejected by the court. In more recent times the My Lai killings in Viet Nam were defended in part on the basis of obedience to orders which would negate the *mens*

*rea* required for the crime of murder. Lieutenant William Calley was charged with premeditated murder based upon the acts committed at My Lai, Viet Nam, during that conflict on March 16, 1968. His defense was that he was acting under orders. However, at his military trial it was stressed that not every order is exonerating. The trial judge's instructions to the military tribunal informed the members as a matter of law that any order received by Calley directing him to kill unresisting Vietnamese within his control or within the control of his troops would have been illegal. The instructions stated:

> A determination that an order is illegal does not, of itself, assign criminal responsibility to the person following the order for acts done in compliance with it. Soldiers are taught to follow orders, and special attention is given to obedience of orders on the battlefield. Military effectiveness depends upon obedience to orders. On the other hand, the obedience of a soldier is not the obedience of an automaton. A soldier is a reasoning agent, obliged to respond, not as a machine, but as a person. The law takes these factors into account in assessing criminal responsibility for acts done in compliance with illegal orders.
>
> *The acts of a subordinate done in compliance with an unlawful order given him by his superior are excused and impose no criminal liability upon him unless the superior's order is one which a man of ordinary sense and understanding would, under the circumstances, know to be unlawful, or if the order in question is actually known to the accused to be unlawful.* [Emphasis added.][19]

Obedience to orders is a defense which strikes at *mens rea;* therefore in logic an obedient subordinate should be acquitted so long as he did not personally know of the order's illegality. In the *Calley* case the members of the military court did not agree with this argument. They said that casting the defense of obedience to orders solely in subjective terms of *mens rea* would operate practically to abrogate those objective restraints which are essential to functioning rules of war. The court members rejected Calley's defense of obedience to orders.

## SELF-DEFENSE

A person is justified in the use of force when he or she has reasonable grounds to believe such conduct is necessary to defend oneself or another person against the imminent use of unlawful force.

The reasonable-cause doctrine means that conduct claimed as in self-defense is justified only when a reasonable man, in confronting the same situation, would believe such conduct was necessary. This doctrine of reasonableness naturally extends to the specific

conduct used for defense: reasonable cause to believe that *such conduct* is necessary.

The heat of conflict and the belief of a person that he is fighting for his life appears to justify an escalation or extension of the necessary defensive conduct. Where a defendant shot the deceased several times and again when the deceased had fallen and was lying on the ground, the Court held such conduct was a question for the jury:

> There was evidence that the last shot was fired after Hermes (the deceased victim) was down. The jury might not believe the defendant's testimony that it was an accidental discharge, but if the last shot was intentional and may seem to have been unnecessary when considered in cold blood, the defendant would not necessarily lose his immunity if it followed close upon the others while the heat of the conflict was on, and if the defendant believed that he was fighting for his life.[20]

Deadly force means force likely to kill. Any weapon which easily and readily can cause death can be classified as a deadly weapon:

> A weapon with which death may be easily and readily produced; anything, no matter what it is, whether it is made for the purpose of destroying animal life, or whether it was not made by man at all, or whether it was made by him for some other purpose, if it is a weapon, or if it is a thing with which death can be easily and readily produced, the law recognizes it as a deadly weapon.[21]

The use of deadly force is only justified, however, under the reasonable belief that such extreme force is necessary to prevent immediate death or serious bodily injury to self or another.

Force likely to cause death or serious injury may, under limited circumstances, be used in defense of property.

> Homicide is justifiable and not unlawful when committed by any person in defense of habitation, property or person against one who manifestly intends or endeavors, by violence or surprise, to commit a felony, or against one who manifestly intends and endeavors, in a violent, riotous or tumultuous manner to enter the habitation of another for the purpose of offering violence to any person therein. However, the circumstances must be sufficient to excite the fears of a reasonable person, and the party killing must have acted under the influence of such fears alone.[22]

The concept is that defense against a felony when the offender manifestly intends or endeavors by violence and surprise to commit a felony restricts such defense to the more serious felonies (involv-

ing violence and surprise). For instance, burglary under all of its possible circumstances does not constitute the forcible and atrocious crime that will justify killing to protect property, and since the character and manner of burglary do not reasonably create a fear of great bodily harm, there is no cause for the exaction of human life in preventing burglary.

A person is not justified in setting a trap gun to protect property. In *People* v. *Ceballos*,[23] the defendant was convicted of assault with a deadly weapon. After a burglary of the defendant's home and a subsequent attempt to break and enter his garage, defendant mounted a loaded twenty-two caliber pistol in the garage aimed at the center of the garage doors and so connected by a wire to one of the doors that the pistol would discharge if the door was opened several inches. A few days after the trap gun was set two boys, one fifteen years old and the other sixteen years old, attempted to enter the garage by prying the doors open; as one of the doors moved outward the trap gun fired and the sixteen-year-old boy was hit in the face with a bullet from the pistol. At trial the defendant argued that had he been present he would have been justified in shooting the injured thief since he was attempting to commit a burglary. The prosecutor argued that a trap gun was inherently excessive force and that the facts of this case did not warrant the use of such deadly force. The California Supreme Court, sitting *en banc, affirmed* the trial jury's guilty verdict.

Deadly force may not be used in crime-prevention situations where it is more serious than the crime threatened. Homicide is justifiable and not unlawful when committed by any person when resisting any attempt to murder any person, or to commit a felony inherently dangerous to human life, or to do some great bodily injury upon any person.[24]

The apparent danger in the developing situation is part of this doctrine of reasonableness: a person claiming justification for a defensive act must not only believe he was in danger, but must make a showing in evidence of reasonable grounds for such belief. This rule of apparent danger was summed up in *Acers* v. *United States*, 164 U.S. 388 (1896):

> There must be some overt act being done by the party which from its character, from its nature, would give a reasonable man, situated as was the defendant, the ground to believe—reasonable ground to believe—that there was danger to his life or of deadly violence to his person, and unless that condition existed then there is no ground upon which this proposition can stand; there is nothing to which the doctrine of apparent danger could apply.

Self-defense as justification to remove criminal responsibility from an act done which would otherwise be criminal is not usually

extended to persons who are the *initial aggressors,* unless there is a withdrawal in good faith clearly indicating a desire to withdraw and terminate the encounter.

This element of withdrawal was present in a case involving an indictment for murder, alleged to have been committed by the defendant, David Rowe, in the Cherokee Nation, Indian Territory, on the thirtieth day of March, 1895, on one Frank Bozeman. The verdict was guilty of manslaughter, and a motion for a new trial having been overruled, the accused was sentenced to imprisonment. The testimony on the part of the prosecution tended to show that on the evening of the thirtieth of March, 1895, the defendant, Rowe, and the deceased, Bozeman, met at a hotel at Pryor's Creek, Indian Territory, and got into an argument. The argument became heated, and the defendant then kicked at deceased, hitting him lightly on the lower part of the leg; that the deceased sprang at defendant, striking him with a knife and cutting him in two places on the face; after the deceased began cutting the defendant the latter drew his pistol and fired, shooting the deceased through the body.

The testimony on the part of the defense tended to show that on the day of the difficulty defendant came into town from his home, about twenty miles distant, with his wife to do some shopping; that he brought his pistol with him and left it at the livery stable where he put up his team, and at supper time went by the stable and got his pistol, fearing that it might be stolen; that defendant did not have anything to say to deceased in the dining-room, but was talking with the father of the deceased, and that defendant was not intoxicated; that when defendant came out in the office deceased started the argument by using abusive language, and after defendant kicked at him, defendant stepped back and leaned up against the counter. The deceased sprang at him and began cutting him with a knife; the deceased cut him in the face and kept on striking at him with the knife. After he was cut in the face the defendant drew his pistol and fired at the deceased, who was in the act of striking him again with the knife.

The appellate court reviewing this case on defendant's appeal noted that the issue was the legal effect of the defendant's initial action toward the deceased related to his defense of self-defense. The majority opinion* noted:

> The first real provocation came from the deceased when he used towards the accused language of an offensive character, and that the accused immediately after kicking at or lightly kicking the deceased, signified by his conduct that he no longer desired controversy with his adversary; whereupon the deceased, despite

---

*Extracts only; footnotes and citations are deleted.

the efforts of the accused to retire from further contest, sprang at the latter, with knife in hand, for the purpose of taking life, and would most probably have accomplished that object, if the accused had not fired at the moment he did. Under such circumstances, did the law require that the accused should stand still, and permit himself to be cut to pieces, under the penalty that if he met the unlawful attack upon him and saved his own life, by taking that of his assailant, he would be guilty of manslaughter? We think not.

*If a person, under the provocation of offensive language, assaults the speaker personally, but in such a way as to show that there is no intention to do him serious harm, and then retires under such circumstances as show that he does not intend to do anything more, but in good faith withdraws from further contest, his right of self-defense is restored when the person assaulted, in violation of law, pursues him with a deadly weapon and seeks to take his life or do him great bodily harm.* [Emphasis added.]

We do not mean to say that the jury ought to have found that the accused, after kicking the deceased lightly, withdrew in good faith from further contest and that his conduct should have been so interpreted. It was for the jury to say whether the withdrawal was in good faith, or was a mere device by the accused to obtain some advantage of his adversary.

The danger in which the accused was, or believed himself to be, at the moment he fired is to some extent indicated by the fact, proved by the government, that immediately after he disabled his assailant (who had two knives upon his person) he said that he, the accused, was himself mortally wounded and wished a physician to be called.[25]

In *reversing* Rowe's manslaughter conviction the appellate court ruled that Rowe was entitled, so far as his right to resist the attack was concerned, to remain where he was, and to do whatever was necessary or what he had reasonable grounds to believe at the time was necessary, to save his life or to protect himself from great bodily harm.

The traditional requirement of *retreat* in the face of an attack is the subject of *Beard* v. *United States*. The *Beard* case was tried in the U.S. Circuit Court for the Western District of Arkansas (before statehood). "Babe" Beard was indicted for the killing of Will Jones. He was tried and *convicted of manslaughter* despite a claim of self-defense.

The facts of the Beard case center on an angry dispute which arose between Beard and three brothers by the name of Jones—Will, John, and Edward—in reference to the ownership of a cow. The

Jones brothers, one of them taking a shotgun with him, went upon the premises of the accused for the purpose of taking the cow away, whether Beard consented or not. They were prevented by the accused from accomplishing that object. He warned them not to come to his place again for such a purpose, informing them that if Edward Jones was entitled to the possession of the cow, he could have it, providing his claim was successfully asserted through legal proceedings instituted by or in his behalf. Will Jones, the oldest of the brothers, and about twenty or twenty-one years of age, publicly avowed his intention to get the cow away from the Beard farm or kill Beard, and of that threat the latter was informed on the day preceding the killing.

In the afternoon of the day on which the Jones brothers were warned by Beard not again to come upon his premises for the cow unless attended by an officer of the law, and in defiance of that warning, they again went to his farm. Beard returned to his home from a town near by—having with him a shotgun that he was in the habit of carrying when absent from home—and went at once from his dwelling into the lot, called the orchard lot, a distance of about fifty or sixty yards from his house and near to that part of an adjoining field or lot where the cow was. Beard ordered the Jones brothers to leave his premises. They refused to leave. Thereupon Will Jones, who was on the opposite side of the orchard fence, ten or fifteen yards only from Beard, moved towards the latter with an angry manner and in a brisk walk, having his left hand (he being, as Beard knew, left-handed) in the left pocket of his trousers. When he got within five or six steps of Beard, the latter warned him to stop, but he did not do so. As he approached nearer the accused asked him what he intended to do, and he replied: "Damn you, I will show you," at the same time making a movement with his left hand as if to draw a pistol from his pocket; whereupon the accused struck him over the head with his gun and knocked him down.

The defendant testified:

Believing from his demonstrations just mentioned that he intended to shoot me, I struck him over the head with my gun to prevent him killing me. As soon as I struck him his brother John, who was a few steps behind him, started towards me with his hands in his pocket. Believing that he intended to take part in the difficulty and was also armed, I struck him and he stopped. I then at once jumped over the fence, caught Will Jones by the lapel of the coat, turned him rather to one side, and pulled his left hand out of his pocket. He had a pistol, which I found in his pocket, grasped in his left hand, and I pulled his pistol and his left hand out together. My purpose in doing this was to disarm him, to prevent him from shooting me, as I did not know how

badly he was hurt. My gun was loaded, having cartridges in the magazine. I could have shot him, but did not want to kill him, believing that I could knock him down with the gun and disarm him and protect myself without shooting him. After getting his (Will Jones's) pistol, John Jones said something to me about killing him, to which I replied that I had not killed him and did not try to do so, for if I had I could have shot him. He said my gun was not loaded; thereupon I shot the gun in the air to show him that it was loaded.

Will Jones died from the effects of the wound given by the defendant; the wound was across the head, rather on the right side, the skull being crushed by the blow.

The United States Supreme Court's decision *reversed* Beard's conviction of manslaughter, saying the accused was on his own premises, where he had a right to be, and was under no compulsion to retreat:

> In our opinion, the court below erred in holding that the accused, while on his premises, outside of his dwelling-house, was under a legal duty to get out of the way, if he could, of his assailant, who, according to one view of the evidence, had threatened to kill the defendant, in execution of that purpose had armed himself with a deadly weapon, with that weapon concealed upon his person went to the defendant's premises, despite the warning of the latter to keep away, and by word and act indicated his purpose to attack the accused. *The defendant was where he had the right to be, when the deceased advanced upon him in a threatening manner, and with a deadly weapon; and if the accused did not provoke the assault and had at the time reasonable grounds to believe and in good faith believed, that the deceased intended to take his life or do him great bodily harm, he was not obliged to retreat, nor to consider whether he could safely retreat, but was entitled to stand his ground and meet any attack made upon him with a deadly weapon, in such way and with such force as, under all the circumstances, he, at the moment, honestly believed, and had reasonable grounds to believe, was necessary to save his own life or to protect himself from great bodily injury.* [Emphasis added.][26]

A quarter century later, the doctrine of *Beard* was restated approvingly and extended:

> The right of a man to *stand his ground and defend himself* when attacked with a deadly weapon, even to the extent of taking his assailant's life, depends upon whether he reasonably believes that he is in immediate danger of death or grievous bodily harm

from his assailant, and not upon the detached test whether a man of reasonable prudence, so situated, might not think it possible to fly with safety or to disable his assailant rather than kill him. [Emphasis added.][27]

# WITHDRAWAL

Withdrawal is a defense against criminal liability based on the criminal conduct of another person in a joint criminal venture. A defendant who withdraws before the commission of the crime or its attempt, or before any of the criminal objectives of the conspiracy had been achieved, may escape liability for the crime.

Withdrawal, to be effectively claimed, requires adequate and timely notice to either the intended victim or a public police agency, as well as such notice to other participants in the crime's planning known to the defendant.

# ENTRAPMENT

Entrapment is an affirmative defense to excuse a person from criminal liability. A person is entrapped to commit a crime when police or their agents persuade him or her to commit an offense. Conduct affording the opportunity to commit a crime is not entrapment. If the defendant is ready and willing (or at least not reluctant) to commit an offense without persuasion, there is no entrapment.[28]

Subjectively, a defendant should demonstrate that *but for* the objectionable police conduct, he or she would not have committed the crime.

*Sorrells* v. *United States* goes back to the days of Prohibition, when whiskey selling was illegal. However, its doctrine on entrapment is applicable to many contemporary crimes, particularly those in which undercover police make "buys" in drug-selling cases. In *Sorells*, the defendant was indicted on two counts (1) for possessing and (2) for selling, on July 13, 1930, a half gallon of whiskey in violation of the National Prohibition Act. He pleaded not guilty. Upon trial he relied upon the defense of entrapment. The court refused to sustain the defense, denying a motion to direct a verdict in favor of defendant and also refusing to submit the issue of entrapment to the jury. The court ruled that "as a matter of law" there was no entrapment. Verdict of guilty followed, motions in arrest and to set aside the verdict as contrary to the law and the evidence were denied, and defendant was sentenced to imprisonment for eighteen months. On appeal to the United States Supreme Court the issue was limited to whether the evidence was sufficient to go to the jury upon the question of entrapment. One Martin, a prohibition agent, testified that having resided for a time in Haywood County, North

Carolina, where he posed as a tourist, he visited defendant's home near Canton, on Sunday, July 13, 1930, accompanied by three residents of the county who knew the defendant well. He was introduced as a resident of Charlotte who was stopping for a time at Clyde. The witness ascertained that defendant was a veteran of the World War and former member of the Thirtieth Division A.E.F. The witness informed defendant that he was also an ex-service man and a former member of the same Division, which was true. Witness asked defendant if he could get the witness some liquor and defendant stated that he did not have any. Later, there was a second request without result. One of those present, one Jones, was also an ex-service man and a former member of the Thirtieth Division, and the conversation turned to the war experiences of the three. After this, witness asked defendant for a third time to get him some liquor, whereupon defendant left his home and after a few minutes came back with a half gallon of liquor for which the witness paid defendant five dollars. Martin also testified that he was "the first and only person among those present at the time who said anything about securing some liquor," and that his purpose was to prosecute the defendant for procuring and selling it. The Government rested its case on Martin's testimony.

Defendant Sorrells called as witnesses the three persons who had accompanied the prohibition agent. In substance, they corroborated the latter's story but with some additions. Jones, a railroad employee, testified that he had introduced the agent to the defendant "as a furniture dealer of Charlotte," because the agent so represented himself; that witness told defendant that the agent was "an old Thirtieth Division man" and the agent thereupon said to defendant that he "would like to get a half gallon of whiskey to take back to Charlotte to a friend of his that was in the furniture business with him," and that defendant replied that he "did not fool with whiskey"; that the agent and his companions were at defendant's home for "probably an hour and a half" and that during such time the agent asked the defendant three or four or probably five times to get him, the agent, some liquor. Defendant said "he would go and see if he could get a half gallon of liquor" and he returned with it after an absence of "between twenty and thirty minutes." Jones added that at that time he had never heard of defendant being in the liquor business, that he and the defendant were "two old buddies," and that he believed "one former war buddy would get liquor for another."

The United States Supreme Court *reversed* Sorrells's conviction. Extracts* from the majority opinion in *Sorrells* set forth the following doctrine on entrapment:

*Extracts only; footnotes and citations are deleted.

It is clear that the evidence was sufficient to warrant a finding that the act for which defendant was prosecuted was instigated by the prohibition agent, that it was the creature of his purpose, that defendant had no previous disposition to commit it but was an industrious, law-abiding citizen, and that the agent lured defendant, otherwise innocent, to its commission by repeated and persistent solicitation in which he succeeded by taking advantage of the sentiment aroused by reminiscences of their experiences as companions in arms in the World War. Such a gross abuse of authority given for the purpose of detecting and punishing crime, and not for the making of criminals, deserves the severest condemnation, but the question whether it precludes prosecution or affords a ground of defense, and, if so, upon what theory, has given rise to conflicting opinions.

It is well settled that the fact that officers or employees of the Government merely afford opportunities or facilities for the commission of the offense does not defeat the prosecution. Artifice and stratagem may be employed to catch those engaged in criminal enterprises. The appropriate object of this permitted activity, frequently essential to the enforcement of the law, is to reveal the criminal design; to expose the illicit traffic, the prohibited publication, the fraudulent use of the mails, the illegal conspiracy, or other offenses, and thus to disclose the would-be violators of the law. A different question is presented when the criminal design originates with the officials of the Government, and they implant in the mind of an innocent person the disposition to commit the alleged offense and induce its commission in order that they may prosecute.

While this Court has not spoken on the precise question, the weight of authority in the lower federal courts is decidedly in favor of the view that in such cases as the one before us the defense of entrapment is available.

Considerations of mere convenience must yield to the essential demands of justice. The argument is pressed that if the defense is available it will lead to the introduction of issues of a collateral character relating to the activities of the officials of the Government and to the conduct and purposes of the defendant previous to the alleged offense. For the defense of entrapment is not simply that the particular act was committed at the instance of government officials. That is often the case where the proper action of these officials leads to the revelation of criminal enterprises. The predisposition and criminal design of the defendant are relevant. But the issues raised and the evidence adduced must be pertinent to the controlling question whether the defendant is a person otherwise innocent whom the Government is seeking to punish for an alleged offense which is the product of the cre-

ative activity of its own officials. If that is the fact, common justice requires that the accused be permitted to prove it. The Government in such a case is in no position to object to evidence of the activities of its representatives in relation to the accused, and if the defendant seeks acquittal by reason of entrapment he cannot complain of an appropriate and searching inquiry into his own conduct and predisposition as bearing upon that issue. If in consequence he suffers a disadvantage, he has brought it upon himself by reason of the nature of the defense.

*We are of the opinion that upon the evidence produced in the instant case the defense of entrapment was available and that the trial court was in error in holding that as a matter of law there was no entrapment and in refusing to submit the issue to the jury.* [Emphasis added.][29]

The defense of entrapment assumes that the act which is labeled criminal was committed and that the defendant committed that act. The defense is, therefore, one of negating the *mens rea* or criminal or evil mind. The defense must involve the determination by expression or implication of the predisposition of the defendant to commit the crime and not merely the fact of committing the act. Also involved and relevant is evidence of who originated the design of the crime, the officer or the defendant, and what degree of persuasion was used by the officer to induce the commission of the act by the defendant. The officer must not seduce an innocent person into a criminal act or career.

In *United States* v. *Russell,*[30] an undercover narcotics agent offered the defendant and his confederates an essential ingredient which was difficult to obtain though legally available sources for their illicitly manufactured drug. The defendant and his group had made the drug before and after the agent's activities.

The Court in *Russell* agreed with the earlier decision of *Sorrells* and did not find an intolerable degree of governmental participation in the criminal enterprise, but instead found that the agent merely afforded an opportunity or facility for the defendant. Here there was ample evidence of defendant's predisposition. Excessive persuasion is improper but mere asking or affording is not fatal to a prosecution. A trap for the unwary criminal is excellent police work, but a trap for the unwary innocent citizen is overreaching police activity, and thus entrapment.

## NEGATION OF SPECIFIC INTENT

A claim of mistake of fact or law due to ignorance may negate the existence of the mental state (*mens rea*) required for prosecution of a crime requiring a specific intent. The claim of "diminished capacity" may negate the *mens rea* required in such crimes. Dimin-

ished capacity is less than a claim of insanity, but it is a claim of mental and/or physical impairment due to mental illness, disease, or defect. Self-induced intoxication may also be claimed as a defense to crimes requiring specific intent, and the term refers to the intake of drugs as well as alcohol and resultant impairment of mental and physical capacities. In claims of lack of the required specific intent because of diminished capacity or intoxication the essence of the claim is that the defendant's mental state was seriously affected and he or she could not form the specific intent required by statute.

Ignorance or mistake becomes a defense when it tends to negate the purpose, knowledge, or intent required by the statute. If the only intent necessary for the crime is the intent to do the act then there may be no defense if the mistake was not to the doing of the act. If the intent necessary is a wrongful intent or wrongful knowledge, then a mistake as to its wrongfulness may be a defense. In *People* v. *Hernandez*,[31] the appellate court allowed the defense of a good-faith belief that a girl was of an age of consent (i.e., over the age of eighteen years) even though in fact the girl was of an age where consent was no defense. The key of this mistake is a good-faith belief based upon a reasonable interpretation of the apparent facts.

The mistake must be of a material fact and the identity of the object may not be a defense. Where the defendant intended to stab and kill one but mistook the identity of another for that of the intended victim, and did stab and kill the wrong person, the defense of mistake was not available. The object is not material as the intent is the important issue for the defense.[32] Identity of intended harm and the actual harm inflicted is the material question. Bad aim is also immaterial if the intended harm is identical.[33] However, if the intended harm is different from the harm accomplished, a defense of mistake may be available. If the defendant throws a rock at a person with intent to injure him, but instead misses and damages property, a defense of lack of intent to a charge of property damage may be available unless the trier of fact can find a sufficient degree of recklessness to show the defendant should have known the consequences.

The claim of ignorance of law has rarely been allowed as a defense and the common saying "ignorance of the law is no excuse" is more right than not.

## CONSENT

A defense of consent by the "victim" may be a defense if legally recognized. There are criminal offenses which are defined as being acts "against the will of" or "without consent of" the victim. Where the crime charged includes as an element the lack of consent, an affirmative showing of such consent excludes the criminal liability.

The crime of robbery includes the element of "against the will" of the victim; burglary may require an entry without consent of the owner; theft is a taking of property without the consent of the owner; rape is sexual intercourse against the will of the victim. These offenses and others where consent is an expressed or a necessarily implied element require an affirmative showing of non-consent by the prosecution.

The prosecution for other crimes is not affected even though consent may be shown affirmatively. In *People* v. *Samuels*, the defendant was charged with preparing and distributing obscene matter, two counts of assault by means of force likely to cause great bodily harm, and sodomy. The aggravated assault charges were based upon a film depicting a sado-masochistic beating (with a riding crop) of a person by the defendant. In appealing his conviction of the assault charge, Samuels claimed that the recipient of the whipping had consented to it, and argued that such consent was an absolute defense to the assault charge. The appellate court *affirmed* Samuels's conviction, saying:

> It is a matter of common knowledge that a normal person in full possession of his mental faculties does not freely consent to the use, upon himself, of force likely to produce great bodily injury. Even if it be assumed that the victim in the film did in fact suffer from some form of mental aberration which compelled him to submit to a beating which was so severe as to constitute an aggravated assault, defendant's conduct in inflicting that beating was no less violative of a penal statute obviously designed to prohibit one human being from severely or mortally injuring another. It follows that the trial court was correct in instructing the jury that consent was not a defense to the aggravated assault charge.[34]

It is not in the power of a victim to give an effectual consent to that which amounts to a breach of the peace so that it is a bar to a criminal prosecution, unless the bodily harm inflicted or threatened is not serious or is a forseeable hazard of joint participation in a lawful sports contest.

## NOTES

1. 10 Clark & Fin. 200 (1843).
2. *Leland* v. *Oregon*, 343 U.S. 790 (1951).
3. M'Naghten's Case, 10 Clark and Fin. 200 (1843).
4. *People* v. *Wolff*, 394 P. 2d 959 (1964, Calif.).
5. See *California Jury Instructions, Criminal*, 3rd ed. (St. Paul, Minn.: West Publishing Co., 1970).
6. *People* v. *Kelly*, 516 P. 2d 875 (1973).
7. *State* v. *Pike*, 40 N.H. 399 (1870, N.H.).
8. *Durham* v. *United States*, 214 F. 2d 862 (1954).

9. 312 F. 2d 847 (1962).

10. *Washington* v. *United States*, 390 F. 2d 444 (1967).

11. *United States* v. *Brawner*, 471 F. 2d 969 (1972).

12. 312 F. 2d 847 (1962).

13. *United States* v. *Brawner*, 471 F. 2d 969 (1972).

14. *United States* v. *Currens*, 290 F. 2d 751 (1961).

15. *Model Penal Code*, 1962 Draft (Philadelphia: American Law Institute), Section 2.09.

16. *Regina* v. *Dudley and Stephens*, 14 Q.B.D. 273 (1884).

17. *People* v. *Lovercamp*, 43 Cal. App. 3d 823 (1974).

18. *People* v. *Lovercamp*, 43 Cal. App. 3d 823 (1974).

19. *United States* v. *Calley*, 46 C.M.R. 1131 (1973, Military Review Court).

20. *Brown* v. *United States*, 256 U.S. 335 (1920).

21. *Acers* v. *United States*, 164 U.S. 388 (1896).

22. *California Jury Instructions, Criminal*, Section 5.11; California Penal Code, Sections 197 (2)–198.

23. 116 *Cal. Rptr.* 233 (1974).

24. *California Jury Instructions: Criminal*, Section 5.10; California Penal Code, Section 197 (1).

25. *Rowe* v. *United States*, 164 U.S. 546 (1896).

26. *Beard* v. *United States*, 158 U.S. 550 (1895).

27. *Brown* v. *United States*, 256 U.S. 335 (1920).

28. *United States* v. *Russell*, 411 U.S. 423 (1973).

29. *Sorrells* v. *United States*, 287 U.S. 435 (1932).

30. 411 U.S. 423 (1973).

31. 393 P. 2d 673 (1964, Calif.).

32. *McGee* v. *State*, 62 Miss. 772 (1885).

33. *People* v. *Weaver*, 163 P. 2d 456 (1945, Calif.).

34. *People* v. *Samuels*, 250 Cal App. 2d 501 (1967).

# 8

# CRIME: INTENT, ACT, CAUSATION

## OBJECTIVES

*The objectives of this chapter are to further develop the concept of* mens rea *as criminal intent and to describe its role as an element of specific crimes; to examine the wrongful act or omission that makes the action done or not done a criminal act; and to explore the doctrine of proximate cause.*

## LEGAL TERMS

Malum in se. *A* malum in se *crime is one inherently evil, wrong in itself; an act immoral in its nature and injurious in its consequences.*

Malum prohibitum. *A wrongful act because prohibited; an act not inherently evil, wrong, or immoral, but one expressly forbidden by statutory law.*

Scienter. *Knowingly, guilty knowledge.*

Respondeat superior. *Responsibility of master or principal: master may be liable for wrongful acts of servant, principal for wrongful acts of agent.*

Supra. *Above. Used to indicate that the citation of a legal case has been previously given.*

Sine qua non. *Without which; an indispensable factor.*

## QUESTIONS FOR STUDY

*1. What are the differences between specific and general intent? Differences between* malum in se *and* malum prohibitum *crimes?*

*2. Develop the theme that crime is a compound concept with some concurrence of mind and act.*

*3. What is the role, if any, of* respondeat superior *in criminal cases?*

*4. Describe the "but for" aspect of criminal causation.*

*5. Define proximate cause. How is proximate cause determined?*

6. *What is an intervening cause? When is it a defense to an accusation of crime?*

7. *Within the orbit of legislative intent to prevent public harm, is there a violation of statutory law when the harm the legislature intended to prevent is not done?*

---

**A**ll crimes entail harm. When the harm the legislature intended to prevent is not done, then there is no violation of the statute.

A crime against the United States is conduct forbidden by the United States Code. Within a state, a criminal offense is conduct prohibited by state law.

Crimes are within the orbit of sanction law: they are specific acts or omissions which, upon conviction, are punishable by death, imprisonment, and fine.

There is an interrelationship in the circumstances that spell out a crime: the general or specific intent, the act done or not done, and the causation factor that brings about the result.

## CRIMINAL INTENT

*Mens rea* means a guilty mind. It is usually synonymous with criminal intent. It may be aligned with a requirement that a specified mental element is required to spell out the particular crime; or it may be implied from knowledge.

A survey of Title 18 of the U.S. Code indicates that the vast majority of the crimes designated by that title require, by express language, proof of the existence of a certain mental state, in words such as *knowingly, maliciously, wilfully, with the purpose of, with intent to,* or combinations or permutations of these and synonymous terms. The existence of a *mens rea* is the rule of, rather than the exception to, the principles of Anglo-American criminal jurisprudence.[1]

Although objective facts may be proved directly, intent or purpose requires that the state of a man's mind must be inferred from the things he says or does. Of course, courts cannot ascertain the thought that has had no outward manifestation, but courts and juries every day pass upon knowledge, belief, and intent—the state of men's minds—having before them no more than evidence of their words and conduct, from which, in ordinary human experience, mental condition may be inferred.

Where a particular mental state is in issue, it must be proved by outward manifestations. In the absence of such manifestations or overt acts, there can be no successful prosecution.[2]

Most legal commentaries divide *mens rea* into two basic types of intent: specific intent, and general intent.

Specific intent indicates that there is a particular mental state or purpose required by the law. Burglary involves two things: an entry into the dwelling of another; and the implied mental state which the common law or statutory provisions require requisite to a purpose or intent to commit a felony (or theft). The crime of assault with intent to kill requires, in addition to the mental state necessary for an assault, the particular purpose or intent to kill the person assaulted. A study of the elements of the particular crime will disclose whether a particular purpose (specific intent) is required.

General intent is usually the general notion of *mens rea*. It is often stated or implied in terms of knowledge.

The general rule at common law was that a guilty knowledge (general intent) was a necessary element in the proof of every crime, and this was followed in regard to statutory crimes even where the statutory definition did not in terms include it. However, there has been a modification of this view in respect to prosecutions under statutes the purpose of which would be obstructed by such a requirement. Whether or not a statute requires *mens rea* is a question of legislative intent to be construed by the court.

In 1943 Samuel Greenbaum[3] delivered cans of rotten eggs in violation of a Federal Food and Drug Act. The pleading did not charge that he knew that the eggs were rotten nor was there any proof offered of guilty knowledge. The issue was sharply drawn as to whether *mens rea* was necessary for "due process" or was implied when the statute was silent as to that element.

The court answered the first question by saying: "The Constitutional requirement of due process is not violated merely because *mens rea* is not a required element of a proscribed crime."[4] (Due process has to do with procedure and clarity in criminal statutes rather than with legislatively declared elements of a crime.)

As to the second question, the court said that where the statute does not express the legislative intent as to *mens rea* the courts will attempt to discover the legislative intent.

There are some activities which the legislature seems to intend to punish regardless of their lack of knowledge or willfullness. This occurs when the offenses prohibited and made punishable are capable of inflicting widespread injury and where the requirement of proof of the offender's guilty knowledge and wrongful intent renders enforcement of the prohibition difficult if not impossible. In such instances the legislative intent to dispense with *mens rea* as an element of the offense has a justifiable basis. This reasoning is particularly apparent in offenses which deal with adulterated food, drugs, and traffic matters.

Courts have indicated that in determining legislative intent concerning statutes which do not expressly require *mens rea* a determination is required whether the offense is *malum in se* or

*malum prohibitum. Malum in se* crimes are those in which the act is bad in and of itself (basically the common-law crimes). *Malum prohibitum* crimes are those in which the acts are not bad in and of themselves but are crimes only because of legislative action (regulatory-type offenses).

In *Morissette* v. *United States*[5] the defendant took some old shell casings piled in a government bombing range, believing them to be abandoned. The trial court would not allow the evidence of defendant's belief, ruling that the federal statute[6] did not require a criminal or evil intent since the statute did not express such necessary intent. The U.S. Supreme Court *reversed* the trial court's ruling. The majority opinion discussed the distinctions between crimes requiring *mens rea* and those not requiring such intent, as the following selected excerpts show:

> In *United States* v. *Behrman*, 258 U.S. 280, and *United States* v. *Balint*, 258 U.S. 250, this Court did construe mere omission from a criminal enactment of any mention of criminal intent as dispensing with it. If they be deemed precedents for principles of construction generally applicable to federal penal statutes, they authorize this conviction. Indeed, such adoption of the literal reasoning announced in those cases would do this and more—it would sweep out of all federal crimes, except when expressly preserved the ancient requirement of a culpable state of mind.
>
> The contention that an injury can amount to a crime only when inflicted by intention is no provincial or transient notion. It is as universal and persistent in mature systems of law as belief in freedom of the human will and a consequent ability and duty of the normal individual to choose between good and evil. A relation between some mental element and punishment for a harmful act is almost as instinctive as the child's familiar exculpatory "But I didn't mean to," and has afforded the rational basis for a tardy and unfinished substitution of deterrence and reformation in place of retaliation and vengeance as the motivation for public prosecution.* Unqualified acceptance of this doctrine by English common law in the Eighteenth Century was indicated by Blackstone's sweeping statement that to constitute any crime there must first be a "vicious will." Common-law commentators of the Nineteenth Century early pronounced the same principle, although a few exceptions not relevant to our present problem came to be recognized.
>
> *In *Williams* v. *New York*, 337 U.S. 241, 248, we observed that "Retribution is no longer the dominant objective of the criminal law. Reformation and rehabilitation of offenders have become important goals of criminal jurisprudence." We also there referred to "a prevalent modern philosophy of penology that the punishment should fit the offender and not merely the crime." Id., at 247. Such ends would seem illusory if there were no mental element in crime.

Crime, as a compound concept, generally constituted only from concurrence of an evil-meaning mind with an evil-doing hand, was congenial to an intense individualism and took deep and early root in American soil. As the states codified the common law of crimes, even if their enactments were silent on the subject, their courts assumed that the omission did not signify disapproval of the principle but merely recognized that intent was so inherent in the idea of the offense that it required no statutory affirmation. Courts, with little hesitation or division, found an implication of the requirement as to offenses that were taken over from the common law. The unanimity with which they have adhered to the central thought that wrongdoing must be conscious to be criminal is emphasized by the variety, disparity and confusion of their definitions of the requisite but elusive mental element. However, courts of various jurisdictions, and for the purposes of different offenses, have devised working formulae, if not scientific ones, for the instruction of juries around such terms as "felonious intent," "criminal intent," "malice aforethought," "guilty knowledge," "fraudulent intent," "wilfulness," "*scienter*," to denote guilty knowledge, or "*mens rea*," to signify an evil purpose or mental culpability. By use of combinations of these various tokens, they have sought to protect those who were not blameworthy in mind from conviction of infamous common-law crimes.

However, the *Balint* and *Behrman* offenses belong to a category of another character, with very different antecedents and origins. The crimes there involved depend on no mental element but consist only of forbidden acts or omissions. This, while not expressed by the Court, is made clear from examination of a century-old but accelerating tendency, discernible both here and in England, to call into existence new duties and crimes which disregard any ingredient of intent. The industrial revolution multiplied the number of workmen exposed to injury from increasingly powerful and complex mechanisms, driven by freshly discovered sources of energy, requiring higher precautions by employers. Traffic of velocities, volumes and varieties unheard of came to subject the wayfarer to intolerable casualty risks if owners and drivers were not to observe new cares and uniformities of conduct. Congestion of cities and crowding of quarters called for health and welfare regulations undreamed of in simpler times. Wide distribution of goods became an instrument of wide distribution of harm when those who dispersed food, drink, drugs, and even securities, did not comply with reasonable standards of quality, integrity, disclosure and care. Such dangers have engendered increasingly numerous and detailed regulations which heighten the duties of those in control of particular industries,

trades, properties or activities that affect public health, safety, or welfare.

While many of these duties are sanctioned by a more strict civil liability, lawmakers, whether wisely or not, have sought to make such regulations more effective by invoking criminal sanctions to be applied by the familiar technique of criminal prosecutions, based on statutes or administrative regulations, for what have been aptly called "public welfare offenses." These cases do not fit neatly into any of such accepted classifications of common-law offenses, such as those against the state, the person, property, or public morals. Many of these offenses are not in the nature of positive aggressions or invasions, with which the common law so often dealt, but are in the nature of neglect where the law requires care, or inaction where it imposes a duty. Hence, legislation applicable to such offenses, as a matter of policy, does not specify intent as a necessary element. The accused, if he does not will the violation, usually is in a position to prevent it with no more care than society might reasonably expect and no more exertion than it might reasonably exact from one who assumed his responsibilities. Also, penalties commonly are relatively small, and conviction does no grave damage to an offender's reputation. Under such considerations, courts have turned to construing statutes and regulations which make no mention of intent as dispensing with it and holding that the guilty act alone makes out the crime. This has not, however, been without expressions of misgiving.

It was not until recently that the Court took occasion more explicitly to relate abandonment of the ingredient of intent, not merely with considerations of expediency in obtaining convictions, nor with the *malum prohibitum* classification of the crime, but with the peculiar nature and quality of the offense. We referred to "a now familiar type of legislation whereby penalties serve as effective means of regulation," and continued, "such legislation dispenses with the conventional requirement for criminal conduct—awareness of some wrongdoing. In the interest of the larger good it puts the burden of acting at hazard upon a person otherwise innocent but standing in responsible relation to a public danger." But we warned: Hardship there doubtless may be under a statute which thus penalizes the transaction though consciousness of wrongdoing be totally wanting." *United States* v. *Dotterweich*, 320 U.S. 277.

Neither this Court nor, as far as we are aware, any other has undertaken to delineate a precise line or set forth comprehensive criteria for distinguishing between crimes that require a mental element and crimes that do not. We attempt no closed definition,

for the law on the subject is neither settled nor static. The conclusion reached in the *Balint* and *Behrman* cases has our approval and adherence for the circumstances to which it was there applied. *A different question here is whether we will expand the doctrine of crimes without intent to include those charged here.* [Emphasis added.]

Stealing, larceny, and its variants and equivalents, were among the earliest offenses known to the law that existed before legislation; they are invasions of rights of property which stir a sense of insecurity in the whole community and arouse public demand for retribution, the penalty is high and, when a sufficient amount is involved, the infamy is that of a felony, which, says Maitland, is "as bad a word as you can give to man or thing." State courts of last resort, on whom fall the heaviest burden of interpreting criminal law in this country, have consistently retained the requirement of intent in larceny-type offenses. If any state has deviated, the exception has neither been called to our attention nor disclosed by our research.

Congress, therefore, omitted any express prescription of criminal intent from the enactment before us in the light of an unbroken course of judicial decision in all constituent states of the Union holding intent inherent in this class of offense, even when not expressed in a statute. Congressional silence as to mental elements in an Act merely adopting into federal statutory law a concept of crime already so well defined in common law and statutory interpretation by the states may warrant quite contrary inferences than the same silence in creating an offense new to general law, for whose definition the courts have no guidance except the Act. Because the offenses before this Court in the *Balint* and *Behrman* cases were of this latter class, we cannot accept them as authority for eliminating intent from offenses incorporated from the common law. Nor do exhaustive studies of state court cases disclose any well-considered decisions applying the doctrine of crime without intent to such enacted common-law offenses, although a few deviations are notable as illustrative of the danger inherent in the Government's contentions here.

The Government asks us by a feat of construction radically to change the weights and balances in the scales of justice. The purpose and obvious effect of doing away with the requirement of a guilty intent is to ease the prosecution's path to conviction, to strip the defendant of such benefit as he derived at common law from innocence of evil purpose, and to circumscribe the freedom heretofore allowed juries. Such a manifest impairment of the immunities of the individual should not be extended to common-law crimes on judicial initiative.

The spirit of the doctrine which denies to the federal judiciary power to create crimes forthrightly admonishes that we should not enlarge the reach of enacted crimes by constituting them from anything less than the incriminating components contemplated by the words used in the statute. And where Congress borrows terms of art in which are accumulated the legal tradition and meaning of centuries of practice, it presumably knows and adopts the cluster of ideas that were attached to each borrowed word in the body of learning from which it was taken and the meaning its use will convey to the judicial mind unless otherwise instructed. In such case, absence of contrary direction may be taken as satisfaction with widely accepted definitions, not as a departure from them.

*We hold that mere omission from Section 641 of any mention of intent will not be construed as eliminating that element from the crimes denounced.* [Emphasis added.]

In view of the care that has been bestowed upon the subject, it is significant that we have not found, nor has our attention been directed to, any instance in which Congress has expressly eliminated the mental element from a crime taken from the common law.[7]

Mere silence on intent by the legislature is not enough to impose an absolute liability. Some courts are moving away from the concept of conviction in the absence of culpability. In a 1964 case an appellate court allowed a good-faith belief as to the age of the girl as a defense to the crime of sexual intercourse with a girl under the age of eighteen years (statutory rape).[8]

Guilt without culpability has taken the additional course of vicarious liability. Vicarious liability theories have no basis in the common law. At common law, criminal responsibility was personal and individual, there was no agency or *respondant superior* theory of culpability.

In *Commonwealth* v. *Koczwara* the defendant owned a bar. His bartender served minors in violation of the Pennsylvania Liquor Code. There was no evidence that the defendant was present at any time his bartender served minors beer. The defendant was convicted, fined and sentenced to county jail for three months. The Pennsylvania Supreme Court said:

We, therefore, must determine the criminal responsibility of a licensee of the Liquor Control Board for acts committed by his employees upon his premises, without his personal knowledge, participation, or presence, which acts violate a valid regulatory statute passed under the Commonwealth's police power.

While an employer in almost all cases is not criminally responsible for the unlawful acts of his employees, unless he con-

sents to, approves, or participates in such acts, courts all over the nation have struggled for years in applying this rule within the framework of "controlling the sale of intoxicating liquor." See Annotation, 139 A.L.R. 306 (1942). At common law, any attempt to invoke the doctrine of *respondeat superior* in a criminal case would have run afoul of our deeply ingrained notions of criminal jurisprudence that guilt must be personal and individual. In recent decades, however, many states have enacted detailed regulatory provisions in fields which are essentially noncriminal, e.g., pure food and drug acts, speeding ordinances, building regulations, and child labor, minimum wage and maximum hour legislation. Such statutes are generally enforceable by light penalties, and although violations are labeled crimes, the considerations applicable to them are totally different from those applicable to true crimes, which involve moral delinquency and which are punishable by imprisonment or another serious penalty. Such so-called statutory crimes are in reality an attempt to utilize the machinery of criminal administration as an enforcing arm for social regulations of a purely civil nature, with the punishment totally unrelated to questions of moral wrongdoing or guilt. It is here that the social interest in the general well-being and security of the populace has been held to outweigh the individual interest of the particular defendant. The penalty is imposed despite the defendant's lack of a criminal intent or *mens rea.* The question here raised is whether the legislature *intended* to impose vicarious criminal liability on the licensee-principal for acts committed on his premises without his presence, participation or knowledge.

As the defendant has pointed out, there is a distinction between the requirement of a *mens rea* and the imposition of vicarious absolute liability for the acts of another. It may be that the courts below, in relying on prior authority, have failed to make such a distinction. In any case, we fully recognize it. Moreover, we find that the intent of the legislature in enacting this Code was not only to eliminate the common law requirement of a *mens rea,* but also to place a very high degree of responsibility upon the holder of a liquor license to make certain that neither he nor anyone in his employ commit any of the prohibited acts upon the licensed premises. Such a burden of care is imposed upon the licensee in order to protect the public from the potentially noxious effects of an inherently dangerous business. We, of course, express no opinion as to the *wisdom* of the legislature's imposing vicarious responsibility under certain sections of the Liquor Code. There may or may not be an economic-sociological justification for such liability on a theory of deterrence. Such determination is for the legislature to make, so long as the constitutional requirements are met.

Can the legislature, consistent with the requirements of due process, thus establish absolute criminal liability? Were this the defendant's first violation of the Code, and the penalty solely a minor fine of from $100–$300, we would have no hesitation in upholding such a judgment. Defendant, by accepting a liquor license, must bear this financial risk. Because of a prior conviction for violations of the Code, however, the trial judge felt compelled under the mandatory language of the statute, Section 494(a), to impose not only an increased fine of five hundred dollars, but also a three month sentence of imprisonment. *Such sentence of imprisonment in a case where liability is imposed vicariously cannot be sanctioned by this Court consistently with the law of the land clause of Section 9, Article I of the Constitution of the Commonwealth of Pennsylvania.* [Emphasis added.]

The Courts of the Commonwealth have already strained to permit the legislature to carry over the civil doctrine of *respondeat superior* and to apply it as a means of enforcing the regulatory scheme that covers the liquor trade. We have done so on the theory that the Code established petty misdemeanors involving only light monetary fines. It would be unthinkable to impose vicarious criminal responsibility in cases involving true crimes. Although to hold a principal criminally liable might possibly be an effective means of enforcing law and order, it would do violence to our more sophisticated modern-day concepts of justice. Liability for all true crimes, wherein an offense carries with it a jail sentence, must be based exclusively upon personal causation. It can be readily imagined that even a licensee who is meticulously careful in the choice of his employees cannot supervise every single act of the subordinates. A man's liberty cannot rest on so frail a reed as whether his employee will commit a mistake in judgment.

This Court is ever mindful of its duty to maintain and establish the proper safeguards in a criminal trial. To sanction the imposition of imprisonment here would make a serious change in the substantive criminal law of the Commonwealth, one for which we find no justification. We have *no* case in any jurisdiction which has permitted a *prison term* for a vicarious offense. The Supreme Court of the United States has had occasion only recently to impose due process limitations upon the actions of a state legislature in making unknowing conduct criminal. *Lambert* v. *California*, 355 U.S. 225 (1957). Our own courts have stepped in time and again to protect a defendant from being held criminally responsible for acts about which he had no knowledge and over which he had little control. We would be utterly remiss were we not to so act under these facts.

In holding that the punishment of imprisonment deprives the defendant of due process of law under these facts, we are not

declaring that Koczwara must be treated as a first offender under the Code. He has clearly violated the law for a second time and must be punished accordingly. Therefore, we are only holding that so much of the judgment as calls for imprisonment is invalid, and we are leaving intact the five hundred dollar fine imposed by Judge Hoban under the subsequent offense section.[9]

Criminal negligence may be an alternative to *mens rea*. Statutory crimes may require negligent acts or omissions or allow criminal negligence to satisfy an expressed element of *mens rea*. The vehicle offenses of "reckless driving" and "vehicle manslaughter" express elements which substitute a form of negligence for the concept of *mens rea*. "Reckless driving" requires a reckless disregard for the safety of others, or a knowledge that the driver's method of driving creates an unreasonably high degree of risk to others. "Vehicle manslaughter" in order to be felonious must involve "gross negligence" together with an unlawful act which causes a death. If there is a misdemeanor vehicle manslaughter, ordinary negligence will satisfy that element.

Murder of the second degree also allows a degree of negligence as a substitute for an intent to kill or malice aforethought. The "abandoned-and-malignant-heart" alternative to show malice aforethought may be shown by a reckless disregard for human life together with an act inherently dangerous to life. When a defendant fires two shots at a caboose and engine of a moving train, and there is no intent to kill (actual malice), it still may be a murder. Since the act was unlawful and inherently dangerous to life and done with disregard for the safety of human life it supplies the necessary malice for murder.[10]

In *People* v. *Crenshaw* the defendant and the deceased argued and the defendant threatened to kill the deceased, then hit him with his fist and walked away. The deceased died as a result of a broken neck. Crenshaw was *convicted* of murder. On appeal, the appellate court *reversed** on the grounds of insufficient evidence to justify conviction for murder:

> The circumstances which distinguish murder from manslaughter have been passed upon by this court in many cases. Malice necessary to constitute a killing murder is presumed where the act is deliberate and is likely to be attained with dangerous or fatal consequences. Death or great bodily harm must be the reasonable or probable consequences of the act to constitute murder. The striking of a blow with the fist on the side of the face or head is not likely to be attended with dangerous or fatal consequences, and no inference of an intent to kill is war-

*Extracts only; footnotes and citations are deleted.

ranted from the circumstances disclosed by the proof in this case. The act of defendant in striking deceased was unlawful, but it is clear from the evidence that it was not delivered with the intent of causing death. The People contend that proof of defendant's statement to deceased that if he would go with him he would kill him, or that for two cents he would kill him right there, shows the intent of the defendant was murder. Even though it may be said to indicate a desire on the part of the defendant to take the life of deceased, his act in striking with the bare fist was not committed for the purpose of carrying into effect any intention of that kind which the defendant may have had in mind. The defendant is presumed to have intended the reasonable and probable consequence of his act, but death not being a reasonable or probable consequence of a blow with the bare fist he is not presumed to have intended it to produce that result, and if he did not, the crime would be manslaughter and not murder. In *People* v. *Mighell*, 254 Ill. 53, defendant was indicted for murder. The death resulted from a blow from the bare fist. The defendant was attempting to administer punishment to the deceased for insulting remarks made to a lady relative of defendant. The court said there was not the slightest reason to suppose defendant contemplated death or serious injury to the deceased; that the act would not, in its consequences, naturally tend to destroy life or that such a result could reasonably be anticipated. It was held the crime could not be murder but was manslaughter. That case, in principle, cannot be distinguished from this.

The People argue that the difference in the size of the two men was such that the blow was likely to be attended with fatal consequences. Defendant was five or six inches taller and about fifty pounds heavier than deceased. There might be a case in which the disparity in size and strength of the parties might be so great that a blow delivered with a bare fist might reasonably be expected to result in dangerous or fatal consequences, but there was no such difference in the two men in this case that a blow with the fist by the larger man would naturally or probably cause death. *The evidence was insufficient to warrant the conviction for murder*. [Emphasis added.][11]

# THE CRIMINAL ACT

The key to culpability for the criminal act is voluntary conduct. Such voluntary behavior may require a specific intent, guilty knowledge, or criminal negligence, but these accompany the conduct. A person acts voluntarily when he performs the act described in the statute with intent to perform that act or fail to perform it.

Voluntary conduct requires only that the offender intends to engage in the prohibited conduct; excluded are such acts as those

committed in an unconscious reflex action during sleep or unconsciousness, or while under hypnosis.

In order that a crime be committed, both a wrongful act (or omission) and a wrongful intent must come together. The act is the effect produced through a conscious exertion of will.

A wrongful intent or purpose alone will not constitute a crime; there must be an act or omission where there is a legal duty to act. The act must be conscious and voluntary. Voluntary is used in the sense of a conscious manifestation of will.

A status is not an act but rather a personal condition. It is a condition of being rather than acting. Conditions such as vagrancy have often been upheld as crimes in the past. However, a growing body of authority is to the effect that statutes making a status (condition) a crime are unconstitutional.[12]

In *Tenster* v. *Leary*,[13] the New York Court of Appeals ruled* that New York's vagrancy statute[14] was invalid as it denied constitutional due process to alcoholic derelicts and other unfortunates:

> The crime of common-law vagrancy, which is what subdivision 1 of our statute involves, contains three elements: (1) being without visible means of support, (2) being without employment, and (3) being able to work but refusing to do so. In a more homely fashion our statute has been described as directed against the "loafer or lazy man, the one who hangs about streets and public places without employment or visible means of support when he could with effort obtain something to do." (*People* v. *Sohn*, 199 N.E. 501.) Such statutes have their origins in feudal laws aimed against runaway serfs and the English "poor laws" and were originally designed as a means of regulating the economic life of the populace. The modern emphasis or stated justification for retaining such laws has shifted, however, to the prevention or control of crime and common-law vagrancy remains a crime in virtually all American jurisdictions.
>
> As a number of commentators have observed, common-law vagrancy, in contrast to most other crimes recognized in our law, is not defined in terms of an *act* or *acts* but in terms of a *status* or *condition of being*. The essential element of this crime, as well as of other *status* crimes, is "the accused's having a certain personal condition or being a person of a specified character." Other crimes of *status* would include "gangster statutes" (such as was involved in *Lanzetta* v. *State of New Jersey*, 306 U.S. 451) or statutes making it criminal to be a narcotics addict (such as was involved in *Robinson* v. *State of California*, 370 U.S. 660). Under our own section 887 a number of other "personal conditions" are

*Extracts only; footnotes and citations are deleted.

declared to make one a vagrant and thus subject to imprisonment, e.g., that of being a prostitute or panderer (Section 887, subd. 4), or of being a beggar on the public ways (Section 887, subd. 5). Such statutes cannot stand if they would make criminal a condition, such as one resulting from illness, over which the accused has no control or if the class of persons coming within their ambit is so vaguely defined as to make it unclear to potential violators just what conduct will subject them to criminal liability and what will not. Such constitutional problems would not appear to be directly involved in the instant case, however, as under our *Sohn* decision (*supra*) it seems clear that physical or even psychological inability to work would bar conviction as a vagrant and plaintiff does not appear to attack the statute as void for vagueness (for which reason we need not reach this point). Another constitutional problem, of major proportions, does, however, appear in this case, namely, whether our statute constitutes a valid exercise of the police power.

Initially, it must be observed that a strong presumption of validity attaches to statutes and that the burden of proving invalidity is upon those who challenge their constitutionality to establish this beyond a reasonable doubt, but it must likewise be noted that a statute whose effect is to curtail the liberty of individuals to live their lives as they would and whose justification is claimed to lie in the exercise of the police power of the State must bear a reasonable relationship to, some proportion to, the alleged public good on account of which this restriction on individual liberty would be justified.

The Attorney-General of New York cites to us various statements from our own decisions and from the decisions of our lower courts in support of vagrancy statutes as a valid exercise of the police power. The general thrust of these decisions is that the able-bodied poor may be made, subject to the sanctions of the criminal law, to accept available employment. This view of the matter does, of course, raise the possibility of interesting Thirteenth Amendment problems, and plaintiff strenuously urges these as ground for reversal, and it also raises an interesting "equal protection" question as to whether persons of means are entitled any more than the poor to enjoy the allegedly debilitating effects of idleness, but, on a more fundamental level, we feel the statute is defective on the ground that, whatever purpose and role it may or may not have served in an earlier day, and however valid or invalid may be the proposition that the able-bodied unemployed poor are a likely source of crime, in this era of widespread efforts to motivate and educate the poor toward economic betterment of themselves, it is obvious to all that the vagrancy laws have been abandoned by our governmental authorities as a means of "persuading" unemployed poor persons to seek work

(the Attorney-General does not even suggest that the vagrancy laws would be invoked against such people today). *It is also obvious that today the only persons arrested and prosecuted as common-law vagrants are alcoholic derelicts and other unfortunates*, whose only crime, if any, is against themselves, and whose main offense usually consists in their leaving the environs of skid row and disturbing by their presence the sensibilities of residents of nicer parts of the community, or suspected criminals, *with respect to whom the authorities do not have enough evidence to make a proper arrest or secure a conviction on the crime suspected.* As to the former, it seems clear that they are more properly objects of the welfare laws and public health programs than of the criminal law and, as to the latter, *it should by now be clear to our governmental authorities that the vagrancy laws were never intended to be and may not be used as an administrative short-cut to avoid the requirements of constitutional due process in the administration of criminal justice.* If it is only to allow arrests and criminal prosecutions for vagrancy to continue against individuals such as these that the Attorney-General would have us uphold the statute, then it must fall. And despite certain fairly recent cases upholding similar statutes we can, in fact, see no other purpose in our statute today and, therefore, find it *invalid.* [Emphasis added.][15]

## CAUSATION: RESULT

Causation in fact means causation *sine qua non*. If the harm or injury caused would not have happened *but for* the act, then the act caused the harm or injury. Direct causation exists where there is no intervening force—that is, no human or animal action occurred between the act done by the offender and the resultant injury or harm. The term cause or causation includes all acts which contribute to the result.

The legal phrase *proximate cause* is used frequently in criminal cases. Its definition is as follows: proximate cause is that cause which, operating in natural and continuous sequence, unbroken by any preceding independent intervening cause, produces the result complained of, and without which the result would not have occurred.[16]

Determining proximate cause, however, is not subject to a precise definition which fits all circumstances: it is not a remote cause; there should be a nearness in the causal relationship; it is a relationship of fact and degree.

Conduct is the cause of a result when it is an antecedent but for which the result in question would not have occurred; and the relationship between the conduct and result satisfies any additional causal requirements imposed by the law defining the offense.[17]

Causation becomes a problem where there are two or more

"causes" or when one act causes another act which causes the harm or injury which violates the statute.

The Indiana Supreme Court, in *Stephenson* v. *State*, took up the problem in an unusual situation: defendant Stephenson forced a woman friend (Madge Oberholzer) to get drunk and to accompany him and friends to Chicago. In the train sleeping compartment he forcibly undressed her and committed bizarre acts of sexual perversion including chewing and other mutilation. The next day the woman purchased and took poison. She died about four weeks later. Stephenson was convicted of murder, causing death of another while engaged in an attempted rape. The appellate court *affirmed* the trial court's action, noting several precedents in its opinion*:

> In the case of *State* v. *Preslar*, the defendant in the nighttime fought with his wife, and she left to go to the home of her father. When she reached a point about two hundred yards from her father's home, she, for some reason, did not want to go in the house till morning, laid down on a bed cover, which she had wrapped around her, till daylight. The weather was cold and the next morning she could not walk, but made herself known. She afterwards died. The court held that the wife without necessity exposed herself, and the defendant was not guilty. In the case of *Rex* v. *Donovan*, the defendant struck his wife, and she went to the window to call for help and fell out. Defendant was charged with throwing his wife out of the window with intent to kill. The court held that the evidence must show that by his treatment he intended to make her jump out of the window. In the case of *Gipe* v. *State*, the defendant broke into a house with intent to rob. The deceased ran out of the house and jumped into a well and remained there, and died from exposure. The indictment charged death by violence, to wit, beating and striking. The court held that the evidence did not show the killing was by force and violence as charged, and did not follow the allegations in the indictment, and for that reason the cause was reversed. In *Treadwell* v. *State*, the defendant shot the deceased, who lived from November till the following September. A few weeks before his death he had a heart attack and convulsions. The court found that he died from heart attacks, and the wounds inflicted by defendant had nothing to do with the death. In the case of *State* v. *Shelledy*, the defendant with others went in a body to the home of one W. armed with revolvers, and forcibly took possession of W. and bound his arms so as to render him helpless, and in the presence of W. avowed their purpose to kill W. and placed him in a hack and started to the timber with him, and when on the banks of

---

*Extracts only; footnotes and citations are deleted.

the Iowa river he leaped from the wagon into the water, and they permitted him to drown, while standing by, and made no effort to rescue the said W., where by reasonable effort they might have done so. The court held that the defendant would be guilty of murder under these circumstances. In *Bush* v. *Commonwealth*, the defendant wounded one V. who was taken to the hospital and treated by a physician who communicated to her scarlet fever from which disease she died. The court held in that case, that if the wound is not dangerous, and when in the natural course of events a new and intervening cause appears and causes the death, there is no guilt. If death was not connected with the wound in the regular chain of cause and consequence, there ought not to be any responsibility. If a new and wholly independent instrumentality interposed and produced death, the wound is not the proximate cause. The principle laid down in the last case is well supported by decided cases and textbook writers, and we agree that the reasoning is sound and that it was properly applied in those cases. It is quite clear that in the *Bush* case there was no causal connection between the wound inflicted and the death. But we do not believe that the rule stated in the above case is controlling here.

In the case of *Rex* v. *Beech*, the prosecutrix was the village nurse and lived alone. At 11:45 P.M. on an evening in November, the appellant came to her house when she was in bed. He entered the house by breaking a window and went upstairs to the bedroom occupied by the prosecutrix. The door was locked, and the appellant threatened to break it open if the prosecutrix would not let him in. She refused, and the appellant then tried to burst open the door. The prosecutrix called out that if he got in he would not find her in the room, and, as the appellant continued his attack upon the door, the prosecutrix jumped out of the window sustaining injuries. The prosecutrix also testified that the appellant had attempted to interfere with her on a previous occasion when she had threatened to take poison if he touched her. The court approved the proposition as stated by the lower court as follows: "Whether the conduct of the prisoner amounted to a threat of causing injury to the young woman; was the act of jumping the natural consequence of the conduct of the prisoner and was the grievous bodily harm the result of the conduct of the prisoner?" The court held that, if these questions were answered in the affirmative, he would be guilty. In *Rex* v. *Valade*, where the accused induced a young girl under the age of consent to go along with him to a secluded apartment, and there had criminal sexual intercourse with her, following which she jumped from a window to the street to get away from him, and was killed by the fall. The accused was held guilty of murder. Bishop in his work

on Criminal Law, vol. 2 (9th Ed.), page 484, says: "When suicide follows a wound inflicted by the defendant his act is homicidal, if deceased was rendered irresponsible by the wound and as a natural result of it." We do not understand that by the rule laid down by Bishop, that the wound which renders the deceased mentally irresponsible is necessarily limited to a physical wound. We should think the same rule would apply if a defendant engaged in the commission of a felony such as rape or attempted rape, and inflicts upon his victim both physical and mental injuries, the natural and probable result of which would render the deceased mentally irresponsible and suicide followed, we think he would be guilty of murder.

In the case at bar, appellant is charged with having caused the death of Madge Oberholtzer while engaged in the crime of attempted rape. The evidence shows that appellant, together with Earl Gentry and the deceased, left their compartment on the train and went to a hotel about a block from the depot, and there appellant registered as husband and wife, and immediately went to the room assigned to them. This change from their room on the train to a room in the hotel is of no consequence, for appellant's control and dominion over the deceased was absolute and complete in both cases. The evidence further shows that the deceased asked for money with which to purchase a hat, and it was supplied her by "Shorty" (appellant's chauffeur), at the direction of appellant, and that she did leave the room and was taken by Shorty to a shop and purchased a hat and then, at her request, to a drug store where she purchased the bichloride of mercury tablets, and then she was taken back to the room in the hotel, where about 10:00 A.M. she swallowed the poison. Appellant argues that the deceased was a free agent on this trip to purchase a hat, etc., and that she voluntarily returned to the room in the hotel. This was a question for the jury, and the evidence would justify them in reaching a contrary conclusion. Appellant's chauffeur accompanied her on this trip, and the deceased had, before she left appellant's home in Indianapolis, attempted to get away, and also made two unsuccessful attempts to use the telephone to call help. She was justified in concluding that any attempt she might make, while purchasing a hat or while in the drug store to escape or secure assistance, would be no more successful in Hammond than it was in Indianapolis. We think the evidence shows that the deceased was at all times from the time she was entrapped by the appellant at his home on the evening of March 15 till she returned to her home two days later, in the custody and absolute control of appellant. Neither do we think the fact that the deceased took the poison some four hours after they left the drawing-room on the train or after the crime of attempted rape had

been committed necessarily prevents it from being a part of the attempted rape. Suppose they had not left the drawing-room on the train, and, instead of the deceased taking poison, she had secured possession of appellant's revolver and shot herself or thrown herself out of the window of the car and died from the fall. We can see no vital difference. At the very moment Madge Oberholtzer swallowed the poison she was subject to the passion, desire, and will of appellant. She knew not what moment she would be subjected to the same demands that she was while in the drawing-room on the train. What would have prevented appellant from compelling her to submit to him at any moment? The same forces, the same impulses, that would impel her to shoot herself during the actual attack or throw herself out of the car window after the attack had ceased, was pressing and overwhelming her at the time she swallowed the poison. The evidence shows that she was so weak that she staggered as she left the elevator to go to the room in the hotel, and was assisted by appellant and Gentry; that she was very ill, so much so that she could not eat, all of which was the direct and proximate result of the treatment accorded her by appellant. We think the situation no different here than we find in the *Beech* case or the *Valade* case. *To say that there is no causal connection between the acts of appellant [Stephenson] and the death of Madge Oberholtzer, and that the treatment accorded her by appellant had no causal connection with the death of Madge Oberholtzer would be a travesty on justice.* [Emphasis added.][18]

The court's decision in the above case points out that an intervening cause—one which comes between the antecedent cause and the consequence—is a defense if it is independent of the defendant's antecedent act. If the intervening cause is dependent on the defendant's antecedent act, then it will be no defense for the defendant.

The basic question in cases such as the above is did the defendant kill someone?

If the immediate cause of death was an independent intervening cause then the defendant is not responsible for the death. Illustration: D. knocks out V. and leaves him on the lawn in front of his house. V.'s wife drags V. out into the road and leaves him. V. is run over and killed by a motorist.[19]

Where two persons deliver mortal wounds and each contribute to the death then each is responsible for the death.[20] If the victim languishes because of the defendant's acts and another act produces death, then the defendant is not responsible for the death.[21]

If the intervening act is dependent on the act of the defendant then the defendant is responsible for the death. Illustration: D. gave V. poison sufficient to cause death. V. fell as a result of consuming

the poison. The fall caused a head injury which was the cause of death.[22]

# NOTES

1. *Dennis* v. *United States*, 341 U.S. 494 (1950).
2. *American Communications Association C.I.O.* v. *Douds*, 339 U.S. 382 (1949).
3. *United States* v. *Greenbaum*, 138 F. 2d 437 (1943).
4. *See United States* v. *Balint*, 258 U.S. 250 (1921).
5. 342 U.S. 246 (1952).
6. Title 18, U.S. Code, Section 641.
7. *Morissette* v. *United States*, 342 U.S. 246 (1952).
8. *People* v. *Hernandez*, 393 P. 2d 673 (1964, Calif.).
9. *Commonwealth* v. *Koczwara*, 155 A. 2d 825 (1959, Penna.).
10. *Banks* v. *State*, 211 S.W. 217 (1919, Texas).
11. *People* v. *Crenshaw*, 131 N.E. 576 (1921, Ill.).
12. *Robinson* v. *California*, 370 U.S. 660 (1962).
13. 229 N.E. 2d 426 (1967 N.Y.).
14. New York Code of Criminal Procedure, Section 887, Subdivision 1.
15. *Tenster* v. *Leary*, 229 N.E. 2d 426 (1967, N.Y.).
16. *City of West Plains* v. *Loomis*, 279 F. 2d 564 (1960 Cir.).
17. *Model Penal Code*, 1962 Draft (Philadelphia: American Law Institute), Section 2.03.
18. *Stephenson* v. *State*, 179 N.E. 633 (1932, Ind.).
19. *People* v. *Thomas*, 156 P. 2d 7 (1945, Calif.).
20. *People* v. *Lewis*, 57 P. 470 (1899, Calif.).
21. *People* v. *Lewis*, 57 P. 470 (1899, Calif.).
22. *People* v. *Cobler*, 2 Cal. App. 2d 375 (1934).

# 9

# CLASSIFICATION OF CRIMES

## OBJECTIVES

*Chapter Nine will indicate the grounds for classifying crimes as serious, less serious, and minor; will show the transition from common-law felonies and infamous crimes to contemporary classification of felonies, misdemeanors, and minor offenses or infractions; and will indicate as a primary factor in determining the seriousness of crime the potential in each category of crime for physical injury to the victim(s).*

## LEGAL TERMS

Crimen falsi. *An offense characterized by fraud through concealment, untruthfulness, false weights, forgery, and like crimes. Usually the offense involves such gross untruthfulness as to affect the administration of justice injuriously.*

Ex parte. *On behalf of one party only; in the absence of the opposing party.*

Utter. *To offer. To utter counterfeit coin or a forged writing means to offer it with the representation that it is genuine.*

Ejusdem generis. *Of the same kind; where general words in legislation follow a designation of particular subjects, classes, or persons, the meaning of the general words will ordinarily be presumed to be restricted, unless there is a clear manifestation of a contrary purpose.*

Barratry. *The purchase or sale of office or preferment in church or state.*

Tort-feasor. *One who commits a tort.*

## QUESTIONS FOR STUDY

1. *What is the origin of the felony crime classification?*
2. *Define infamous crime. What is a "high crime"?*
3. *What is the meaning of the term* moral turpitude? *What is the impact, if any, of conviction of a crime involving moral turpitude?*
4. *When is a crime a felony? A misdemeanor?*
5. *What is the justification for legislative action dividing felonies into several degrees or classes?*
6. *What is the rationale for terming some prohibited acts infractions or minor offenses?*
7. *Develop the theme that the social-harm factor inherent in certain types of crimes is linked to grading such crimes as serious offenses.*
8. *What is the legislative reaction to the use of firearms in crime?*

---

**C**rimes have been classified by their identification in the common law (felonies and transgressions); as infamous (crimes which barred the convict as a future witness); as bad in themselves (*malum in se*); or as "bad" because they are prohibited by statutory law (*malum prohibitum*). Contemporary legislatures classify serious crimes as felonies, less serious criminal offenses as misdemeanors, and minor offenses as infractions. Social harm is generally a primary consideration in legislative classification.

## COMMON-LAW FELONIES

Early common law dealt with indictable offenses. The serious crimes were treason and felonies; lesser crimes were transgressions or trespass. Treason and other felonies were heinous offenses and often resulted in forfeiture of the convicted offender's property, as well as death sentences or lengthy terms of imprisonment.

The term *felony* dates back to feudal times when the act done was a breach of the fidelity and loyalty of the feudal relationship (lord and man). In the Middle Ages, any listing of felonies was brief and headed by treason, accounting for the term *treason and other felonies*. The so-called common-law felonies are: treason, murder, manslaughter, larceny, robbery, burglary, rape.[1] However, what is a felony "at common law" depends to some extent on when the question is asked, for the common law did not remain static. Some definitions would add mayhem and arson to the foregoing listing.[2]

Non-felonious crimes were prosecuted in thirteenth-century England in a manner similar to the trials of torts which were civil cases. Matters that were no more than an action for damages were not considered as an indictable trespass; but matters that would

support a charge of trespassing could be formed into an indictment constituting a non-felony crime, a misdemeanor.[3]

# INFAMOUS CRIMES

At common law an infamous crime was one without fame, and common-law felonies were viewed as so heinous in early England that conviction of treason and other felonies, as well as *crimen falsi*, was linked with infamy and the convicted defendant was deemed unworthy of credit as a witness.

The language of the Fifth Amendment to the United States Constitution is a heritage of this infamous crime classification, as well as of the mode of prosecution of infamous crimes, in its declaration: "No person shall be held to answer for a capital, or otherwise infamous crime, unless on a presentment or indictment of a Grand Jury. . . ."

In this amendment, the leading word "capital" describes crime by its punishment only (death). Therefore, the associated words *or otherwise infamous crime* must be held to include any crime subject to an infamous punishment or which was infamous at common law.[4]

In *Ex parte Wilson,* the United States Supreme Court held that a crime punishable by imprisonment for a term of years at hard labor was an infamous crime. The Court reviewed* the fact that there were two kinds of infamy: one founded in the opinions of the people as to the mode of punishment; and the other in the construction of law respecting the future credibility of a person convicted of an infamous crime:

1. *Punishment*

Infamous punishments cannot be limited to those punishments which are cruel or unusual; because, by the Eighth Amendment of the Constitution, "cruel and unusual punishments" are wholly forbidden, and cannot therefore be lawfully inflicted even in cases of convictions upon indictments duly presented by a grand jury.

By the first Crimes Act of the United States, forgery of public securities, or knowingly uttering forged public securities with intent to defraud, as well as treason, murder, piracy, mutiny, robbery, or rescue of a person convicted of a capital crime, was punishable with death; most other offenses were punished by fine and imprisonment; whipping was part of the punishment of stealing or falsifying records, fraudulently acknowledging bail, larceny of goods, or receiving stolen goods; disqualification to hold office was part of the punishment of bribery; and those convicted of perjury or subornation of perjury, besides being fined and impris-

*Extracts only; footnotes and citations are deleted.

oned, were to stand in the pillory for one hour, and rendered incapable of testifying in any court of the United States.

By that act, no provision was made for imprisonment at hard labor. But the punishment of both fine and imprisonment at hard labor was prescribed by later statutes, as, for instance, for counterfeiting coin, or uttering or importing counterfeit coin; and for perjury, subornation of perjury, forgery and counterfeiting, uttering forged securities or counterfeit money, and other grave crimes. Since the punishments of whipping and of standing in the pillory were abolished, imprisonment at hard labor has been substituted for nearly all other ignominious punishments, not capital. And by the act of March 3, 1825, any sentence of imprisonment at hard labor may be ordered to be executed in a State prison or penitentiary.

What punishments shall be considered as infamous may be affected by the changes of public opinion from one age to another. In former times, being put in the stocks was not considered as necessarily infamous. And by the first Judiciary Act of the United States, whipping was classed with moderate fines and short terms of imprisonment in limiting the criminal jurisdiction of the District Courts to cases "where no other punishment than whipping, not exceeding thirty stripes, a fine not exceeding one hundred dollars, or a term of imprisonment not exceeding six months, is to be inflicted." But at the present day either stocks or whipping might be thought an infamous punishment.

Among the punishments "that consist principally in their ignominy," Sir William Blackstone classes "hard labor, in the house of correction or otherwise," as well as whipping, the pillory or the stocks. 4 Bl. Com. 377. And Mr. Dane, while treating it as doubtful whether confinement in the stocks or in the house of correction is infamous, says, "Punishments, clearly infamous, are death, gallows, pillory, branding, whipping, confinement to hard labor, and cropping." 2 Dane Ab. 569, 570.

The same view has been forcibly expressed by Chief Justice Shaw. Speaking of imprisonment in the State prison, which by the statutes of Massachusetts was required to be at hard labor, he said: "Whether we consider the words 'infamous punishment' in their popular meaning, or as they are understood by the Constitution and laws, a sentence to the State prison, for any term of time, must be considered as falling within them. The convict is placed in a public place of punishment, common to the whole State, subject to solitary imprisonment, to have his hair cropped, to be clothed in conspicuous prison dress, subjected to hard labor without pay, to hard fare, coarse and meagre food, and to severe discipline.

For more than a century, imprisonment at hard labor in the

State prison or penitentiary or other similar institution has been considered an infamous punishment in England and America.

### 2. *Credibility*

Infamy which disqualified a convict to be a witness depended upon the character of his crime, and not upon the nature of his punishment. The disqualification to testify appears to have been limited to those adjudged guilty of treason, felony, forgery, and crimes injuriously affecting by falsehood and fraud the administration of justice, such as perjury, subornation of perjury, suppression of testimony by bribery, conspiring to accuse one of crime, or to procure the absence of a witness; and not to have been extended to cases of private cheats, such as the obtaining of goods by false pretenses, or the uttering of counterfeit coin or forged securities. *Fox* v. *Ohio,* 5 How. 410.

But the object and the very terms of the provision in the Fifth Amendment show that incompetency to be a witness is not the only test of its application.

Whether a convict shall be permitted to testify is not governed by a regard to his rights or to his protection, but by the consideration whether the law deems his testimony worthy of credit upon the trial of the rights of others.[5]

Modern law does not disqualify a person from testifying because of a prior conviction of any crime. A distinction is made between those who will not be allowed to testify (disqualified) and those who may testify even though a jury may consider factors which concern the degree of belief they will ascribe to the testimony.

Disqualification may rest on:
1. The witness's lack of personal knowledge.
2. Refusal to take the oath or affirmation to tell the truth.
3. If the witness is the judge presiding at the trial or a juror at the trial.[6]

Credibility of a witness who has testified may be tested by such factors as:
1. Character and conduct.
2. Evidence of conviction of a felony crime, or a crime or offense involving dishonesty.[7]
3. The capacity and opportunity to perceive, recollect or communicate.
4. The existence of bias, interest, or other motive to be untruthful.
5. Inconsistent prior statements.
6. Admission of untruthfulness.
7. Attitude toward the action.[8]

In 1966 the California Supreme Court dealt with the complexities of the classification of infamous crime in *Otsuka* v. *Hite* and

then defined it as crimes involving moral corruption and dishonesty. The majority opinion* stated:

> The term "infamous crime" first appeared in our Constitution of 1849, which similarly declared in Article II, Section 5, that "no idiot or insane person, or person convicted of any infamous crime, shall be entitled to the privileges of an elector." "Infamous crime" was not further defined in the Constitution, but the first session of the Legislature soon filled the gap. Article II of "An Act to Regulate Elections," passed on March 23, 1850, dealt with the qualifications and disabilities of electors. Section 12 thereof was identical with the just-quoted provision of 1849; and Section 14 declared, "A crime shall be deemed infamous which is punishable by death or by imprisonment in the state prison." (Comp. Laws of Cal. (1850–1853), ch. 140, p. 775.)
>
> For 22 years that definition of "infamous crime" remained on the statute books. In 1872, however, the election laws of 1850 and intervening years were superseded by the new Political Code. Section 1084 of that code restated the general disqualification that "no idiot or insane person, or person convicted of any infamous crime, is entitled to the privilege of an elector." But the statutory definitions of "infamous crime" was not reenacted in the new code, nor was any substitute definition provided.
>
> Seven years later the adoption of the Constitution of 1879 further complicated matters. Article II, Section 1, of the new Constitution repeated the now-familiar general language denying the right to vote to persons "convicted of any infamous crime," but then extended the disqualification to the additional category of persons "hereafter convicted of the embezzlement or misappropriation of public money." This was despite the fact that in 1879 a conviction of embezzlement or misappropriation of public money was a conviction of felony (Pen. Code, Section 424), just as it is today; indeed, it has been a felony in this state since the Constitution of 1849 commanded our Legislature to "pass a law providing for the punishment of such embezzlement, or defalcation, as a felony" (Art. IV, Section 22), and the Legislature swiftly complied (Comp. Laws of Cal. (1850–1853) ch. 125, sections 66, 67, pp. 648–649). It follows that if "infamous crime" is deemed to mean "any felony," then Article II, Section 1, declares a voting disqualification applicable on its face to "any person convicted of the felony of embezzling public money." It is difficult to ascribe such a redundancy to the drafters of our fundamental organic law.
>
> Still another complication is presented by Article XX, Section 11, of the Constitution of 1879 (based on Article XI, Section

*Extracts only; footnotes and citations are deleted.

18, of the Constitution of 1849), which directs that "Laws shall be made to exclude from office, serving on juries, and from the right of suffrage, persons convicted of bribery, perjury, forgery, malfeasance in office, *or other high crimes*." [Emphasis added.] What is a "high crime"? The Legislature has not further defined the term but has responded to the command of this section, at least with regard to the right of suffrage, by simply declaring that "Every person who qualifies under the provisions of Section 1 of Article II of the Constitution of this State" and who is duly registered is entitled to vote. (Elec. Code. section 100.) Yet if reasonably possible, every provision of the Constitution should be given meaning and effect, and related provisions should be harmonized. (*Wheeler* v. *Herbert* 92 P. 353.) It would seem that under the rule of construction *ejusdem generis*, the term "high crimes" should be deemed to refer to criminal conduct evidencing the kind of moral corruption and dishonesty inherent in the listed offenses of "bribery, perjury, forgery, malfeasance in office." Harmonizing this definition with the more general language of Article II, Section 1, it would follow that "infamous crime" as used in the latter section should be deemed to refer to offenses evidencing such moral corruption and dishonesty.[9]

## CRIMEN FALSI

In the common law, *crimen falsi* was a crime involving deceit, fraud, or falsehood (perjury, subornation of perjury, forgery, etc.). More recently it appears to be a special classification for misdemeanors.

The Pennsylvania Supreme Court has reviewed the issue whether previous criminal convictions less than felonies in the nature of *crimen falsi* could be admitted to attack a witness's credibility in the case of *Commonwealth* v. *Jones*. This opinion* links infamous crimes with *crimen falsi* misdemeanors, and defines *crimen falsi*:

> The general rule is that the record of previous convictions which are admissible to attack the credibility of a defendant in a criminal case, who has testified in his own behalf, are such only as affect credibility, that is to say, conviction of a felony or a misdemeanor in the nature of a *crimen falsi*. "Conduct derogatory to a witness' character for veracity may be proved by showing by other witnesses that he has been convicted of an infamous offense. No collateral issue of fact is thus raised, as the record establishes the fact; only crimes of felony or a misdemeanor in the nature of *crimen falsi* are admissible to affect credibility." Com[monwealth] v. *Williams*, 160 A. 602, 607; Com[mon-

---

*Extracts only; footnotes and citations are deleted.

*wealth*] v. *Schambers*, 167 A. 645, 646. In the latter case it was said:

The term (*crimen falsi*) involves the element of falsehood, and includes everything which has a tendency to injuriously affect the administration of justice by the introduction of falsehood and fraud. It has been held to include, also, forgery, perjury, subornation of perjury, suppression of testimony by bribery or conspiracy to procure the absence of a witness, barratry, the fraudulent making or alteration of a writing to the prejudice of another man's right.[10]

## MORAL TURPITUDE

Crimes involving moral turpitude are those in which the behavior of the offender is base, vile, or depraved; or contrary to honesty, modesty, or morality.

The term *moral turpitude* has deep roots in the law. The presence of moral turpitude has been used as a test in a variety of situations, including legislation governing the disbarment of attorneys.[11]

Moral turpitude also has found judicial employment as a criterion in disqualifying or impeaching witnesses, in determining the measure of contribution between joint tort-feasors, and in deciding whether certain language is slanderous. Without exception, federal and state courts have held that a crime in which fraud is an ingredient involves moral turpitude. A court of appeals has stated that fraud has ordinarily been the test to determine whether crimes not of the gravest character involve moral turpitude.[12]

The phrase *crime involving moral turpitude* has also been used for many years as a criterion in a variety of statutes. No case has been decided holding that the phrase is vague, nor is there any trace of judicial expression which hints that the phrase is so meaningless as to be a deprivation of due process.

The Unites States Supreme Court has also construed the phrase *crime involving moral turpitude*. An alien had been convicted of counterfeiting government obligations with intent to defraud, and one question of the case was whether the crime of counterfeiting involved moral turpitude. This question was raised by the parties and discussed in the briefs. The Court treated the question without hesitation, stating that the crime of counterfeiting obligations of the United States was "plainly a crime involving moral turpitude."[13]

In a case concerned with the deportation of an alien because he was twice convicted of crimes allegedly involving moral turpitude (tax evasion), the Court recognized the grave nature of deportation (the equivalent of banishment), but held that crimes in which fraud was an ingredient have always been regarded as involving moral turpitude. The phrase *crime involving moral turpitude* has without exception been construed to embrace fraudulent conduct.[14]

# MALUM IN SE vs. MALUM PROHIBITUM

*Malum in se* crimes are those acts which are evil or "bad" according to natural law, morality, or the general public opinion in a community. This classification would include the common-law felonies, most of the infamous crimes, and any crime involving moral turpitude (depravity, vileness, dishonesty, etc.).

*Malum prohibitum* crimes are acts prohibited by law, not basically evil or "bad" standing alone, and not involving any moral turpitude.

Despite the fact that *malum prohibitum* crimes are not evil by the nature of the transaction or transgression and are of little detriment to society at large, there is a measure of "blameworthiness" in these offenses. The criminal liability is founded on some blameworthiness due to failure to obey the statute, despite the fact that the conduct described as forbidden is not linked to acts usually identified as criminal. The obvious example of *malum prohibitum* offenses are the vehicle-code prohibitions as well as regulatory offenses found in codes other than the penal code.

# FELONIES, MISDEMEANORS, AND INFRACTIONS

Felonies are usually so termed or defined by statute. State laws describe felonies as those crimes punishable by death or confinement in a state prison. Some jurisdictions identify felonies as crimes punishable by death or imprisonment for a term in excess of one year (the traditional year-and-a-day rule). Federal laws describe as felonies all crimes against the United States, and within the scope of the U.S. Code, which are punishable by imprisonment for one year or more.

Some crimes which are termed felonies have provisions which allow for an alternative sentence less than commitment to a state prison. In such cases, the offense is deemed a felony only when the convicted offender is sent to state prison. If sentenced to county jail or probation, the offense is a misdemeanor. These crimes are commonly termed "wobblers."

Misdemeanors are the lesser crimes, those that are not classified as felonies. Normally, they are less serious crimes, but in many states so-called high misdemeanors call for penalties that would normally place them in a felony classification.

Some states now or in the future may divide felonies into degrees or classes. There are felonies from Class A to C in New York's Penal Code, and there are felonies of the first to fifth degree in a proposed California Penal Code revision.[15] In these penal codes each crime is then specified as being a felony of a specific degree or class, this identification determining the penalty for the crime. Each degree or class of felony has specific imprisonment limits and minimum, maximum, and minimum parole eligibility. The California

proposed penal code revision also divides its misdemeanors into degrees. First-degree misdemeanors may lead to a term of imprisonment not exceeding one year; second degree, not exceeding six months. When the degree is not specified in the section covering the elements of the crime, it is to be considered a misdemeanor of the second (lesser) degree.

The Model Penal Code suggests dividing misdemeanors in a similar fashion: misdemeanors, and petty misdemeanors.[16]

In some instances, misdemeanors can become felonies when the convicted offender is shown to have a prior conviction for the same type of crime. Such statutes are constitutional; they are not *ex post facto* laws, nor do they conflict with the doctrine of double jeopardy, deny equal protection of the laws or due process of law, or impose a penalty on crimes outside the jurisdiction. The punishment is for the new crime, but it is more severe where there is proof of the required prior conviction.[17]

Infractions or minor offenses are violations of law less than a crime. This classification of prohibited acts usually concern the regulation of non-criminal behavior, such as some violations of the vehicle code. An infraction or minor offense is punishable by fine only and not imprisonment.

## THE SOCIAL-HARM FACTOR

There has been some classification of crimes as to their social harm or "seriousness." Classically, crimes against people or directed against the habitation (home, residence) were believed to be more serious than crimes against property or the public order. Of the seven major crimes in the Federal Bureau of Investigation's *Uniform Crime Reports*, four are crimes against people: murder, aggravated assault (use of weapons, infliction of serious injury), rape, and robbery.

Crimes having a social-harm factor are those in which there is a face-to-face confrontation between the offender and the victim(s); or in which the victim is physically injured or such physical injury is threatened or possible.

The National Advisory Commission on Criminal Justice Standards and Goals recommends that police chiefs identify those crimes on which police resources will be concentrated, and suggests the highest priority be given to:

1. Most serious crimes.
2. Crimes that stimulate the greatest fear.
3. Crimes resulting in the greatest economic loss.[18]

There is a strong legislative reaction to the use of firearms in crime. Penal codes often deny probation and/or increase the usual sentence when a robber, rapist, burglar, kidnapper, or arsonist is armed with a firearm or other deadly weapon at the time of the

crime. This reaction to the social harm inherent in firearms use by such criminals is being extended in some jurisdictions to additional penalties for persons found to be armed with a concealable firearm at the time of arrest. This emerging policy is that criminals with guns threaten physical harm to victims and police, and crimes in which the offender is armed should be considered most serious crimes.

California statutes provide:

### Committing felony while carrying dangerous weapons.

Any person who commits or attempts to commit any felony within this state while armed with any of the deadly weapons, as defined by subdivision (f) of Section 3024,* upon conviction of such felony or of an attempt to commit such felony, shall in addition to the punishment prescribed for the crime of which he has been convicted, be punishable by imprisonment in a state prison for not less than five nor more than 10 years. Such additional period of imprisonment shall commence upon the expiration or other termination of the sentence imposed for the crime of which he is convicted and shall not run concurrently with such sentence.

Upon a second conviction under like circumstances the additional period of imprisonment shall be for not less than 10 years nor for more than 15 years, and upon a third conviction under like circumstances the additional period of imprisonment shall be for not less than 15 nor for more than 25 years, such terms of additional imprisonment to run consecutively.

Upon a fourth or subsequent conviction under like circumstances the person so convicted may be imprisoned for life or for a term of not less than 25 years, within the discretion of the court in which the fourth or subsequent conviction was had.[19]

### Use of firearm in robbery, assault with deadly weapon, etc: Additional punishment: Subsequent convictions.

Any person who uses a firearm in the commission or attempted commission of a robbery, assault with a deadly weapon, murder, rape, burglary, or kidnapping, upon conviction of such crime, shall, in addition to the punishment prescribed for the crime of which he has been convicted, be punished by imprisonment in the State prison for a period of not less than five years. Such additional period of imprisonment shall commence upon expiration or other termination of the sentence imposed for the

*The words *deadly weapon* are defined in Section 3024 to include any instrument or weapon of the kind commonly known as a blackjack, slingshot, billy, sandclub, sandbag, metal knuckles; any dirk, dagger, pistol, revolver, or any other firearm; any knife having a blade longer than five inches; any razor with an unguarded blade; and any metal pipe or bar used or intended to be used as a club.

crime of which he is convicted and shall not run concurrently with such sentence.

Upon a second conviction under like circumstances, the additional period of imprisonment shall be for a period of not less than 10 years, and upon a third conviction under like circumstances the additional period of imprisonment shall be for a period of not less than 15 years, such terms of additional imprisonment to run consecutively.

Upon a fourth or subsequent conviction under like circumstances, the defendant may be imprisoned for life or a period of not less than 25 years, in the discretion of the court.

This section shall apply even in those cases where the use of a weapon is an element of the offense.[20]

# NOTES

1. Theodore F.T. Plucknett, *A Concise History of the Common Law* (Boston: Little, Brown and Co., 1956), pp. 442–54.
2. *Otsuka* v. *Hite*, 414 P. 2d 412 (1966, Calif.).
3. Plucknett, pp. 455–58.
4. *Mackin* v. *United States*, 117 U.S. 348 (1886).
5. *Ex parte Wilson*, 114 U.S. 417 (1884).
6. Rules of Evidence for the United States Courts and Magistrates, effective July 1, 1973, Rule 601 *et. seq. See also* California Evidence Code, Section 701 *et. seq.*
7. Rules of Evidence for the United States Courts and Magistrates, Rules 608–9.
8. California Evidence Code, Section 780.
9. *Otsuka* v. *Hite*, 414 P. 2d 412 (1966, Calif.).
10. *Commonwealth* v. *Jones*, 5 A. 2d 804 (1939, Penna.).
11. *In re Kirby*, 73 N.W. 92 (1897, S.D.); *Bartos* v. *United States District Court*, 19 F. 2d 722 (1927).
12. *United States ex rel. Berlandi* v. *Reimer*, 113 F. 2d 429 (1940).
13. *United States ex rel. Volpe* v. *Smith*, 289 U.S. 422 (1933).
14. *Jordan* v. *De George*, 341 U.S. 223 (1951).
15. Assembly Bill 565, 1975.
16. *Model Penal Code*, 1962 Draft (Philadelphia: American Law Institute), Sections 1.04 (3) and (4).
17. *People* v. *Calderon*, 23 Cal. Rptr. 62 (1962).
18. U.S. National Advisory Commission on Criminal Justice Standards and Goals, *Report on Police* (Washington, D.C.: U.S. Government Printing Office, 1973), p. 12.
19. California Penal Code, Section 12022.
20. California Penal Code, Section 12022.5.

# 10

# JURISDICTION

## OBJECTIVES

The two major objectives of Chapter Ten are to present jurisdiction as the power, authority, and rights of courts to act; and to reveal the many factors that determine jurisdiction. Secondary objectives are to link jurisdiction with venue; to spell out the differences between trial and appellate jurisdiction; to describe the jurisdiction of the federal government as opposed to state-wide jurisdiction; and to indicate the statute of limitations as a possible bar to establishing jurisdiction.

## LEGAL TERMS

Venue. *The geographic division in which a court with jurisdiction to adjudicate is located.*

De novo. *Over again; a second time.*

Vicinage. *Neighborhood; vicinity; area.*

Voir dire. *This term is usually linked to the preliminary examination of a juror or witness; it is oriented to seeking the true facts about a juror's or witness's competency or interest.*

Lex loci delicti (lex loci delictus, lex delicti). *The law of the place where the crime was committed.*

## QUESTIONS FOR STUDY

1. How is the sovereignty of the federal government expressed in the area of jurisdiction? State governments?

2. Define original jurisdiction. Appellate jurisdiction.

3. How is venue linked with jurisdiction?

4. What is the rationale for prosecution and trial in the place or district in which the crime was committed?

5. What is the maritime jurisdiction of the federal government? Its jurisdiction over aircraft?

6. *Are federal laws giving federal courts subject matter rather than territorial jurisdiction, as in bank robberies and unlawful flight, necessary and proper legislation? Why?*

7. *Describe the rule of* lex loci delicti.

8. *What factors establish larceny as a continuing crime?*

9. *Does a state have any extra-territorial jurisdiction?*

10. *What factors determine whether a statute of limitations in a specific crime has run its term?*

---

**S**overeign governments—federal, state, county, and municipal—within the scope of their police power make and enforce the substantive criminal law within their territorial jurisdiction.

Federal courts have jurisdiction over federal-law offenses codified in the U.S. Code; state courts have jurisdiction over offenses codified in their state criminal or penal code. In addition, federal courts have an appellate or *habeas corpus* jurisdiction whenever a person seeks a legal remedy and can develop a "federal question" —a pleading to move his or her appeal or petition from the jurisdiction of the state courts into the federal courts.

On federal "lands" the authority of the United States government is equal to the power of state governments as to lands within the state. Federal "lands" include territories such as Puerto Rico and Washington, D.C.; military bases and facilities; and federal buildings. A similar authority exists in the "maritime" jurisdiction of the federal government, such as conduct aboard ships of American registry or ships of any registry in "American" waters. This authority has been extended to aircraft in "American" airspace.

## COURTS: JURISDICTION

Jurisdiction is the authority, power, and right of courts to act; it is the legal authority by which judges exercise their control over the behavior of individuals.

Courts, in a broad division of jurisdiction by subject matter, assign civil cases to one portion of a court system and criminal cases to another.

In an equally broad division of jurisdiction, courts are assigned original or appellate jurisdiction.

Original jurisdiction means the right and power of a court to hear and determine a case in the first instance.

Appellate jurisdiction is the right and power to review cases tried and determined in lower courts; it is jurisdiction to revise or correct judgments of courts of original jurisdiction.

In some court systems, courts with original jurisdiction in felonies may be assigned appellate jurisdiction in cases appealed from

lower courts of original jurisdiction in which lesser crimes are tried.

A court system might have a tiered organization which gives the lowest tier of courts the original jurisdiction to try and sentence persons charged and convicted of misdemeanor crimes. The next tier would have the dual character of original jurisdiction to try and sentence persons charged and convicted of felony crime, and an appellate jurisdiction to hear appeals from convictions of misdemeanors. Added to these two tiers may be one or more purely appellate court levels. A court of appeals is one to which all persons convicted of felony crimes have a right to appeal; and a supreme court is one which, at its discretion, accepts cases by petition after a hearing at the appellate court (retaining control of the number and types of cases it will decide).

The basic federal court system for territorial jurisdiction is comprised of judicial districts and circuits. Small or less populated states are usually one judicial district; other states are divided into two or more districts. The circuits are made up of groups of states, and includes United States territories (Guam, Puerto Rico, etc.) and Washington, D.C.[1]

The federal court system is also tiered. Commissioners (magistrates) within a federal district handle the minor or misdemeanor cases for trial and sentence. District courts have original jurisdiction over felony crimes as well as over the commissioners within their district. There is a circuit court of appeal which has the primary appellate jurisdiction only, and a United States Supreme Court which chooses the cases it will hear and decides and rejects those petitions it determines are not of sufficient importance to warrant a hearing at this, the highest level of the United States court system.

States divide their territory by counties or groups of counties, or judicial districts, for territorial jurisdiction, with some special provisions for lower courts at the municipal level to serve highly urban areas.[2]

## VENUE

Venue at common law meant the county in which the criminal proceeding was to be tried. It now designates the county or other geographic division in which a court with jurisdiction to adjudicate the case is located, and within whose territorial jurisdiction a trial jury will be selected. It refers initially to such courts as have territorial authority over crimes occurring within a particular geographic area.

Venue can be changed by a court of original jurisdiction upon a motion alleging the defendant cannot obtain a fair trial in the place of territorial jurisdiction. There is a need for an affirmative showing on this motion that the potential jurors have been prejudiced by publicity or other factors and could not arrive at a verdict free from such prejudice.

It is not always necessary to begin the trial or complete the trial in order to obtain a change of venue. It is often preferable to determine the place of trial prior to the actual trial of the case rather than afterwards in order to prevent duplication of the trial. There are jurisdictions which authorize and suggest a pre-trial motion and appellate petition (for writ of mandate) to determine prior to trial whether the place of trial should be changed because of prejudice.

This procedure allows the appellate court to review the evidence of prejudice and make a decision *de novo* whether there is a "reasonable likelihood that a fair trial cannot be had in the present forum."[3] If there is a "reasonable likelihood," the appellate court will order the trial moved to a different geographical area.

Venue can be allocated by legislation in the case of crimes with "continuing" characteristics such as kidnapping, awarding venue to either the place where the initial crime occurred or any county into which the victim of the crime was transported. Conspiracies have a "continuing" factor inasmuch as they are usually triable wherever the conspiracy was maintained: wherever any overt act in furtherance of the conspiracy was done, or wherever one or more of the conspirators spent a considerable portion of his or her time during the conspiracy.

Indictments or information containing the accusation of crime must allege sufficient facts to establish venue in the court in which it is filed; and this geographical placing of the crime must be identified as, and in fact be, in the territorial jurisdiction of such court.

State statutes must insure, in criminal prosecutions, trial by a jury of the *vicinage*. The Constitution makes clear that determination of proper venue in a criminal case requires determination of where the crime was committed.[4] This principle is enacted in numerous statutory enactments, which provide that except as otherwise permitted, "the prosecution shall be had in a district in which the offense was committed..." The provision for trial in the vicinity of the crime is a safeguard against the unfairness in investigating at long distance and hardship in producing witnesses at a distant court.[5]

The basic constitutional guarantee of a trial by jury calls for trial by an impartial jury. The case of *Rideau* v. *Louisiana* illustrates local prejudicial publicity requiring a change of venue as the best means of insuring trial by an impartial jury.

In *Rideau*, the petitioner Wilbert Rideau was arrested and lodged in the parish (similar to county in other states) jail, no more than a few hours after a man robbed a bank in Lake Charles, Louisiana, kidnapped three of the bank's employees and killed one of them. The next morning a motion picture film with a sound track was made of an "interview" in the jail between petitioner and the sheriff of the parish. This "interview" lasted approximately twenty

minutes and consisted of interrogation by the sheriff and admissions by petitioner that he had perpetrated the bank robbery, kidnapping, and murder. Later the same day and on the succeeding two days, the filmed "interview" was broadcast over the local television station and was seen and heard by many people in the parish. Subsequently, petitioner was arraigned on charges of armed robbery, kidnapping, and murder, and two lawyers were appointed to represent him. They promptly filed a motion for change of venue; this was denied and petitioner was convicted in the trial court of the parish and *sentenced to death on the murder charge.*

The United States Supreme Court *reversed* Rideau's conviction, ruling that it was a denial of due process of law for the trial court to refuse the request for a change of venue after the people of the parish had been exposed repeatedly and in depth to the spectacle of the petitioner personally confessing in detail to the crimes with which he was later to be charged. The majority opinion concluded:

> We do not hesitate to hold, without pausing to examine a particularized transcript of the *voir dire* examination of the members of the jury, that due process of law in this case required a trial before a jury drawn from a community of people who had not seen and heard Rideau's televised "interview."[6]

Experience has shown that verdicts in the jurisdiction where prejudice is high are different from verdicts obtained in a different geographical area in which prospective jurors are uninfluenced by the local prejudice of the community in which the trial would have normally been held. In the *Fain* case[7] the local court and jury found the defendant guilty and imposed the penalty of death for the crime committed. After reversal and the subsequent change of venue to a different geographical area, a new jury, uninfluenced by any local bias, also found Fain guilty but imposed the alternate sentence of life rather than the extreme penalty of death.

## FEDERAL JURISDICTION

The criminal jurisdiction of the federal government is stated in Title 18, U.S. Code, Section 7:

**SPECIAL MARITIME AND TERRITORIAL JURISDICTION OF THE UNITED STATES DEFINED:**
The term "special maritime and territorial jurisdiction of the United States," as used in this title, includes:

(1) The high seas, any other waters within the admiralty and maritime jurisdiction of the United States and out of the jurisdiction of any particular State, and any vessel belonging in whole or in part to the United States or any citizen thereof, or to any corporation created by or under the laws of the United States,

or of any State, Territory, District, or possession thereof, when such vessel is within the admiralty and maritime jurisdiction of the United States and out of the jurisdiction of any particular State.

(2) Any vessel registered, licensed, or enrolled under the laws of the United States, and being on a voyage upon the waters of any of the Great Lakes, or any of the waters connecting them, or upon the Saint Lawrence River where the same constitutes the International Boundary Line.

(3) Any lands reserved or acquired for the use of the United States, and under the exclusive or concurrent jurisdiction thereof, or any place purchased or otherwise acquired by the United States by consent of the legislature of the State in which the same shall be, for the erection of a fort, magazine, arsenal, dockyard, or other needful building.

(4) Any island, rock, or key containing deposits of guano, which may, at the discretion of the President, be considered as appertaining to the United States.

(5) Any aircraft belonging in whole or in part to the United States, or any citizen thereof, or to any corporation created by or under the laws of the United States, or any State, Territory, District, or possession thereof, while such aircraft is in flight over the high seas, or over any waters within the admiralty and maritime jurisdiction of the United States and out of the jurisdiction of any particular State.

Subdivisions 2, 3, and 4 define the general territorial jurisdiction of the federal government within the nation's boundaries; subdivisions 1 and 5 describe the extraterritorial jurisdiction of the federal government and particularly concerns vessels and aircraft.

Laws of states are assimilated in particular federal enclaves. Courts have held that Congress may lawfully declare that the criminal law of a state as it exists at the time shall be the law of the United States in particular portions of United States territory subject to the latter's exclusive jurisdiction.[8] Section 13, Title 18, U.S. Code, is often described as the Assimilative Criminal Act. It reads:

**LAWS OF STATES ADOPTED FOR AREAS WITHIN FEDERAL JURISDICTION:** Whoever within or upon any of the places now existing or hereafter reserved or acquired as provided in Section 7 of this title, is guilty of any act or omission which, although not made punishable by any enactment of Congress, would be punishable if committed or omitted within the jurisdiction of the State, Territory, Possession, or District in which such place is situated, by the laws thereof in force at the time of such act or omission, shall be guilty of a like offense and subject

to a like punishment. (Section 7 of Title 18, U.S. Code, specifies the territorial and extra-territorial jurisdiction of the federal government.)

Federal laws now give federal courts jurisdiction over persons accused of crimes such as bank robbery and thefts committed against a federally insured bank; transporting a stolen vehicle over state lines; flight across state lines to avoid state prosecution; and interstate kidnapping. At the time these and similar laws were enacted it was believed to be necessary and proper legislation.

In 1819, when the state of Maryland contested federal legislation under this *necessary and proper* clause of the Constitution,[9] the United States Supreme Court ruled in favor of the national government, and the Court's comment on this constitutional principle was:

> In ascertaining the sense in which the word "necessary" is used in this clause of the Constitution, we may derive some aid from that with which it is associated. Congress shall have power "to make all laws which shall be *necessary and proper* to carry into execution" the powers of the government. If the word "necessary" was used in that strict and rigorous sense for which the counsel for the State of Maryland contend, it would be an extraordinary departure from the usual course of the human mind, as exhibited in composition, to add a word, the only possible effect of which is to qualify that strict and rigorous meaning; to present to the mind the idea of some choice of means of legislation not straightened and compressed within the narrow limits for which gentlemen contend.
>
> But the argument which most conclusively demonstrates the error of the construction contended for by the counsel for the State of Maryland, is founded on the intention of the Convention, as manifested in the whole clause. To waste time and argument in proving that, without it, Congress might carry its powers into execution, would be not much less idle than to hold a lighted taper to the sun. As little can it be required to prove, that in the absence of this clause, Congress would have some choice of means. That it might employ those which, in its judgment, would most advantageously effect the object to be accomplished. That any means adapted to the end, any means which tended directly to the execution of the constitutional powers of the government, were in themselves constitutional. This clause, as construed by the State of Maryland, would abridge, and almost annihilate this useful and necessary right of the legislature to select its means. That this could not be intended, is, we should think, had it not been already controverted, too apparent for controversy. We think so for the following reasons:

*1st*. The clause is placed among the powers of Congress, not among the limitations on those powers.

*2nd*. Its terms purport to enlarge, not to diminish the powers vested in the government. It purports to be an additional power, not a restriction on those already granted. No reason has been, or can be assigned for thus concealing an intention to narrow the discretion of the national legislature under words which purport to enlarge it. The framers of the Constitution wished its adoption, and well knew that it would be endangered by its strength, not by its weakness. Had they been capable of using language which would convey to the eye one idea, and, after deep reflection, impress on the mind another, they would rather have disguised the grant of power, than its limitation. If, then, their intention had been, by this clause, to restrain the free use of means which might otherwise have been implied, that intention would have been inserted in another place, and would have been expressed in terms resembling these. "In carrying into execution the foregoing powers, and all others," etc, "no laws shall be passed but such as are necessary and proper." Had the intention been to make this clause restrictive, it would unquestionably have been so in form as well as in effect.

The result of the most careful and attentive consideration bestowed upon this clause is, that if it does not enlarge, it cannot be construed to restrain the powers of Congress, or to impair the right of the legislature to exercise its best judgment in the selection of measures to carry into execution the constitutional powers of the government. If no other motive for its insertion can be suggested, a sufficient one is found in the desire to remove all doubts respecting the right to legislate on that vast mass of incidental powers which must be involved in the Constitution, if that instrument be not a splendid bauble.

We admit, as all must admit, that the powers of the government are limited, and that its limits are not to be transcended. But *we think the sound construction of the Constitution must allow to the national legislature that discretion, with respect to the means by which the powers it confers are to be carried into execution, which will enable that body to perform the high duties assigned to it, in the manner most beneficial to the people. Let the end be legitimate, let it be within the scope of the Constitution, and all means which are appropriate, which are plainly adapted to that end, which are not prohibited, but consistent with the letter and spirit of the Constitution, are constitutional.* [Emphasis added.][10]

The extraterritorial jurisdiction of the federal government has been judicially reviewed. In the case of *United States* v. *Flores*, the

issue centered around whether the criminal jurisdiction of the United States was based solely on the territorial principle and could not be extended to include crimes in the territorial waters of a foreign sovereignty. The case concerned an American citizen indicted for murdering another American citizen in foreign territorial waters aboard the *S.S. Padnsay,* an American vessel, while in a foreign port. In *Flores* the Supreme Court stated:*

It is true that the criminal jurisdiction of the United States is in general based on the territorial principle, and criminal statutes of the United States are not by implication given an extraterritorial effect. But that principle has never been thought to be applicable to a merchant vessel which, for purposes of the jurisdiction of the courts of the sovereignty whose flag it flies to punish crimes committed upon it, is deemed to be a part of the territory of that sovereignty, and not to lose that character when in navigable waters within the territorial limits of another sovereignty.

In view of the wide recognition of this principle of extraterritorial jurisdiction over crimes committed on merchant vessels and its explicit adoption in *United States* v. *Rodgers, supra* [150 U.S. 249 (1893)], we cannot say that the language of the present statute punishing offenses on United States vessels out of the jurisdiction of a State, "when committed within the admiralty and maritime jurisdiction of the United States," was not intended to give effect to it. If the meaning of the statute were doubtful, the doubt would be resolved by the report on these sections by the Special Joint Committee on the Revision of the Laws, 60th Congress, in which it was pointed out that the jurisdiction extends to vessels of the United States when on navigable waters within the limits of a foreign state, and "all cases arising on board such vessels while on any such waters, are clearly cases within the admiralty and maritime jurisdiction of the United States."

*In the absence of any controlling treaty provision, and any assertion of jurisdiction by the territorial sovereign, it is the duty of the courts of the United States to apply to offenses committed by its citizens on vessels flying its flag, its own statutes, interpreted in the light of recognized principles of international law. So applied the indictment here sufficiently charges an offense within the admiralty and maritime jurisdiction of the United States.* [Emphasis added.][11]

At one time crimes aboard American-owned aircraft were not within federal jurisdiction as they were not crimes committed on an American "vessel" or on the "high seas."[12] However, the addi-

---

*Extracts only; footnotes and citations are deleted.

tion of subdivision 5 to Section 7 of Title 18, U.S. Code, by amendment in 1952 corrected the jurisdiction situation in regard to aircraft and air space.

## STATE TERRITORIAL JURISDICTION

State criminal or penal codes provide for territorial and extraterritorial jurisdiction over: (1) crimes committed within the state; and (2) crimes in which part of the criminal transaction happens inside of the state's geographic boundaries.

The rule of *lex loci delicti* is that jurisdiction is at the place of the wrong, where the acts of the offender take effect. Depending on the crime involved, the site of a crime may be where the act or omission was done or the place of the result.

A defendant (Updike) appealed his conviction of fraudulently obtaining $5,000 from one Theodore Zadra. The issue in dispute was whether Colorado courts had jurisdiction in this case. The appellate court *affirmed* Updike's conviction, ruling that Colorado courts did have jurisdiction:

> A crime is an injury to the state where it is committed, and the courts of that state have jurisdiction thereof; this is not disputed. The general rule is that the crime of obtaining money or property by false pretenses is completed where the money or property is obtained, and that, if the pretenses are made within one jurisdiction and the money or property is obtained in another, the person making the representations must be indicted within the latter jurisdiction. The same rule is applicable to the obtaining of money by means of the confidence game. In line with the above, this court has declared that the crime of obtaining money by false pretenses is committed where the property is obtained by the defendant. (*Pepper* v. *People*, 225 P. 846.) It narrows the question to a determination of where the property or thing of value was obtained.

> It does not make a particle of difference whether the fraudulently obtained check ($5,000) was sold by defendant [Updike] in Idaho, as his counsel asserts, or deposited there for collection. The question is not where he sold it, but where he obtained it; and whether he sold it or deposited it for collection, or where or in whatever manner he may have disposed of his booty theretofore obtained, is beside the question. The subsequent history of the travels of the check are only incidental; after the crime was committed, it is immaterial who eventually got the check or its proceeds.

> As we have said, Zadra's check was mailed at Glenwood Springs, Garfield County, Colorado, to defendant. There it was delivered to the postmaster as agent of defendant; then and there defendant so obtained it; it completed the offense, and the venue was properly laid in Garfield county in Colorado.

If we take defendant at his word that it was money as such, instead of a check, which he is charged with obtaining by fraud, it nevertheless means the money which Zadra had on deposit at Glenwood Springs, obtained there, and used to replace that which defendant got on the check from the bank at Boise. He is neither charged nor convicted here with obtaining any money at all in Idaho.

Another ingenious argument is advanced to fix the situs of the crime outside of the state of Colorado. It is suggested that it was committed in Idaho, because Zadra's check did not become a thing of value until it was endorsed, which endorsement was made in the first instance in the latter state. We are compelled to disagree with this viewpoint as to the effect of such endorsement. If Zadra's check had possessed no value beyond its mere indorsement, the drawee bank at Glenwood Springs (Colorado) would have repudiated it and returned it marked "no funds."

*When defendant feloniously by fraudulent pretenses extracted $5,000 of Zadra's money out of the bank at Glenwood Springs [Colorado], we are persuaded that the crime was committed in Colorado fully as much as if defendant had robbed Zadra or the bank with far-reaching tools while he stood in an adjoining state. One may perpetrate an offense against a state or county upon whose soil he never touched foot.* [Emphasis added.] We see no difference in principle from the case at bar if one should stand in one state and shoot at another in a neighboring state. The assailant is presumed to follow up his bullet, and constructively makes the attempt to kill in the State where the bullet strikes. Here, defendant's bullets of fraudulent misrepresentations were shot from Idaho, some of them, in fact, from Colorado, but they all struck the mortal blow to Zadra's bank account in Colorado, where the missiles took effect. We are unable to see any valid distinction on the subject of venue in the absence of statute, between such offenses against the person and against property, when both constitute crimes against the state. If counsel for defendant are correct in their argument, it logically follows that it is no crime in this state to abstract a billfold of traveler's checks from a bank in this jurisdiction by fraud or theft, as long as the miscreant takes the precaution to cash them in any other part of the world. It cannot be so.[13]

Ordinarily a state does not seek jurisdiction over criminal acts done outside of its boundaries. States do exert jurisdiction over crimes committed in part in their states. These statutes provide that whenever a person, with intent to commit a crime, does any act within the state in execution or partial execution of such intent, culminating in commission of a crime, either within or without the state, such person is punishable for such crime in the state in the

same manner as if the crime had been committed in a county within the state. However, these statutes must be construed as applying only where the act(s) done within the state amount to an attempt.

Roy L. Buffum, a physician and surgeon, and Reginald L. Rankin were indicted for and convicted of criminal abortion in that they conspired to use certain means to induce miscarriages.

Evidence at trial indicated that four women who were pregnant went separately to the office of Buffum in Long Beach to solicit his aid in inducing miscarriages. Buffum refused to perform the abortions but took the telephone numbers of three of the women and told each she would receive a call. Rankin later telephoned them, told them the amount they must pay, arranged to meet them at a designated intersection in Long Beach, and indicated that he would transport them to the place where the abortions were to be performed. Buffum gave Rankin's telephone number to the fourth woman, and she called Rankin and made similar arrangements. Rankin met the women at the appointed place and drove them in his automobile to Tijuana, Mexico. There, with the assistance of Rankin, another man performed an operation upon each of them. While in the operating room, three of the women gave money to Rankin. Later the same day Rankin returned the women to Long Beach, where they again went their separate ways. Subsequently three of them required hospitalization. Buffum treated one of them without preliminary examination or inquiry as to the nature of her illness, and reimbursed her family for the hospital bill.

In appealing this conviction Buffum claimed the California courts did not have jurisdiction as neither he nor his co-defendant Rankin committed the crime of criminal abortion in California. The appellate court *reversed* this case:

> The People rely upon subdivision 1 of section 27 of the Penal Code, which provides that persons may be punished "under the laws of this state" if they "commit, in whole or in part, any crime within this state," and also upon section 778a of that code, which provides: "Whenever a person, with intent to commit a crime, does any act within this state in execution or part execution of such intent, which culminates in the commission of a crime, either within or without this state such person is punishable for such crime in this state in the same manner as if the same had been committed entirely within this state."
>
> To read such a statute as authorizing the punishment by one state of acts which do not amount to an attempt but are merely preparatory to the commission of a crime in another state would seem tantamount to an effort to regulate conduct in the other jurisdiction.
>
> Section 778a of the Penal Code should be construed as applying only where the acts done within the state amount to an

attempt. By its terms the section is limited to acts done "in execution or part execution of" an intent to commit a crime, and these words are comparable to the expression "in whole or in part" as used in subdivision 1 of section 27. The statute further requires that what is done in the state must be of such a nature that it "culminates" in the commission of an offense, and this is analogous to the requirement in attempt cases that there must be a "direct" ineffectual act towards consummation of the crime.

Since section 778a and subdivision 1 of section 27 does not apply unless acts are done within the state which amount at least to an attempt, we must next determine whether defendants could properly be convicted of an attempt to violate section 274 upon a showing that they transported the four women from a place in California to a place in Mexico with the intention of performing abortions upon them in that country. Sections 663 and 664 of the Penal Code prescribe punishment for attempts to commit crimes but do not define the offense. This court has held that two elements are necessary to establish an attempt, namely, a specific intent to commit a crime and a "direct" ineffectual act done towards its commission. Preparation alone is not enough, there must be some appreciable fragment of the crime committed, it must be in such progress that it will be consummated unless interrupted by circumstances independent of the will of the attempter, and the act must not be equivocal in nature. *No case has been cited or found which holds that persons can be convicted of an attempt to commit abortions if they do no more within the state than make arrangements for transportation and then take women from California to Mexico for the purpose of performing abortions upon them in that country. It is our opinion that such conduct is merely preparatory and does not constitute a direct, unequivocal act done toward the commission of the offense specified.* [Emphasis added.] There is nothing in the section which indicates that transportation or arrangement therefor has a direct relation to the acts prohibited by the statute.[14]

A state can exercise jurisdiction for crimes committed outside of the state in cases involving larceny if the proceeds of the crime are brought into the state. This is only possible because larceny is a continuing crime in which jurisdiction not only exists at the locale of the actual larceny, but anywhere the theft's proceeds are transported. This is not true of crimes that are completed at their site.

Lyle J. McGowan was *convicted in California* of *burglary* arising from a breaking-and-entering *in Oregon*. Defendant's appeal was based on a lack of jurisdiction of the California courts as the crime of burglary was wholly committed in the adjoining state of Oregon.

The appellate court *reversed*, ruling that the California courts did not have jurisdiction over a crime committed in Oregon:

> By both the common law and the statutes of this state the breaking and entry of the building or structure belonging to another, with intent to commit some crime, is the constituent element of the offense of burglary. It is not necessary that any larceny be committed; it is not necessary that any felony be committed; the breaking and the entry, with intent, constitutes the crime.
>
> *It is unnecessary to cite authorities to the effect that the courts of this state have no jurisdiction over completed offenses committed in other states.* [Emphasis added.] It is only when the offense committed is a continuing offense, or one which reaches across boundary lines, that jurisdiction is given. Thus, if the one who commits the offense of burglary also commits larceny by stealing property, brings that stolen property across the boundary line, the offense of larceny is continued from the adjoining state into this state, and the superior court of any county into which the stolen property is brought may take jurisdiction of the offense committed in such county, to wit, the offense of larceny, not the offense of burglary.[15]

Receiving stolen property is also a continuing crime as it is a taking of the proceeds of a larceny, and jurisdiction can be in the place of receiving the stolen property or any place such property is subsequently transferred. In a Connecticut court, a defendant (Pambianchi)[16] was convicted of receiving stolen goods (an automobile). He appealed, and argued that because the automobile was stolen in New York and received by him in New York, the courts of Connecticut do not have jurisdiction. The reviewing court's ruling in *Pambianchi* was that the crime of receiving and concealing stolen goods, like that of theft, is a continuing one, and the courts of Connecticut have jurisdiction whenever stolen goods actually received in some other state are brought within the territorial limits of Connecticut.

## STATE EXTRATERRITORIAL JURISDICTION

When its action does not conflict with federal legislation, the sovereign authority of a state over conduct of its citizens upon the high seas is analogous to the sovereign authority of the United States over its citizens in like circumstances; and a state may govern the conduct of its citizens upon the high seas with respect to matters in which the state has a legitimate interest.

One Skiriotes appealed from a judgment of the Supreme Court of Florida which affirmed his conviction of using diving equipment in taking sponges from the Gulf of Mexico off the coast of Florida,

arguing that a state's criminal jurisdiction was limited to its territorial boundaries. The United States Supreme Court *affirmed* Skiriotes's conviction and the jurisdiction of Florida courts. The majority opinion stated:

If the United States may control the conduct of its citizens upon the high seas, we see no reason why the State of Florida may not likewise govern the conduct of its citizens upon the high seas with respect to matters in which the State has a legitimate interest and where there is no conflict with acts of Congress. Save for the powers committed by the Constitution to the Union, the State of Florida has retained the status of a sovereign. Florida was admitted to the Union "on equal footing with the original States, in all respects whatsoever." And the power given to Congress by Section 3 of Article IV of the Constitution to admit new States relates only to such States as are equal to each other "in power, dignity, and authority, each competent to exert that residuum of sovereignty not delegated to the United States by the Constitution itself."

There is nothing novel in the doctrine that a State may exercise its authority over its citizens on the high seas. That doctrine was expounded in the case of *The Hamilton* (*Old Dominion S.S. Co.*) v. *Gilmore*, 207 U.S. 398 (1907). There, a statute of Delaware giving damages for death was held to be a valid exercise of the power of the State, extending to the case of a citizen of that State wrongfully killed on the high seas in a vessel belonging to a Delaware corporation by the negligence of another vessel also belonging to a Delaware corporation. If it be said that the case was one of vessels and for the recognition of the formula that a vessel at sea is regarded as part of the territory of the State, that principle would also be applicable here. There is no suggestion that appellant did not conduct his operations by means of Florida boats. That he did so conduct them was assumed by the Circuit Court of Appeals in dealing with appellant's arrest in *Cunningham, Sheriff* v. *Skiriotes*, and that reasonable inference has not in any way been rebutted here.

But the principle recognized in *The Hamilton, supra,* was not limited by the conception of vessels as floating territory. There was recognition of the broader principle of the power of a sovereign State to govern the conduct of its citizens on the high seas. The court observed that "apart from the subordination of the State of Delaware to the Constitution of the United States" there was no doubt of its power to make its statute applicable to the case at bar. And the basic reason was, as the court put it, that when so applied "the statute governs the reciprocal liabilities of two corporations, existing only by virtue of the laws of Delaware, and permanently within its jurisdiction, for the consequences of

conduct set in motion by them there, operating outside the territory of the state, it is true, but within no other territorial jurisdiction." If confined to corporations, "the state would have power to enforce its law to the extent of their property in every case." But the court went on to say that "the same authority would exist as to citizens domiciled within the state, even when personally on the high seas, and not only could be enforced by the state in case of their return, which their domicile by its very meaning promised, but, in proper cases, would be recognized in other jurisdictions by the courts of other states." That is, "the bare fact of the parties being outside the territory, in a place belonging to no other sovereign, would not limit the authority of the state, as accepted by civilized theory." *The Hamilton, supra,* page 403.

When its action does not conflict with federal legislation, the sovereign authority of the State over the conduct of its citizens upon the high seas is analogous to the sovereign authority of the United States over its citizens in like circumstances.

We are not unmindful of the fact that the statutory prohibition refers to the "Gulf of Mexico, or the Straits of Florida or other waters within the territorial limits of the State of Florida." But we are dealing with the question of the validity of the statute as applied to appellant from the standpoint of state power. The State has applied it to appellant at the place of his operations and if the State had power to prohibit the described conduct of its citizen at that place we are not concerned from the standpoint of the Federal Constitution with the ruling of the state court as to the extent of territorial waters. *The question before us must be considered in the light of the total power the State possesses, and so considered we find no ground for holding that the action of the State with respect to appellant transcended the limits of that power.* [Emphasis added.][17]

## STATUTE OF LIMITATIONS

The periods of time within which a person accused of crime must be prosecuted differs between federal and state laws, and between states. Misdemeanor prosecutions must be commenced earlier (1–3 years); felonies within a longer period (3–5 years); and there is no statute of limitations on criminal homicide.

When the statute of limitations has run its term it is a bar to the jurisdiction of the court. In *Waters* v. *United States*,[18] the court stated that the statute of limitations must operate as a jurisdictional limitation upon the power to prosecute and punish.

A statute of limitations for a specific crime is suspended (tolled) when the accused is beyond the territorial jurisdiction of the state in which the crime is to be prosecuted. Conversely, the statute barring a criminal prosecution after a certain span of years might not

commence until discovery of the crime. However, the general rule is that the statute commences on the date the crime is completed.

Appellate courts have been reluctant to extend the time span of a crime, despite the fact that there is often a joint action among crime partners to conceal the fact of a crime to avoid apprehension.

In *Grunewald* v. *United States,* the United States Supreme Court *reversed* the petitioner's conviction because the duration of the crime (conspiracy) was lengthened to allow prosecution after the federal statute of limitations in this case (three years) had run its term from the time the criminal act was committed. The Court's majority opinion noted:

> We cannot accede to the proposition that the duration of a conspiracy can be indefinitely lengthened merely because the conspiracy is kept a secret, and merely because the conspirators take steps to bury their traces, in order to avoid detection and punishment after the central criminal purpose has been accomplished.
>
> By no means does this mean that acts of concealment can never have significance in furthering a criminal conspiracy. But a vital distinction must be made between acts of concealment done in furtherance of the *main* criminal objectives of the conspiracy, and acts of concealment done after these central objectives have been attained, for the purpose only of covering up after the crime. Thus the Government argues in its brief that "in the crime of kidnapping, the acts of conspirators in hiding while waiting for ransom would clearly be planned acts of concealment which would be in aid of the conspiracy to kidnap. So here, there can be no doubt that all acts of concealment, whether to hide the identity of the conspirators or the action theretofore taken, were unquestionably in furtherance of the initial conspiracy." We do not think the analogy is valid. Kidnapers in hiding, waiting for ransom, commit acts of concealment in furtherance of the objectives of the conspiracy itself, just as repainting a stolen car would be in furtherance of a conspiracy to steal; in both cases the successful accomplishment of the crime necessitates concealment. More closely analogous to our case would be conspiring kidnapers who cover their traces after the main conspiracy is finally ended —i.e., after they have abandoned the kidnaped person and then take care to escape detection. In the latter case, as here, the acts of covering up can by themselves indicate nothing more than that the conspirators do not wish to be apprehended—a concomitant, certainly, of every crime since Cain attempted to conceal the murder of Abel from the Lord.
>
> *We hold, therefore, that prosecution was barred by the three-year statute of limitations, since no agreement to conceal*

*the conspiracy after its accomplishment was shown or can be implied on the evidence before us to have been part of the conspiratorial agreement. [Emphasis added.]*[19]

# NOTES

1. Title 28, U.S. Code, Sections 41–132.
2. See *Judicial Administration in Georgia: A Case Study* (Athens, Ga.: University of Georgia Press, 1972).
3. *Fain* v. *Superior Court of Stanislaus County*, 465 P. 2d 23 (1970, Calif.); *Maine* v. *Superior Court of Mendocino County*, 438 P. 2d 372 (1968, Calif.).
4. "The Trial of all Crimes, except in Cases of Impeachment, shall be by Jury; and such Trial shall be held in the State where the said Crimes shall have been committed. . ." (U.S. Const., Art. III, sec. 2, cl. 3.)
"In all criminal prosecutions, the accused shall enjoy the right to a speedy and public trial, by an impartial jury of the State and district wherein the crime shall have been committed. . ." (U.S. Const., Amend. VI.)
5. *United States* v. *Cores*, 356 U.S. 405 (1957).
6. *Rideau* v. *Louisiana*, 373 U.S. 723 (1963).
7. *Fain* v. *Superior Court of Stanislaus County*, 465 P. 2d 23 (1970, Calif.).
8. *United States* v. *Sharpnack*, 355 U.S. 286 (1958).
9. "To make all Laws which shall be necessary and proper for carrying into Execution the foregoing Powers, and all other Powers vested by this Constitution in the Government of the United States or in any Department or Officer thereof." (U.S. Const. Art. I, Sec. 8, cl. 18.)
10. *McCulloch* v. *Maryland*, 17 U.S. 316 (4 Wheat.) (1819).
11. *United States* v. *Flores*, 289 U.S. 137 (1933).
12. *United States* v. *Cordova*, 89 F. Supp. 298 (1950).
13. *Updike* v. *People*, 18 P. 2d 472 (1933, Colo.).
14. *People* v. *Buffum*, 256 P. 2d 317 (1953, Calif.).
15. *People* v. *McGowan*, 14 P. 2d 1036 (1932, Calif.).
16. *State* v. *Pambianchi*, 95 A. 2d 695 (1953, Conn.).
17. *Skiriotes* v. *Florida*, 313 U.S. 69 (1941).
18. 328 F. 2d 739 (1964).
19. *Grunewald* v. *United States*, 353 U.S. 391 (1956).

# PART THREE
## SPECIFIC CRIMES

# 11

# CORPUS DELICTI

## OBJECTIVES
Chapter Eleven describes and defines the essential elements of a crime and examines the proof necessary to establish the corpus delicti in criminal proceedings.

## LEGAL TERMS
Corpus delicti. *The fact that a crime has been committed; the body of a crime.*
Aliunde. *From elsewhere; from another source.*

## QUESTIONS FOR STUDY
1. What are the two essential elements of the corpus delicti?
2. Why is it necessary to prove the corpus delicti *beyond a reasonable doubt to sustain a conviction?*
3. What is the necessary measure of proof in regard to the corpus delicti *when the issue is the admissibility of the defendant's out-of-court confession?*
4. Does motive form any part of the corpus delicti?
5. What is the role of evidence aliunde *in proving the corpus delicti?*
6. Develop the theme that proof of the corpus delicti *does not require identity of the perpetrator. What are the exceptions, if any, to this rule?*
7. In a murder prosecution is it necessary that the body of the victim be found to establish the corpus delicti?

E very definition of crime, whether by common law, statute, or appellate interpretation of statutory language, has within it every element necessary to prove the crime. Each act or mental state is expressed or necessarily implied, and must be proven by the introduction of evidence in order to sustain

a conviction. In the American system of justice each of these elements of the crime must be proved beyond a reasonable doubt or the person accused is not legally guilty of the crime charged. These elements are called the *corpus delicti*.

The *corpus delicti* is the body of the crime or the essential elements of the crime: evidence that a crime was committed. Before the prosecution can present evidence on the issue of a defendant's implication, it is the prosecution's burden to show (1) that there has actually been a public wrong, an injury, *and* (2) that a criminal agency is responsible for this wrong—as opposed to the agencies of accident or misfortune, or natural causes.

The quantum of proof necessary to establish the *corpus delicti* is different depending upon its purpose. The *corpus delicti* (the essential elements of the crime) must be proved beyond a reasonable doubt in order to sustain a conviction; however, if the issue is merely the admissibility of the defendant's confession, admission or statement against interest at the trial, the burden is a *prima facie* proof of the *corpus delicti*.

Proof of the identity of a defendant and his role in the crime are usually separate and distinct from evidence proving the *corpus delicti*.

## LINK-UP: PUBLIC WRONG AND CRIMINAL AGENCY

In establishing the first element of the *corpus delicti*, the prosecution must prove that a public wrong or an injury was committed; that the event could not have resulted solely from the act, or failure to act, of the victim or have come about due to natural causes. For instance, when a death results from a wound, and evidence is presented to show this wound could not have been self-inflicted or the result of accident, the first step of the *corpus delicti* has been established. Since the cause of death is shown to be a wound, natural causes are excluded. Therefore, the only conclusion possible is that the death resulted from the criminal act of another—absent some claim of legal justification which would classify the wounding and resultant death as non-criminal.

In *People* v. *Black*, Gloria Gould Black was convicted in San Diego (Calif.) of manslaughter in the stabbing death of her husband. The appellate court *affirmed* this conviction. The court's opinion noted that testimony excluding accident or natural causes as the cause of death established a *prima facie* case as to the *corpus delicti*:

> It conclusively appears that death occurred as a result of the wound on the left side of the body below the arm pit, death being caused by excessive internal bleeding, and that this wound was caused by the knife found under or near the body. The knife had

pierced the abdominal muscles, the intercostal muscle, the diaphragm, and the wall of the stomach. There was evidence that it would take considerable force to drive the knife in order to cause this wound. The knife went straight in and not at an angle and there was no wound of exit, the knife having been withdrawn.

While there are some inconsistencies in the story told by the defendant, she at all times told essentially the same story to the officers and on the stand. She testified her husband had had two drinks before going to the office that morning; she had pleaded with him not to drink any more because they intended to go to San Diego about noon; he returned about 11:00 A.M. appearing to be under the influence of liquor; he placed some packages in their car and then she noticed him putting a bottle of gin in his pocket; she tried to get the bottle and he pushed her down on the steps; she reminded him he had broken her ribs once and he became angry; he then left in the car; thinking he was in no condition to go to San Diego she changed her clothes, putting on a pair of slacks and a blouse; her husband returned later and she did not know how long he had been gone; she heard a noise in the kitchen like he was "bumping" into something and then he went outside and sat in the patio; she went out and tried to get him to help her with their income tax but he refused to do so; she went into the house and saw her husband going toward the lath house; she saw him take hold of something trying to steady himself; he had been wearing his glasses when she talked to him in the patio; she went into the back bedroom and later heard him come into the kitchen; he said he was going to make a sandwich; his speech was thick and not normal; she heard a rattle when he took a knife from the knife rack; she heard him at the bread drawer and he asked where the mustard was; she knew he was stumbling because of the way he went to the bread drawer; she thought she heard a fall followed by a moment of silence; and she then came into the kitchen and found him on the floor, lying on his side.

She further testified she had not seen the knife at this time and had not turned him over; she had noticed blood on his face and he was breathing; she asked him to get up, thinking he had fainted; she went to the phone and called Dr. Adams' office; just as she was calling the third time the doctor came; Dr. Adams rolled the deceased over on his back and after pushing up his shirt and listening, told her he was dead and that it must have been a heart attack; she threw herself on the body trying to kiss him and was raised up by Dr. Adams; she then observed the wound on his side and called Dr. Adams' attention to it; Dr. Adams felt under the body and came up with the knife in his hand; and she told Dr. Adams her husband had said he was going to make a

sandwich. She denied that she had stuck the knife into Mr. Black's body.

The defendant testified that she had carried on a conversation with her husband all the time after his last return to the house and she knew no one else was present. There was no direct evidence as to the stabbing itself and the case rests largely on circumstantial evidence.

While some doctors expressed the opinion that the wound causing death could have been self-inflicted or could have been accidentally caused by the deceased falling upon the knife, it does not follow that such a thing is probable, especially in view of the other evidence. While a death which results from wounds which could not have been self-inflicted sufficiently discloses a *corpus delicti, People* v. *DuBois,* 16 Cal. App. 2d 81, 60 P. 2d 190, this may be established in other ways. The autopsy surgeon expressed the opinion that the wound was not self-inflicted. From the record, including the exhibits, it seems improbable that the deceased could have inflicted such a wound under his left arm pit while holding the knife in his right hand. It seems equally improbable that, with his right hand holding the knife, he could have fallen in such a manner as to drive this knife straight into his left side, without any angle. That he could have then withdrawn the knife presents a further improbability. There was evidence indicating that the appellant was not telling the truth, and that a considerable amount of cleaning up had been done. Without reviewing the entire evidence it must be held that the circumstantial evidence, with the reasonable inferences therefrom, was sufficient to establish a *corpus delicti* under the established rules, and *that when viewed in connection with all of the evidence the* corpus delicti *was established beyond a reasonable doubt. Conceding that there might have been a possible doubt, the evidence was such as to justify the jury in believing beyond a reasonable doubt that the appellant inflicted the wound which resulted in the death of her husband. We have no doubt that the evidence is sufficient to support the verdict.* [Emphasis added.][1]

Arson, as criminal homicide, also requires the exclusion of accidental or natural causes of burning or charring in addition to proof of a criminal agency as responsible for the occurrence of a fire.[2]

In other crimes, the *corpus delicti* requirement calls for some proof that the crime charged did happen: that a criminal agency *moved* the circumstances of the crime, and that these circumstances total the essential elements of the crime charged.

## QUANTUM OF PROOF FOR *CORPUS DELICTI*

Initially, the prosecution must present evidence establishing a reasonable probability of a public wrong and a linked criminal agency

to develop a *prima facie* showing of the *corpus delicti*. However, to warrant a conviction the *corpus delicti* must be proven beyond a reasonable doubt.

In *People* v. *McMonigle* the appellate court reviewed the facts of a murder *conviction*. McMonigle appealed, challenging the trial judge's instructions to the jury as to the proof necessary to establish the *corpus delicti*. The court's opinion* in this case stated:

> The challenged instruction reads as follows: "The Court instructs you that initially and in the first instance the *corpus delicti* for every criminal case must be proven by satisfactory evidence aside from any statement, confession or admission of the defendant. After the latter, however, have been received in evidence they may strengthen and fortify the proof of the *corpus delicti* to the extent that the evidence may have that effect." This is a correct statement of the law in recognition of the "sharp distinction between the rule governing the *admission* of extrajudicial statements, admissions or confessions and the rule governing the jury in its *consideration* of such evidence after it is admitted." (*People* v. *Selby*, 245 P. 426.) "To warrant a conviction" the *corpus delicti* "must be proven to a moral certainty and beyond a reasonable doubt, but it is not necessary that it should be so proven before other evidence is introduced which corroborates it or strengthens reasonable inferences drawn therefrom." (*People* v. *Ives*, 110 P. 2d 408.)
>
> The leading California case on the question of the establishment of the *corpus delicti* is *People* v. *Selby, supra*. There, after a full discussion of prior decisions in this state on the subject, the court said at page 437: "It is apparent from this review of the cases that the general trend of authority has been to hold that upon *prima facie* proof of the *corpus delicti* the extrajudicial statements, admissions or confessions of the accused may be *admitted* in evidence and having been so properly admitted they may, with the evidence *aliunde*, be considered by the jury in its determination whether or not all the elements of the crime and the connection therewith of the accused have been established to a moral certainty and beyond all reasonable doubt." Consistent with this premise of distinction, it was said in *People* v. *Mason*, 99 P. 2d 567: "Where a confession is freely and voluntarily made, it is admissible as evidence in support of the *corpus delicti* as well as the criminal participation of the accused. Full proof of the *corpus delicti* independently of the confession of the accused is not required." *Prima facie* proof of the *corpus delicti* being sufficient for that purpose. The rule is likewise declared that it is

*Extracts only; footnotes and citations are deleted.

*not* necessary that the jury, in resolving the question of the guilt or innocence of a defendant upon all the evidence in the case, should, before considering for any purpose the extrajudicial statements, admissions or confessions of a defendant, be first satisfied to a moral certainty and beyond a reasonable doubt that the *corpus delicti* has been established by evidence *aliunde*.

When the case is submitted for their verdict the jury may consider *all* the evidence in the case, including the extrajudicial statements, admissions or confessions of the accused, in determining whether or not all the elements of the offense charged and the connection therewith of the accused have been established to a moral certainty and beyond a reasonable doubt. If this were not the correct rule, proof of the extrajudicial statements, admissions or confessions of the accused would have no utility except to connect him with the crime charged. The general rule is that unless evidence is admitted for limited purpose it will be considered for every purpose.[3]

Ray Cullen was convicted in California of first-degree murder, and on the automatic appeal the judgment was *affirmed*. The bodies of the victims were not found. The appellate court's holding, in part, was that in a murder prosecution it is not necessary that the body of the victim be actually found. The defendant in *Cullen* was charged with the murder of his wife, Mary Cullen, and of her father, Daniel T. Boyer. The court's opinion noted:

It is unnecessary to detail the defendant's repetition to the officers the deaths had occurred in the house; his statement he hired a man and truck to take the bodies away for $125; his attempts to bargain for a manslaughter sentence if he told where the bodies were; his statements he knew where they were, it would not take long to find them; he would not plead guilty to a murder charge because he was afraid he would get the death penalty but would consider pleading to second degree; his only hope was that they had no *corpus delicti*; if he told where the bodies were they could hang him for it: "I could have put them in oil drums and hauled them away. I didn't say I did. I said I could have. They can dig up the desert; they can blow up the river, and they will never find them." Toward the end of February, when an officer sought to serve a subpoena, Boyhtari (a neighbor) was found dead in his cabin with a suicide note beside him dated January 17th.

Defendant Cullen took the stand and told the story first related by him and explained or attempted to explain the incriminating details in the foregoing evidence. He testified he had signed the pension check with Boyer's name at the latter's re-

quest and with his authority—a version suggested to him by one of the sheriff's officers. He claimed he was put through a brutal third degree and his arms and legs were twisted in an effort to get him to tell where the bodies were. He did not divulge the location of the bodies nor did he confess guilt.

The principal contention is that the *corpus delicti*, outside of the extrajudicial statements and declarations of the defendant, has not been established; and that the circumstantial evidence is insufficient to prove that Mary Cullen and Daniel Boyer were dead and that their deaths resulted from some criminal agency.

Here the *corpus delicti* consists of two elements, the death of the alleged victims and the existence of some criminal agency as the cause, either or both of which may be proved circumstantially or inferentially.

It is not necessary in order to support the conviction that the bodies actually be found. In *People* v. *Wilkins*, 158 Cal. 530, 536, 111 P. 612, it was said that to require direct and positive proof of the *corpus delicti* would be most unreasonable; that the worst crimes are naturally committed at chosen times, in darkness and secrecy; that human tribunals must act upon such indications as the circumstances admit; that more often than not the attendant and surrounding facts remove all mystery and supply that degree of certainty men are accustomed to regard as sufficient in the most important concerns of life.

It is the function of the jury to draw the proper inferences from the proof of the circumstances. It is not the province of the reviewing court to overturn the jury's verdict when it is supported by substantial evidence including the reasonable inferences to be drawn therefrom. The circumstances in evidence established a *prima facie* showing of the *corpus delicti* sufficient to allow the case, with the defendant's admissions, to go to the jury. The circumstances also pointed to the defendant as the perpetrator and, together with the admissions, unquestionably support the verdicts.[4]

## PROOF OF IDENTITY OF PERPETRATOR

Proof of the *corpus delicti* does not require identity of the perpetrators. It is not necessary that it connect the defendant with the commission of the crime, although it may do so. In fact, proof of the *corpus delicti* does not require proof that the crime was committed by the defendant, or that the identity of the perpetrators of the crime be proved.[5]

Statutory law may, however, expressly require that the identity of the perpetrator be an essential element to the *corpus delicti*. The drunk-driving statute in most jurisdictions requires that the

defendant must have driven the automobile while intoxicated. The elements of intoxication and driving cannot be shown without the identity also being shown. The intoxicated person must also be the driver of the automobile; therefore identity is a necessary element of the *corpus delicti* in drunk-driving cases.

## NOTES

1. *People* v. *Black*, 229 P. 2d 61 (1951, Calif.).
2. Paul B. Weston and Kenneth M. Wells, *Criminal Investigation: Basic Perspectives*, 2nd ed. (Englewood Cliffs, N.J.: Prentice-Hall, Inc., 1974), p. 327; *Kehoe* v. *Commonwealth*, 149 S.W. 818 (1912, Ky.).
3. *People* v. *McMonigle*, 177 P. 2d 745 (1947, Calif.).
4. *People* v. *Cullen*, 234 P. 2d 1 (1951, Calif.).
5. *People* v. *Leary*, 172 P. 2d 41 (1946, Calif.).

# 12

# OVERVIEW: CRIMINAL OFFENSES

## OBJECTIVES

*This chapter will introduce the wide scope of the criminal law; offer a categorization of crimes that follows a natural grouping of offenses; and summarize crimes not described in chapters concerned with major felonies.*

## LEGAL TERMS

In forma pauperis. *As a poor person; a term for a procedure in which a court's permission is sought to submit legal papers without the usual fee or cost.*

Per curiam. *This term is used to indicate an opinion of the whole court as opposed to an opinion written by a single member of the court.*

## QUESTIONS FOR STUDY

1. List the crimes generally included in the category of "crimes against the person."

2. Develop the theme that robbery is a form of aggravated larceny.

3. What is the rationale for a category of crime termed "crimes against the habitation"?

4. What is the justification for grouping the crime of incest with sex crimes rather than crimes against the family?

5. What constitutional guarantees conflict with anti-obscenity law enforcement?

6. What are the similarities and/or differences between "crimes against the government" and "crimes against public order"?

7. What are the essential elements of a criminal conspiracy?

**T**his overview of crimes attempts to sum up those offenses not specifically described in later chapters dealing with specific offenses. While the overview necessarily summarizes many major crimes, it serves as a backdrop for considering the major offenses of criminal homicide, aggravated assault, robbery, kidnapping, arson, burglary, theft, and rape.

A natural grouping of criminal offenses places individual crimes within one of the following categories:

1. Crimes against the person.
2. Crimes against the habitation.
3. Crimes against property.
4. Sex offenses.
5. Crimes against the family.
6. Crimes against public decency.
7. Crimes against the administration of government.
8. Crimes against public order.

## CRIMES AGAINST THE PERSON

Criminal homicide (murder, manslaughter), aggravated or simple assault, and kidnapping are the most common crimes against the person; while robbery is a form of aggravated larceny, it is also considered a crime against the person because of the injury potential inherent in the face-to-face situation characteristic of robbery. These crimes are described in subsequent chapters.

Closely linked with crimes against the person are the criminal offenses involving weapons and destructive devices. At one time the major thrust of weapons legislation was confined to pistols and revolvers and other "concealable" weapons such as sawed-off shotguns and rifles. Some years ago these laws were extended to cover machine guns and silencers, and—more recently—extended to "loaded firearms" in public places, and to destructive devices. As a general rule these statutes exempt from any criminality the standard "authorized person": peace officers (as defined by local statutes) and members of the armed forces of the United States when in the performance of official duty, and persons properly licensed under state law.

## CRIMES AGAINST THE HABITATION

Arson and burglary* are the major crimes against the habitation, the residence. The general crime of trespass also is a crime against habitation when the property entered without consent is the residence or connecting lands of another.

Linked to burglary is the offense of possessing burglar's tools. This is the unlawful possession of any tool or instrument adapted,

*See Chapters 16 and 17, respectively.

designed, or commonly used for opening locked boxes or buildings, with intent to commit burglary.

## CRIMES AGAINST PROPERTY

Theft* is the major crime against property.

Linked to thefts is the crime of receiving stolen property. Any person who receives, retains, or disposes of property knowing that it has been stolen may be guilty of this offense. It may be difficult to uncover evidence of the "knowledge" requirement, but "bargain" buyers and those who do not exercise reasonable inquiry about true ownership of property often acquire stolen property under circumstances that spell out this knowledge.

Offenses involving written instruments also comprise a large segment of crimes against property. A written instrument is: any record of information (including sound and computer tapes); money, money orders, coins, checks, drafts, securities, tokens, and stamps; receipts, orders for the delivery of property, credit cards, memoranda of credit card transactions, tickets, seals, badges, trademarks, or other symbols of value, right, privilege, or identification.

This definition is sufficiently broad so that any of the items named therein could be the subject of forgery. It covers much more than simple writing, including printing, photography, and taping (sound and computer tapes), and any other method of communication capable of being tangibly recorded.

Forgery is a complex crime based on the intent to defraud. Simply, a person is guilty of forgery when, with intent to defraud any person, he or she (1) makes or alters any written instrument so that it purports to be the act of another person who did not authorize such act, (2) induces another person, by deception, to sign or execute a written instrument which is not what it has been represented, or (3) presents or delivers (utters) any written instrument which he or she knows to be forged.

"Bad" or fraudulent checks may be forgery or a particular offense against property usually termed *fictitious checks* or *Not Sufficient Funds (NSF)*. If the check-writer signs a false name with the intent to defraud, the essential elements of a forgery or fictitious check offense are present. On the other hand, if the check-writer signs his or her name to the check it can be no more than the offense of issuing a check without sufficient funds (NSF). A person is guilty of issuing a check without sufficient funds when, with intent to defraud any person, he or she makes or presents a check or draft for the payment of money without a reasonable belief that it will be paid upon its presentation to the bank upon which it is drawn.

Crimes against credit-card organizations have increased to the

*See Chapter 18.

extent that most jurisdictions include the misuse of a credit card in their theft or forgery statutes, or create a new particular offense for unlawful use or possession of credit cards. In credit-card crimes there is a need to show an intent to defraud, but this is usually a natural development from the circumstances concerned with the misuse of the card.

## SEX OFFENSES

Rape is the major sex crime in this category.* Other major sex offenses are incest, deviant sexual conduct, indecency with animals, indecent exposure, sexual offenses against children, and prostitution.

A person commits the crime of incest when he or she marries or has sexual intercourse with a person known to be within the relationship of parent/child, brother/sister, uncle/aunt, or nephew/niece.

Deviant sexual conduct means contact between the penis and the anus; or between the mouth or tongue and the penis, the scrotum, the anus, or the vulva. There is some decriminalization of this type of contact, but it is still forbidden in most jurisdictions as the catch-all offense of sodomy. Soliciting or loitering in any public place for the purpose of soliciting another person to engage in such conduct is generally a crime of a lesser degree.

Indecency with animals involves the act of sexual intercourse or deviant sexual conduct with an animal. It is often termed *bestiality*, a sexual connection between a human being and an animal of the opposite sex.

At common law the crimes of sodomy and bestiality were usually linked in the term *crime against nature*.

A man was convicted in the Criminal Court for Knox County, Tennessee, under a Tennessee statute proscribing "crimes against nature," upon a showing that he had forced a female neighbor to submit to his acts of cunnilingus. Rejecting the man's claim that the statute did not encompass cunnilingus and his claim that the statute was unconstitutionally vague, the Court of Criminal Appeals of Tennessee affirmed the conviction, and the Supreme Court of Tennessee denied review. Thereafter, the constitutional claim was renewed in a petition for a writ of *habeas corpus* in the United States District Court for the Eastern District of Tennessee, and, upon denial of the petition and appeal to the United States Court of Appeals for the Sixth Circuit, the Court of Appeals reversed, holding that the statute failed to give the fair warning necessary to withstand a charge of unconstitutional vagueness (514 F. 2d 570). Granting *certiorari* and a motion to proceed *in forma pauperis*, the United States Supreme Court *reversed*. In a *per curiam* opinion expressing the view of five of the eight members of the court, it was held that

*See Chapter 19.

the Tennessee statute was not unconstitutionally vague in terms of the fair warning requirement, where (1) the phrase *crime against nature* had been considered by the courts of some states to encompass acts of cunnilingus, (2) the broad interpretation of *crime against nature* as encompassing forms of sexual aberration beyond those actions constituting the common-law offense of sodomy was not itself unconstitutionally vague, (3) the Supreme Court of Tennessee, although not specifically holding that cunnilingus fell within the statute, had given clear notice in its decisions that the statute would receive the broader of two plausible interpretations and would be applied to acts of cunnilingus when such a case arose, and (4) there was no possibility of retroactive lawmaking.[1]

Indecent exposure is the act of exposing the private parts for the purpose of arousing or gratifying the exposer's sexual desire. It is the act of *male* persons, referred to as "flashers" or "exhibitionists." However, some of the prosecutions of "topless" dancers have been based on this offense, despite the fact that the exposer is a female and the viewers are not outraged by the act—a condition usually called for in the prosecution of indecent exposure cases.

Sexual offenses against children range from actual sexual contact to child molesting. A person is guilty of sexual abuse of a child when he engages in deviant sexual conduct or has sexual intercourse with a child. This may be punishable as statutory rape,* but the lower age limit than that necessary for the crime of rape of a child may make the sexual abuse of the younger child a more serious crime than statutory rape. Child molesting is the sexual annoying of a child. It is an act such as touching the body of a child, or touching the body of a child through the clothing, with intent to arouse or gratify the sexual desire.

Sexual offenses against children can be aggravated when the child suffers serious bodily injury during the commission of the offense.

Laws forbidding prostitution are legislative mandates against the professionalization of sex. The offense usually is specified as engaging in, or offering to or agreeing to engage in, sexual contact (intercourse or deviant) with another person for a fee. This offense is also being decriminalized in some jurisdictions. In the state of Nevada it is not a crime, unless the local option at county levels makes it illegal. On the other hand, there is strong pressure to punish the prostitute's customer. This is usually punishable within the scope of laws against prostitution, but some localities are spelling it out as the offense of "patronizing a prostitute"—acting out the customer role by paying or agreeing to pay a fee for the purpose of prostitution.

*See Chapter 19.

# CRIMES AGAINST THE FAMILY

At one time the major crime against the family was bigamy; now it may be child abuse (the "battered child").

A person may be guilty of bigamy when, having a living spouse, he or she marries another person. A controlling essential element in this crime is that the accused must have knowledge and enter the subsequent marriage knowing it is wrong. A defense to bigamy is that at the time of the subsequent marriage, the accused reasonably believed that he or she was legally free to remarry.

A person may be guilty of child abuse when he or she subjects a child to cruel mistreatment; or being a parent or other custodian, deserts the child with intent to abandon, or unreasonably causes or permits the physical or emotional health of that child to be endangered.

At one time this type of offense was known as "endangering the health or morals of a minor," but the child-abuse term surfaced when agents of criminal justice noted that parents and other custodians of children were "battering" children.

Serious body injuries and the deaths of battered children have led to special laws and specific reporting requirements in attempts to lessen the incidence of this offense. Reporting persons (such as physicians, nurses, and school and welfare employees) may also be guilty of an offense if they fail to promptly report a non-accidental injury of a child. The report must contain, at the least, the name and location of the child and the character and extent of the injury. The report must be made to the law-enforcement agency having jurisdiction of the territory in which the child is located at the time the injury was discovered.

"Failing to provide" is a traditional crime against the family. The offense concerns persons having a spouse, child, or indigent parent whom they are legally obligated to support, and who knowingly fail to furnish such person with necessary support. A defense to any charge of failure to provide is financial inability, but the burden of proof is on the accused to raise a reasonable doubt about his or her ability to pay.

# CRIMES AGAINST PUBLIC DECENCY

Trafficking in obscenity is the major offense against public decency. This offense is the knowing involvement of a person with obscene materials. The major problem is the actual definition of obscene materials.

*Knowingly* means being aware of the character of the material or of a performance; *involvement* may mean to distribute (transfer possession), prepare, perform, publish, or to direct; and *materials* means anything printed or written, or any picture, drawing, photograph, motion picture, statue or other figure, or any recording.

The claim that suppression of obscene material violates the First Amendment of the United States Constitution has blocked state legislation. The emotional argument is against censorship and for the rights of adults to see and read and express freely.

In *Stanley* v. *Georgia*, the United States Supreme Court dealt* with the Constitutional implications of anti-obscenity law enforcement:

It is now well established that the Constitution protects the right to receive information and ideas. "This freedom of speech and press necessarily protects the right to receive." This right to receive information and ideas, regardless of their social worth, is fundamental to our free society. Moreover, in the context of this case—a prosecution for mere possession of printed or filmed matter in the privacy of a person's own home—that right takes on an added dimension. For also fundamental is the right to be free, except in very limited circumstances, from unwanted governmental intrusions into one's privacy.

Our whole constitutional heritage rebels at the thought of giving government the power to control men's minds.

And yet, in the face of these traditional notions of individual liberty, Georgia asserts the right to protect the individual's mind from the effects of obscenity. We are not certain that this argument amounts to anything more than the assertion that the State has the right to control the moral content of a person's thoughts. To some, this may be a noble purpose, but it is wholly inconsistent with the philosophy of the First Amendment. As the Court said in *Kingsley International Pictures Corp.* v. *Regents*, 360 U.S. 684, 688–689 (1959), "this argument misconceives what it is that the Constitution protects. Its guarantee is not confined to the expression of ideas that are conventional or shared by a majority. And in the realm of ideas it protects expression which is eloquent no less than that which is unconvincing." Cf. *Joseph Burstyn, Inc.* v. *Wilson*, 343 U.S. 495 (1952). Nor is it relevant that obscene materials in general, or the particular films before the Court, are arguably devoid of any ideological content. The line between the transmission of ideas and mere entertainment is much too elusive for this Court to draw, if indeed such a line can be drawn at all. Whatever the power of the State to control public dissemination of ideas inimical to the public morality, it cannot constitutionally premise legislation on the desirability of controlling a person's private thoughts.

Perhaps recognizing this, Georgia asserts that exposure to obscene materials may lead to deviant sexual behavior or crimes of sexual violence. There appears to be little empirical basis for

*Extracts only; footnotes and citations are deleted.

that assertion. But more important, if the State is only concerned about printed or filmed materials inducing antisocial conduct, we believe that in the context of private consumption of ideas and information we should adhere to the view that "among free men, the deterrents ordinarily to be applied to prevent crime are education and punishment for violations of the law. . ."

Given the present state of knowledge, the State may no more prohibit mere possession of obscene matter on the ground that it may lead to antisocial conduct than it may prohibit possession of chemistry books on the ground that they may lead to the manufacture of homemade spirits.[2]

## CRIMES AGAINST THE ADMINISTRATION OF GOVERNMENT

Bribery, perjury, and interfering with the administration of justice are the major offenses against government.

Bribery is an attack on the official function of people in government: decisions, recommendations, votes, or other exercises of discretion by a public official within the scope of real or ostensible authority. The offense of bribery consists of conferring or agreeing to confer money or other pecuniary benefit upon a public official or an authorized emissary pursuant to an understanding that the public servant's future performance of one or more official functions will thereby be influenced. The essential elements of bribery are associated with the corrupt agreement; it is not required that the money or other thing of value actually change hands; that the public official "perform" as agreed; or that the act agreed to violate the duty of the public official.

Perjury is the offense of knowingly making a material false statement while under oath in a public proceeding. Knowledge needs no more than the fact that the statement-maker does not believe what he or she stated is true; and a statement is material when it can or does affect the outcome of the official proceeding.

Interfering with the administration of justice includes subornation of perjury (inducing perjury), intimidating victims or witnesses in a criminal proceeding, and compounding a crime—bribing another not to report a crime. It also extends to falsifying physical evidence, or destroying it; and tampering with a juror in any manner. The essence of these offenses is that the acts done block or threaten the administration of justice in criminal proceedings.

## CRIMES AGAINST PUBLIC ORDER

Offenses against public order begin with the minor offense of "disturbing the peace" and end with the major crime of "riot."

Whatever the local term for acts done to disturb the peace, it

is likely that this offense is one of the most common offenses prosecuted in lower courts. The basic act is fighting or challenging another to fight, but it extends to the use of loud and unreasonable noise, and may include profane or indecent language. The usual test is whether the peace actually was disturbed, or whether the act done was likely to provoke violence.

The definition of riot is a tumultuous occasion which disturbs the peace by three or more persons who have assembled with an intent to mutually assist each other in the execution of an enterprise. "Riotously" implies force and violence. Persons are guilty of rioting when they actively participate in a riot.

At one time lynching was associated with riotous assemblies. This is the taking of any person from custody (peace officer; detention) by the use or threat of force with intent to kill or inflict serious bodily injury upon the seized person.

## CONSPIRACY

The criminal offense of conspiracy is difficult to categorize as it may relate to any of the acts or omissions described as criminal in the foregoing overview. A criminal conspiracy can relate to either a felony or a misdemeanor.

At common law a criminal conspiracy was a misdemeanor; under modern statutory law the grade of conspiracy as a crime depends upon the nature of the conspiracy and its relationship to one of the statutory crimes—felony or misdemeanor.

A conspiracy is a combination of people for an unlawful purpose; a combination of two or more persons to accomplish a criminal act or to perform a lawful act by criminal means.[3]

Essential elements of a criminal conspiracy are:

1. An agreement (two or more co-conspirators) to commit a criminal offense.

2. A specific intent to commit such offense.

3. A subsequent overt act implementing the agreement and intent.

In one Tennessee case the defendants were participants in a labor dispute. As a result of various acts, they were prosecuted under an indictment containing eight counts charging conspiracy. One count in the indictment charged conspiracy to violate an extortion statute, another count charged conspiracy to commit acts injurious to public health as set forth by statute, two counts charged conspiracy to commit the offense of malicious mischief against the property of a named company and named person respectively, and the other counts charged conspiracy to commit the offense of assault and battery.

In reviewing the worth of the indictment in this case the Appellate Court noted:

This Court, speaking through the late Mr. Justice McKinney in *Solomon* v. *State*, 168 Tenn. 180, 76 S.W. 2d 331, 334, discussed at much length and quoted from various authorities on the question of criminal conspiracy. It is there well said among other things that a conspiracy "is a combination between two or more persons to do a criminal or an unlawful act or a lawful act by criminal or unlawful means."

It is easily seen that the object of any conspiracy is the crime which the defendants conspire to commit. We are not looking for the personal motives and expectations of the conspirators as these are in no wise material to the prosecution and as all of us know such things are generally secret. This being true it would be a practical impossibility for a Grand Jury to state in an indictment what each defendant expected to gain as the fruits of his unlawful conduct. It seems to us that the objectives of these conspiracies are stated with far more clarity and precision than the authorities require.[4]

Criminal conspiracy has an open-end potential for prosecutors. It is a prosecution option in any crime when the perpetrator has one or more crime partners.[5]

## NOTES

1. *Rose* v. *Locke*, 46 L.Ed. 2d 185 (1975).
2. *Stanley* v. *Georgia*, 394 U.S. 557 (1969).
3. *People* v. *Heredia*, 65 Cal. Rptr. 402 (1968).
4. *State* v. *Smith*, 273 S.W. 2d 143 (1954, Tenn.).
5. *Gebardi* v. *United States*, 287 U.S. 112 (1932).

# 13

# CRIMINAL HOMICIDE AND ASSAULT

## OBJECTIVES

*The primary objective of this chapter is to examine the law regarding physical attacks upon one human being by another. Secondary objectives are to show the division of crimes concerned with fatal attacks into murder and manslaughter; and the division of crimes dealing with non-fatal attacks into aggravated assault and assault.*

## LEGAL TERMS

Felony murder. *A criminal homicide committed while perpetrating or attempting a felony.*

Capital murder. *A term used to indicate first-degree murder punishable by death or life imprisonment due to special circumstances written into the statutory laws of some states in the period following the United States Supreme Court's decision in* Furman v. Georgia, *408 U.S. 238 (1972).*

## QUESTIONS FOR STUDY

1. *How does criminal homicide differ from excusable homicide? From justifiable homicide?*

2. *Define malice aforethought (malice, maliciously). How can such malice be proved in criminal homicide cases?*

3. *List and describe the various circumstances of first-degree murder.*

4. *What is the rationale for one or more of the foregoing circumstances constituting the crime of "capital murder"?*

5. *What is the difference, if any, between the premeditation and deliberation requirements of first-degree murder?*
6. *What is the scope of the felony-murder rule?*
7. *What are the essential elements of voluntary manslaughter?*
8. *What are the essential elements of aggravated assault?*
9. *What are the common defenses in criminal homicides and assaults?*

---

**H**omicide is the killing of one human being by another. When a homicide is not excusable or justified, it is a *criminal homicide*. When a human being is killed and investigation discloses no criminal responsibility (criminal agency) for the death, as one which resulted from an accident or other misfortune, it is termed excusable homicide. Justifiable homicide is the killing of a human being by command of the law in the execution of justice, or in the lawful defense of self or habitation.

Criminal homicide is usually divided by statute into murder in the first degree, murder in the second degree, and manslaughter. Murder in the first degree is well defined by statute, but second-degree murder is frequently defined as any murder which is not first-degree murder, and manslaughter may be defined as any criminal homicide which cannot be legally classified as murder.

## *CORPUS DELICTI* **OF CRIMINAL HOMICIDE**

The *corpus delicti* of *all* criminal homicide is:
1. An evidentiary showing of the death of a human being.
2. An evidentiary showing of a criminal agency.
3. An evidentiary showing that the criminal agency was the proximate cause of the death.

The death must be of a human being and occur within a certain period of time after the act causing the injury. The time may vary in different jurisdictions from one to three years.

The requirement that the victim be a *human being* raises questions as to whether the death of an unborn child is a criminal homicide. Courts have interpreted *human being* to require the baby to be born alive[1]; or, the mother must be "quick with child"—that is, have a living child within the womb.[2] Independent circulation, the feeling of movement inside the mother, or breathing may be evidence of a live human being. To alleviate the controversy around the subject of when the fetus becomes a living human being, states have passed statutes directed particularly to the destruction of the fetus. For instance:

(a) Murder is the unlawful killing of a human being, or a fetus, with malice aforethought.

(b) This section shall not apply to any person who commits an act which results in the death of a fetus if any of the following apply:

(1) The act complied with the Therapeutic Abortion Act, Chapter II (commencing with Section 25950) of Division 20 of the Health and Safety Code.

(2) The act was committed by a holder of a physician's and surgeon's certificate, as defined in the Business and Professions Code, in a case where, to a medical certainty, the result of child-birth would be death of the mother of the fetus or where her death from childbirth, although not medically certain, would be substantially certain or more likely than not.

(3) The act was solicited, aided, abetted, or consented to by the mother of the fetus.

(c) Subdivision (b) shall not be construed to prohibit the prosecution of any person under any other provision of law.[3]

However, the controversy still rages in the arguments for or against abortion, and in the interpretation of the time at which the embryo becomes a fetus.

At the other end of the scale the mere fact that a person is in a dying condition prior to the act which kills him is no defense to the charge of criminal homicide. An act which hastens death satisfies the *corpus delicti* of a criminal homicide.

The *criminal agency* means that the death was caused by another person's unlawful act or omission. The form, manner, means, or instrument are not material. A failure to act where a duty exists may provide the unlawfulness. A physical touching is not necessary. The only requirement is that the act (or omission), manner, or means be unlawful.

The proximate cause is that cause which produces a result without the aid of any intervening cause: the direct cause.[4]

The *corpus delicti* of homicide is an essential element of homicide and must be proved beyond a reasonable doubt before any conviction may stand.

## MURDER AND MALICE AFORETHOUGHT

State statutes uniformly describe murder as the willful and intentional killing of a human being with malice aforethought.

Except where the felony-murder doctrine applies, an essential element of murder is malice in addition to proof of the *corpus delicti*.

Malice aforethought (malice, maliciously) denotes a particular state of mind on the part of the criminal agent. It is an inexcusable, unjustified, and unmitigated person-endangering state of mind. At common law, *malice aforethought* meant the intentional killing of

one human being by another without legal excuse or without circumstances which would reduce the offense to manslaughter.

The essential element of malice aforethought may be proved in several different ways:

1. The specific intent to cause death or grievous bodily harm.
2. Knowledge that the act will cause death or grievous bodily harm (use of a deadly weapon).
3. The specific intent to commit any felony.
4. Resisting arrest or escape from arrest or custody.[5]

*Malice* does not necessarily import an ill will towards the victim but at the least it must include a general malignant recklessness toward the lives and safety of others. Usually it is an intention to commit the act and a concurrent appreciation of the likely result. The malice must preexist the act and can be implied from the character of the act.

Malice aforethought is shown "where the defendant for a base, anti-social purpose, does an act which involves a high degree of probability that it will result in death."[6] The specific determinations to satisfy this definition are:

1. Was the act (or acts) done for a base anti-social purpose?
2. Was the accused aware of the duty imposed upon him not to commit acts which involve the risk of grave injury or death (or was there diminished capacity)?
3. If so, did he or she act despite that awareness?

Modern statutes define malice aforethought. For example:

> Such malice may be express or implied. It is expressed when there is manifested a deliberate intention unlawfully to take away the life of a fellow human being. It is implied when no considerable provocation appears, or when the circumstances attending the killing show an abandoned and malignant heart.[7]

Malice aforethought should not be confused or equated with deliberation and premeditation, which are additional elements necessary to find a murder to be in the first degree.

A defendant Banks and a friend shot into a moving train. They did not know or try to hit anyone in the train but a bullet from the defendant's gun killed a brakeman in the caboose. Banks and his crime partner were convicted of murder. The appellate court *affirmed* the trial court's action, and in its opinion defined malice:

> One who deliberately uses a deadly weapon in such reckless manner as to evince a heart regardless of social duty and fatally bent on mischief, as shown by firing into a moving railroad train upon which human beings necessarily are, cannot shield himself from the consequences of his acts by disclaiming malice. Malice may be toward a group of persons as well as toward an individual.

It may exist without former grudges or antecedent menaces. *The intentional doing of any wrongful act in such manner and under such circumstances as that the death of a human being may result therefrom is malice.* [Emphasis added.]

The evidence shows a deliberate unprovoked shooting into a moving train, an act which could reasonably result in the destruction of human life. No excuse or justification is pleaded, or shown in the evidence for the act.[8]

In a Pennsylvania case, a seventeen-year-old defendant named Malone went to a movie with a revolver in his pocket. There was one cartridge in the revolver. After the movie Malone met William Long. While they were eating at a lunch counter Malone suggested that they play "Russian Poker."[*] Long said he didn't care and to go ahead. Malone put the revolver against Long's side and pulled the trigger three times. The third pull resulted in the fatal wound. Malone said he did not expect the gun to go off because he thought the cartridge was the first one to the right of the firing chamber. Malone was *convicted* of murder. On appeal Malone claimed he had no intention of hurting Long, who was a friend. The appellate court *affirmed* Malone's conviction, noting in its opinion that the facts in this case spelled out the malice essential to murder:

A specific intent to take life is, under our law, an essential ingredient of murder in the *first* degree. At common law, the "grand criterion" which "distinguished murder from other killing" was malice on the part of the killer and this malice was not necessarily "malevolent to the deceased particularly" but "any evil design in general; the dictate of a wicked, depraved, and malignant heart"; 4 Blackstone 199. Among the examples that Blackstone cites of murder is "coolly discharging a gun among a multitude of people," causing the death of someone of the multitude.

In Pennsylvania, the common law crime of murder is divided into two degrees, and murder of the *second* degree includes every element which enters into first degree murder except the intention to kill. When an individual commits an act of gross recklessness for which he must reasonably anticipate that death to another is likely to result, he exhibits that "wickedness of disposition, hardness of heart, cruelty, recklessness of consequences, and a mind regardless of social duty" which proved that there was at that time in him "the state or frame of mind termed malice." This court has declared that if a driver "wantonly, recklessly, and

---

[*]"Russian Poker" or "Russian Roulette" is a game in which the participants, in turn, place a single cartridge in one of the five chambers of a revolver cylinder, give the latter a quick twirl, place the muzzle of the gun against the temple and pull the trigger, leaving it to chance whether or not death results to the trigger puller.

in disregard of consequences" hurls "his car against another, or into a crowd" and death results from that act "he ought to face the same consequences that would be meted out to him if he had accomplished death by wantonly and wickedly firing a gun."

In the instant case if the defendant had by some negligent, unintentional act, caused Long to fall off the stool at which he was sitting in the store and if, as a result of that fall, Long had sustained a fatal injury, *both* the *initial act* and the *death* might be correctly characterized as accidental. But when the defendant knowing that a revolver had at least one loaded cartridge in it, pressed the muzzle of that revolver to the side of Long and pulled the trigger three times, his *act* cannot be characterized as accidental, even if his statement that he had *no intention to kill* Long is accepted (as the jury accepted it).

The killing of William H. Long by this defendant resulted from an act intentionally done by the latter, in reckless and wanton disregard of the consequences which were at least sixty per cent certain from his thrice attempted discharge of a gun known to contain one bullet and aimed at a vital part of Long's body. *This killing was, therefore, murder, for malice in the sense of a wicked disposition is evidenced by the intentional doing of an uncalled-for act in callous disregard of its likely harmful effects on others. The fact that there was no motive for this homicide does not exculpate the accused. In a trial for murder proof of motive is always relevant but never necessary.* [Emphasis added.][9]

## FIRST-DEGREE MURDER

Most jurisdictions specify that the circumstances of a first-degree murder should additionally include deliberation and premeditation. (See Figure 10.)

A significant number of states list one or more of the following circumstances which will also prove a first-degree murder:

1. Poison used.
2. Lying in wait (ambush).
3. Torture involved.
4. Act greatly dangerous to life.
5. Use of a destructive device (bomb, grenade, etc.).
6. Killing of a law enforcement officer.
7. Killer(s) hired.
8. Killer(s) previously convicted of murder.
9. Killer(s) serving life sentence.
10. Killing of a witness.
11. Killing in the commission of specified felonies (robbery, burglary, arson, etc.). (See Figures 10 and 11.)

*Premeditation* and *deliberation* denote a willful and specific purpose and design to kill. *Deliberate* means a full and conscious

knowledge of the purpose to kill. *Premeditated* means a design which must precede the killing, no matter how short the time between the design and the killing.

In a Maryland case a defendant named Elliot shot and killed his ex-wife's fiance with one shot from a shotgun which hit the deceased in the head and shoulder. Elliott was *convicted* of first-degree murder. The statute for murder in Maryland, at that time, provided: "All murder which shall be perpetrated by means of poison, or lying in wait, or by *any kind* of wilful, deliberate and premeditated killing shall be murder in the first degree." Elliot appealed, arguing that the prosecution did not prove the deliberation and premeditation necessary to first-degree murder. The appellate court *affirmed* Elliot's murder-one conviction, and in these selected extracts of its opinion related the facts of the case to the state's burden of proof:

> Where the law divides murder into grades, as it does in this State, such a homicide is presumed to be murder in the second degree and the burden is on the State to show that the killing was wilful, deliberate and premeditated, if the offense is to be elevated to murder in the first degree under Section 494. To be "wilful" there must be a specific purpose and design to kill. To be "deliberate" there must be full and conscious knowledge of the purpose to kill. To be "premeditated" the design must have preceded the killing by a sufficient length of time, even though short, to be deliberate.
>
> *In order to justify a conviction of murder in the first degree in this case, the trial court must have found (i) that the defendant had an actual intent to kill, (ii) that he had fully formed a purpose to kill, and (iii) that he had enough time to deliberate and premeditate the killing. We think there was sufficient evidence for the trial court to have found the existence of all three elements.* [Emphasis added.] *Even according to defendant's own statement he had watched the deceased [the fiance of his former common-law wife] from the door of his aunt's house, and, after getting the shotgun and loading it, he resumed watching the deceased come across, first Ogston, and then Bradley Streets, into the range of the shotgun, when he stood in front of the doorway, took aim and fired. If the defendant had not deliberated before, there was time enough to consider and plan the killing between the deceased's act of leaving 504 Ogston Street and his coming within range of the assassin's shotgun on Bradley Street. As we have already stated, the State produced other evidence, not only of deliberation and premeditation, but also of the actual intent and fully formed purpose to kill.* [10]

In the District of Columbia a federal trial court *convicted* one Bullock of the murder of a police officer. On appeal Bullock chal-

*(continued on page 188)*

| | KILLING OF HUMAN BEING | WILFUL INTENTION | DELIBERATE | MALICE | PREMEDITATED | POISON | LYING IN WAIT | TORTURE | ACT GREATLY DANGEROUS TO LIFE | DESTRUCTIVE DEVICE | LAW ENFORCEMENT OFFICER | MURDER FOR HIRE | PREVIOUSLY CONVICTED OF MURDER | SERVING A LIFE SENTENCE | WITNESSES |
|---|---|---|---|---|---|---|---|---|---|---|---|---|---|---|---|
| Alabama | X | X | X | X | X | X | | X | | | | | | | |
| Alaska | X | X | X | X | X | X | | | | | | | | | |
| Arizona | X | X | X | X | X | X | X | | | | | | | | |
| Arkansas | X | X | X | X | X | X | X | | | | | | | | |
| California | X | X | X | X | X | X | X | | X | | | | | | |
| Colorado | X | X | | X | X | | | X | X | | | | | | |
| Connecticut* | X | X | | | | | | | X | X | | | | | |
| Delaware | X | X | | | | | | | X | X | | | | | |
| Florida* | X | X | | X | | | | | X | | | | | | |
| Georgia* | X | X | X | | | | | | | | | | | | |
| Hawaii* | X | X | | | | | | | | | | | | | |
| Idaho | X | X | | X | X | X | X | X | | X | | | | | |
| Illinois* | X | X | | | | | | X | | | | | | | |
| Indiana | X | X | X | X | X | X | | | X | X | X | X | | | |
| Iowa | X | X | X | X | X | X | | | | | | | | | |
| Kansas | X | X | X | X | | | | | | | | | | | |
| Kentucky* | X | X | | | | | | X | | | | | | | |
| Louisiana | X | X | | | | | | | | X | X | X | | | |
| Maine* | X | | X | | | | | | | | | | | | |

**VARIOUS CIRCUMSTANCES OF FIRST-DEGREE MURDER BY STATES**

| State | | | | | | | | | | | | | | |
|---|---|---|---|---|---|---|---|---|---|---|---|---|---|---|
| Maryland | X | X | X | X | | | X | | X | | | | | |
| Massachusetts | X | X | X | | | | | | | | | | | |
| Michigan | X | X | X | X | | | | | | | | | | |
| Minnesota | X | X | | X | | | | | | | | | | |
| Mississippi* | X | | | | X | | | | | | | | | |
| Missouri | X | X | | X | | | X | | | | | | | |
| Montana | X | X | | | | | | | | | | | | |
| Nebraska | X | X | | X | | | X | | | | | | | |
| Nevada | X | X | | X | | | X | | X | X | | | | |
| New Hampshire | X | X | X | | | | X | | X | X | | | | |
| New Jersey | X | X | | X | | | X | | X | | | | | |
| New Mexico | X | X | | X | X | | X | | X | | | | | |
| New York | X | X | | | | | | | X | | X | | | |
| North Carolina | X | X | | X | | | X | X | | | | | | |
| North Dakota | X | X | | X | | | X | X | | | | | | |
| Ohio | X | X | | X | | | | | | | | | | |
| Oklahoma | X | X | | X | | | X | | X | X | | X | | |
| Oregon | X | X | | | | X | | | | | | | | |
| Pennsylvania | X | X | | | | | | | | | | | | |
| Rhode Island | X | X | | X | | | X | | | | | | | |
| South Carolina* | X | X | | X | | | X | | | | | | | |
| South Dakota | X | X | | | X | | | | | | | | | |
| Tennessee | X | X | | X | | | X | | X | X | | | | |
| Texas | X | X | | | X | | | | X | X | | | | |
| Utah | X | X | | | X | | | | X | X | X | | X | |
| Vermont | X | X | | X | X | | X | | | | | | | |
| Virginia | X | X | | X | X | | X | | X | | | | | |
| Washington | X | X | | X | | X | | | | | | | | |
| West Virginia | X | X | | X | X | | X | | | | | | | |
| Wisconsin | X | X | | | | | | | | | | | | |
| Wyoming | X | X | X | X | | X | X | X | X | X | X | | | |

*Based on a developing "capital murder" doctrine; first-degree murder punishable by death or life imprisonment.

**Figure 10. VARIOUS CIRCUMSTANCES OF FIRST-DEGREE MURDER BY STATES.**

| State | RAPE | ROBBERY | BURGLARY | ARSON | MAYHEM | KIDNAPPING | SEXUAL OFFENSES | LARCENY | DRUG SALES | AIRCRAFT PIRACY | SODOMY | ESCAPE | COMMISSION OF A FELONY |
|---|---|---|---|---|---|---|---|---|---|---|---|---|---|
| Alabama | X | X | X | | | | | | | | | | |
| Alaska | X | X | X | | | | | | | | | | |
| Arizona | X | X | X | | | | | | | | | | |
| Arkansas | X | X | X | X | | | | | | | | | |
| California | X | X | X | X | | | X | | | | | | |
| Colorado | X | X | X | | X | X | | | | | | | |
| Connecticut | X | X | X | | X | X | | X | | | X | X | |
| Delaware | X | X | X | | X | X | | | | | X | X | |
| Florida | X | X | X | | X | | | X | X | X | | X | |
| Georgia | X | X | | | | | | | | | | | |
| Hawaii | X | X | X | | X | | | | | | | X | |
| Idaho | X | | | | | | | | | | | | |
| Illinois | X | | | | | | | | | | | | |
| Indiana | X | X | X | | X | | | | X | | | X | |
| Iowa | X | X | X | X | | | | | | | | | |
| Kansas | X | X | X | | | | | | | | | | |
| Kentucky | X | X | X | | | | | | | X | | X | |
| Louisiana * | X | X | | X | X | | | | | | X | | |
| Maine | X | | X | | | | | | | | | | |
| Maryland | X | X | X | X | X | | | | | X | X | | |
| Massachusetts | X | X | | | | | | | | | | | |
| Michigan | X | X | X | | X | | X | | | | | X | |
| Minnesota | X | | | | | | | | X | | | | |
| Mississippi | X | X | X | | | | | | | | | X | |

| State | | | | | | | | | | |
|---|---|---|---|---|---|---|---|---|---|---|
| Montana | X | X | X | X | | | | | | X |
| Nebraska | X | X | X | | | | | | | |
| Nevada | X | X | X | | X | | | | X | |
| New Hampshire | X | X | X | | | | | X | | |
| New Jersey | X | X | X | X | | | X | | | |
| New Mexico | X | | | | | | | | | X |
| New York* | X | X | X | X | | X | X | X | X | |
| North Carolina | X | X | X | X | | | | | | |
| North Dakota | X | X | X | X | | | X | | | |
| Ohio | X | X | X | X | | | | | X | |
| Oklahoma | X | | X | X | X | | | | | |
| Oregon | X | X | X | X | | | X | | | X |
| Pennsylvania | | | | | | | | | | X |
| Rhode Island | X | X | X | | | | | | | |
| South Carolina | X | X | X | X | | | | | | X |
| South Dakota | X | | | | | | | | | X |
| Tennessee | X | X | X | X | X | | | | | |
| Texas | X | X | X | X | | | | X | | |
| Utah | X | X | X | X | X | | X | | | |
| Vermont | X | X | X | | | | | | | |
| Virginia | X | X | X | X | X | | | | | |
| Washington | X | X | X | | | X | | | | |
| West Virginia | X | X | X | | | | | | | |
| Wisconsin** | X | X | | | | | | | | |
| Wyoming | X | X | X | X | | | X | | | X |

**Figure 11. THE FELONY-MURDER RULE BY STATES.**

*2nd degree murder: First requires specific intent to kill.
**3rd degree murder.

lenged the trial judge's instructions to the jury that deliberation and premeditation sufficient for murder in the first degree did not take any appreciable length of time to form. The appellate court *reversed* Bullock's conviction, and in its opinion* discussed this time factor:

> ... To speak of premeditation and deliberation which are instantaneous, or which take no appreciable time, is a contradiction in terms. It deprives the statutory requirement of all meaning and destroys the statutory distinction between first and second degree murder. At common law there were no degrees of murder. If the accused had no overwhelming provocation to kill, he was equally guilty whether he carried out his murderous intent at once or after mature reflection. Statutes like ours, which distinguish deliberate and premeditated murder from other murder, reflect a belief that one who meditates an intent to kill and then deliberately executes it is more dangerous, more culpable or less capable of reformation than one who kills on sudden impulse; or that the prospect of the death penalty is more likely to deter men from deliberate than from impulsive murder. The deliberate killer is guilty of first-degree murder; the impulsive killer is not.
>
> We all think the evidence insufficient to show that the killing was deliberate and premeditated. When the victim, a police officer, came on the scene, appellant was engaged in a drunken quarrel with another person and had a loaded revolver in his hand. There is no sufficient evidence that appellant was facing in the officer's direction, or knew of his presence, until he spoke. The officer asked, "What's the trouble around here?" or "What's all this racket about?" The prosecutor, in his opening statement to the jury, conceded that "as soon as the officer spoke, defendant shot him." Shortly before the close of the trial the court said: "The way it impresses me from the evidence is that the officer was right on top of them, and almost momentarily the man pulled the revolver and shot him." In denying a motion for a new trial the court said: "My view is that the defendant did not realize a police officer was nearby until the officer called out the question 'What's the trouble around here?' and that it was a matter of only a second or two before the defendant fired the two shots in rapid succession which resulted in the death of the police officer." The evidence overwhelmingly supports these statements of the prosecutor and the judge. Accordingly it does not support a conviction of first degree murder. *There is nothing deliberate and premeditated about a killing which is done within a second or two after the accused first thinks of doing it; or, as we think*

---

*Extracts only; footnotes and citations are deleted.

*the evidence shows, instantaneously, as appellant, interrupted in his quarrel, turned and fired.* [Emphasis added.][11]

The law does not undertake to measure the length of the period during which a thought must be pondered before it can ripen into an intent to kill which is deliberate and premeditated, and the true test is not the duration of time but the extent of the reflection.[12]

The words *willful, deliberate and premeditated* indicate that the legislature meant, by reiteration, to emphasize its intent to ensure considerably more reflection than the mere amount of thought necessary to form intention.[13] If not, every intention to kill would be first-degree murder. There must be more than malice for a finding of first-degree murder.

## THE FELONY-MURDER RULE

The felony-murder rule imposes a particular criminal liability upon the perpetrator of a felony for a death that occurred during the commission of that felony.[14] The attack resulting in the killing must be done while the crime is in progress, and not after it is over.

A limitation on felony murder is the merger doctrine, that the felony must be independent of the killing. Robbery would be an independent felony. Aggravated assault would not be independent since the attack (assault and battery) merges with and is an essential step toward the killing. The purpose of the rule is to deter felons from killing in the course of their crime. The killing during the commission of the felony needs no further proof of malice, but is itself sufficient proof of malice.

The felon must be the agent of the killing. Thus the felony-murder rule may not extend to a case in which the police officer shoots the defendant's crime partner while they are fleeing the robbery scene.[15]

However, apart from the felony-murder doctrine, but in similar circumstance, a participant in a felony could be found guilty of murder on a theory of vicarious liability or implied malice:

> When the defendant or his accomplice, with a conscious disregard for life, intentionally commits an act that is likely to cause death, and his victim or a police officer kills in reasonable response to such act, the defendant is guilty of murder. In such a case, the killing is attributable, not merely to the commission of a felony, but to the intentional act of the defendant or his accomplice committed with conscious disregard for life. Thus, the victim's self-defensive killing or the police officer's killing in the performance of his duty cannot be considered an independent intervening cause for which the defendant is not liable, for it is a reasonable response to the dilemma thrust upon the victim or the

policeman by the intentional act of the defendant or his accomplice.[16]

Most states class felony murder as first-degree murder; a major percentage of states specify rape, robbery, burglary, and arson as the felonies essential to the first-degree felony-murder rule; a few states expand the specified felonies to such offenses as mayhem (maiming), kidnapping, sexual offenses, larceny, sodomy, illegal drug sales, aircraft piracy, and escape; and some jurisdictions simply state "during the commission of a felony." (See Figure 11.)

## SECOND-DEGREE MURDER

Murder in the second degree is best described as a criminal homicide committed with malice aforethought but without the elements of deliberation and premeditation. Second-degree murder may be committed without intent to kill, and in the course of any felony inherently dangerous to human life.[17]

## MANSLAUGHTER

Manslaughter may be divided into degrees by number or by name. A common division is the following: voluntary manslaughter, involuntary manslaughter, and vehicle manslaughter.

Voluntary manslaughter is an unlawful killing (*corpus delicti*) without malice, during a sudden quarrel or heat of passion, upon adequate provocation. There is also a hidden but most important element: an intent to kill. This intent to kill is an essential element of voluntary manslaughter, and must be formed during a sudden quarrel or heat of passion. If the intent was so formed the law will presume the absence of malice. Malice is, of course, actually present but the law will presume it is absent where, because of human infirmity and with sufficient provocation, the defendant acts rashly and with his reason obscured. Anger, sudden resentment, jealousy or terror may render the mind incapable of cool reflection and may reduce the degree of crime to manslaughter. On the other hand, revenge will never reduce murder to manslaughter.

One M.F. Fraley walked up to Dan Parker, said, "Hello Dan," and without further warning fired two shots into Parker. Parker fell, and Fraley shot him four more times. Fraley then said, "You damned son of a bitch! I told you I'd kill you. You killed my boy." Parker had, nine or ten months before, shot and killed Fraley's son. Parker died from Fraley's gunshots. Fraley was arrested, tried, and *convicted* of murder. On appeal, the appellate court *affirmed* Fraley's murder conviction, and in its opinion* discussed the difference between a heat-of-passion killing and a revenge slaying:

*Extracts only; footnotes and citations deleted.

It is urged here that, when the petitioner saw the deceased on this occasion, the recollection of that event must have engendered in him a passion which overcame him, that the killing was committed in the heat of such passion, was without premeditation, and therefore not murder. To this we cannot assent, even if we could take the statement of counsel as a proper substitute for testimony tending to prove the facts stated. In *Ragland* v. *State*, 27 South 983, four hours intervening between the provocation and the killing was held as a matter of law to be sufficient cooling time to preclude the reduction of a homicide to manslaughter. *Perry* v. *State*, 30 S.E. 903, and *Rockmore* v. *State*, 93 Ga. 123, 19 S.E. 32, each hold three days as a matter of law sufficient cooling time. *Commonwealth* v. *Aiello*, 36 A. 1079, holds from 1 to 2 hours sufficient, and *State* v. *Williams*, 53 S.E. 823, holds 15 minutes sufficient. And the authorities are all agreed that the question is not alone whether the defendant's passion in fact cooled, but also was there sufficient time in which the passion of a reasonable man would cool? If in fact the defendant's passion did cool, which may be shown by circumstances, such as the transaction of other business in the meantime, rational conversations upon other subjects, evidence of preparation for the killing, etc., then the length of time intervening is immaterial. But if in fact it did not cool, yet if such time intervened between the provocation and the killing that the passion of an average man would have cooled, and his reason have resumed its sway, then still there is no reduction of the homicide to manslaughter.

If the fatal wound be inflicted immediately following a sufficient provocation given, then the question as to whether the defendant's passion thereby aroused had in fact cooled, or as to whether or not such time had elapsed that the passion of a reasonable man would have cooled, is a question of fact to be determined upon a consideration of all the facts and circumstances in evidence; but, when an unreasonable period of time has elapsed between the provocation and the killing, then the court is authorized to say as a matter of law that the cooling time was sufficient.

Ordinarily one day, or even half a day, is in law much more than a sufficient time for one's passion to cool; and *a killing committed upon provocation given some 9 or 10 months before is not, on account of that provocation or any passion, engendered thereby, reduced to manslaughter. A deliberate killing committed in revenge for an injury inflicted in the past, however near or remote, is murder.* [Emphasis added.][18]

In order for a killing to be voluntary manslaughter, there must be both heat of passion (or sudden quarrel) and adequate provoca-

tion. Words alone will not furnish adequate provocation. The determination of whether the circumstances offered to the defendant were sufficient provocation is determined by applying an objective standard: would it have created the passion offered in mitigation in the ordinary man of average disposition? It is a "reasonable-man" standard.

An additional modern factor has been created by the courts. Mental mitigation through intoxication, mental disease, or defect may cause an unlawful killing to be deemed manslaughter rather than murder:

> If because of mental defect, disease, or intoxication the defendant is unable to comprehend his duty to govern his actions in accord with the duty imposed by law, he does not act with malice aforethought and cannot be guilty of murder.[19]

This test is something less than legal insanity, yet it is a sufficient mental disturbance to reduce the homicide to manslaughter. It is the imposition of a specific subjective test on the otherwise objective determination of manslaughter.

By law the presence or absence of malice aforethought distinguishes murder from manslaughter; in practice the degree of provocation distinguishes murder from manslaughter. Now, in addition, a mental state may distinguish murder and manslaughter.

Involuntary manslaughter is an unlawful or negligent killing without malice and without the intent to kill necessary for voluntary manslaughter.

A mother of four children, Mrs. Rodriguez was *convicted* of involuntary manslaughter under strange circumstances. A neighbor heard children calling for their mother and for fifteen or twenty minutes paid little attention. When the cries became more shrill she looked out her window and saw smoke coming from the Rodriguez home, a one-family house. She and others pulled three of the children out of the house. The baby, Carlos, died in the fire. Mrs. Rodriguez was not at the house at the time of the fire. The appellate court *reversed* Mrs. Rodriguez's conviction for involuntary manslaughter, and in its opinion* observed:

> It appears from the record that guilt was predicated on the alleged "commission of a lawful act which might produce death, in an unlawful manner, or without due caution and circumspection." Penal Code, Section 192 (Involuntary Manslaughter).
>
> In *People* v. *Penny*, 285 P. 2d 926, the defendant was convicted of involuntary manslaughter. While engaged in the practice of "face rejuvenation" she applied a formula containing

---

*Extracts only; footnotes and citations are deleted.

phenol to the skin. Death was caused by phenol poisoning. The trial court charged the jury that ordinary negligence was sufficient to constitute lack of "due caution and circumspection" under Penal Code, Section 192. The court said: "It has been held that without 'due caution and circumspection' is the equivalent of 'criminal negligence.' "

It is generally held that an act is criminally negligent when a man of ordinary prudence would foresee that the act would cause a high degree of risk of death or great bodily harm. The risk of death or great bodily harm must be great. Whether the conduct of defendant was wanton or reckless so as to warrant conviction of manslaughter must be determined from the conduct itself and not from the resultant harm. Criminal liability cannot be predicated on every careless act merely because its carelessness results in injury to another. The act must be one which has knowable and apparent potentialities for resulting in death. Mere inattention or mistake in judgment resulting even in death of another is not criminal unless the quality of the act makes it so. The fundamental requirement fixing criminal responsibility is knowledge, actual or imputed, that the act of the accused tended to endanger life.

It clearly appears from the definition of criminal negligence stated in *People* v. *Penny, supra,* that knowledge, actual or imputed, that the act of the slayer tended to endanger life and that the fatal consequences of the negligent act could reasonably have been foreseen are necessary for negligence to be criminal at all. Must a parent never leave a young child alone in the house on risk of being adjudged guilty of manslaughter if some unforeseeable occurrence causes the death of the child? The only reasonable view of the evidence is that the death of Carlos was the result of misadventure and not the natural and probable result of a criminally negligent act. There was no evidence from which it can be inferred that defendant realized her conduct would in all probability produce death. There was no evidence as to the cause of the fire, as to how or where it started. There was no evidence connecting defendant in any way with the fire. *There was no evidence that defendant [Mrs. Rodriguez] could reasonably have foreseen there was a probability that fire would ignite in the house and that Carlos would be burned to death. The most that can be said is that defendant may have been negligent; but mere negligence is not sufficient to authorize a conviction of involuntary manslaughter.* [Emphasis added.][20]

The critical issue is usually the degree of negligence involved. Defined in other ways, the requisite negligence must be gross negligence: negligence amounting to a reckless disregard of the con-

sequences and of the rights of others.[21] It is not mere negligence or carelessness; it is an extreme or gross negligence, tantamount to a wanton disregard for the safety of life and limb.

There is an additional definition of involuntary manslaughter which is similar to the felony-murder rule: if a death is the result of an unlawful act not amounting to a felony (misdemeanor) it is involuntary manslaughter. Knowledge of potential danger is not necessary in this definition. Gross negligence is imputed by the doing of the unlawful act.[22]

It is well to keep in mind that the *corpus delicti* of a criminal homicide is an essential element of the crime of manslaughter as well as murder.

Vehicle manslaughter is similar to involuntary manslaughter: a vehicle-caused death resulting from an unlawful act not amounting to a felony which is the proximate cause of death. If there is gross negligence (entire failure to exercise care or such a slight degree of care as to show indifference) the manslaughter may be tried as a felony. If there is mere negligence it may be deemed a misdemeanor.[23]

The rise in the number of deaths caused by the operators of vehicles has caused the lawmakers of many states to enact specific vehicle-homicide laws. The Uniform Vehicle Code proposed by the National Committee on Uniform Traffic Laws and Ordinances suggests the following:

(a) Whoever shall unlawfully and unintentionally cause the death of another person while engaged in the violation of any state law or municipal ordinance applying to the operation or use of a vehicle or to the regulation of traffic shall be guilty of homicide when such violation is the proximate cause of said death.

(b) Any person convicted of homicide by vehicle shall be fined not less than $500 nor more than $2,000, or shall be imprisoned in the county jail not less than three months nor more than one year, or may be so fined and so imprisoned, or shall be imprisoned in the penitentiary for a term not less than one year nor more than five years.[24]

The laws of most states and of the District of Columbia specifically mention homicide caused by the operation of a vehicle which is comparable to the offense and penalties set forth above.

## ASSAULT

An assault is an unlawful attempt, coupled with the present ability, to commit an injury on the person of another. In other words, it is an attempt to commit a battery: an unlawful beating or other wrongful physical harm inflicted on a human being without his or her consent.

Assault with a deadly weapon (ADW) is defined as an unlawful attack by one person upon another for the purpose of inflicting severe bodily injury by the use of a weapon or other means likely to produce death or serious bodily harm. It is not necessary that an injury result or physical contact be made when a gun, knife, or other weapon is used which could and probably would result in serious personal injury if the crime were successfully completed.

Assault and assault with a deadly weapon are general intent crimes; *mens rea* is established by showing intent to perform an act of a nature declared punishable as a criminal offense.

One Rocha, the defendant, was charged with and convicted of assault with a deadly weapon. He was drinking with a friend at a bar. The victim of the assault, Pete Piceno, was in the bar, drinking. He went to the restroom and upon his return to the barroom discovered that Rocha was occupying the bar stool that Piceno had previously been using. An argument concerning the seat ensued and Rocha invited Piceno to accompany him out the back door of the bar. Once outside, the defendant unexpectedly turned and swung at Piceno with a knife, succeeding in stabbing Piceno four times. Rocha fled. Rocha appealed his conviction on the grounds that assault is a specific intent crime. The appellate court *affirmed* Rocha's ADW conviction and ruled that such assaults are general intent crimes:

The principal question raised by this appeal is whether a violation of Penal Code Section 245 (a) (assault with a deadly weapon) is a crime requiring proof of general or specific intent. In holding that only a general criminal intent must be demonstrated, we hopefully eliminate the confusion on this issue which has developed throughout the courts of this state.

Rocha's principal contention is that assault with a deadly weapon is a specific intent crime. In *People* v. *Hood,* 462 P. 2d 370, the issue of whether simple assault and assault with a deadly weapon are general or specific intent offenses was reexamined. Faced with the assertion that voluntary intoxication should be a defense to those crimes, we declined to categorize the intent requirement as either general or specific, but ruled that the "nature of the requisite intent is such that it is not susceptible to negation through a showing of voluntary intoxication."

In *People* v. *Hood, supra,* it was recognized that the terms, general and specific intent, are often indistinguishable when viewed in contexts other than the applicability of the defense of voluntary intoxication. Policy considerations, not the specific intent-general intent dichotomy, were the principal basis of that opinion. Since alcohol is so often a factor inducing simple assaults and assaults with a deadly weapon it would be anomalous

to permit exculpation because of intoxication. However, an additional factor was the variance between the nature of the intent to commit a battery which has always been deemed a general intent and the intent to commit an assault for the purpose of causing a particular additional result (e.g., assault with intent to murder or rape). The latter intent has been labeled a specific intent.

The legislative history of Penal Code Section 245 indicates that the Legislature differentiated assault with a deadly weapon from specific intent crimes. When the Penal Code was adopted in 1872, Section 245 read, "Every person who, with intent to do bodily harm," commits an assault with a deadly weapon is guilty of a felony. All reference to intent was deleted from the section in 1873 when it was amended to its present form.

Traditionally, simple assault and assault with a deadly weapon have been referred to as "general intent" crimes. The *mens rea* of such offenses is established by showing "an intent to perform an act of such a nature that the law declares its commission punishable as a criminal offense." The act must be committed wilfully but knowledge that it is unlawful or a belief that it is wrong need not be proven. We adhere to those cases that hold that assault with a deadly weapon is a general intent crime. It remains to define what that intent is.

An assault is an unlawful attempt, coupled with the present ability, to commit a violent injury on the person of another, or in other words, it is an attempt to commit a battery. Accordingly the intent for an assault with a deadly weapon is the intent to attempt to commit a battery, a battery being any wilful and unlawful use of force or violence upon the person of another. *We conclude that the criminal intent which is required for assault with a deadly weapon and set forth in the instructions in the case at bench, is the general intent to wilfully commit an act the direct, natural and probable consequences of which if successfully completed would be the injury to another.* [Emphasis added.] Given that intent it is immaterial whether or not the defendant intended to violate the law or knew that his conduct was unlawful. The intent to cause any particular injury, to severely injure another, or to injure in the sense of inflicting bodily harm is not necessary.

In the case at bench there was ample evidence from which the jury could infer that the defendant had the intent to commit a battery upon the victim, Piceno, and the instructions given clearly informed the jury of the elements of assault with a deadly weapon.

The instruction provides: "An assault with a deadly weapon is an unlawful attempt, coupled with a present ability, to commit

a violent injury upon the person of another with a deadly weapon. Any object, instrument or weapon, when used in a manner capable of producing and likely to produce death or great bodily injury, is then a deadly weapon. To constitute an assault with a deadly weapon, actual injury need not be caused. The characteristic and necessary elements of the offense are the unlawful attempt, with criminal intent, to commit a violent injury upon the person of another, the use of a deadly weapon in that attempt, and the then present ability to accomplish the injury. If an injury is inflicted, that fact may be considered by the jury, in connection with all the evidence, in determining the means used, manner in which the injury was inflicted, and the type of offense committed."[25]

## PROSECUTION PROBLEMS AND COMMON DEFENSES

For both prosecutor and defender, the inquiry should include: (1) Did the defendant cause the death of the deceased (proximate cause)? (2) If so, is defendant criminally responsible for this homicide (justification-excuse-capacity-criminal agency)? (3) If so, what is the grade or degree of guilt (first degree, second degree, manslaughter)? The complexity of the law on criminal homicide and the variety of factual situations make this a most difficult crime to prosecute. A look at an outline of the elements will show the number of possibilities involved which a prosecutor must consider, prove, or foreclose.

The defense may attack any one or more of the many essential elements of homicide, particularly in involuntary manslaughter situations. Malice aforethought, the intent, and premeditation and deliberation are often difficult to prove and are prime targets for the defense in a murder charge.

Defenses of insanity and diminished capacity (mental mitigation) may be affirmatively advanced by the defense. Such defenses must be considered and foreclosed when possible by prosecution investigation and expert witnesses.

Self-defense is an often-used defense and may be offered with the alternative of provocation and heat of passion to mitigate a murder charge. Defense of habitation and of other persons are also available under special circumstances. Conspiracy, accomplice, and transferred-intent situations further complicate the prosecution.

Similar problems and defenses occur in assault and aggravated assault cases. Oftentimes the onset of the criminal act is the same —the only difference may be that the injury is not fatal.

Probably the most difficult problem for either the prosecution or defense is to explain the theory of their case and relate the law

to the facts in a sufficiently clear manner so the lay jurors can understand and apply the proper rules of law.

# NOTES

1. *Morgan* v. *State*, 256 S.W. 433 (1923, Tenn.).
2. *State* v. *Forte*, 23 S.E. 2d 842 (1943, N.C.).
3. California Penal Code, Section 187.
4. *See* Ch. 8, "Crime: Intent, Act, Causation," for a detailed discussion of causation in crime.
5. *Turner* v. *Commonwealth*, 180 S.W. 768 (1915, Ky.).
6. *People* v. *Podder*, 518 P. 2d 342 (1974, Calif.). *See People* v. *Gonzales*, 269 N.E. 783 (1968, Ill.).
7. California Penal Code, Section 188.
8. *Banks* v. *State*, 211 S.W. 217 (1919, Tex.).
9. *Commonwealth* v. *Malone*, 47 A. 2d 445 (1946, Penna.).
10. *Elliott* v. *State*, 137 A. 2d 130 (1957, Md.).
11. *Bullock* v. *United States*, 122 F. 2d 213 (1941, D.C.).
12. *People* v. *Thomas*, 156 P. 2d 7 (1945, Calif.).
13. *People* v. *Caldwell*, 279 P. 2d 539 (1955, Calif.).
14. *People* v. *Ireland*, 450 P. 2d 580 (1969, Calif.).
15. *People* v. *Washington*, 402 P. 2d 130 (1965, Calif.).
16. *People* v. *Gilbert*, 408 P. 2d 365 as quoted in *Taylor* v. *Superior Court of Alameda County*, 477 P. 2d 131 (1970, Calif.).
17. *People* v. *Ireland*, 450 P. 2d 580 (1969, Calif.).
18. *Ex parte Fraley*, 109 P. 295 (1910, Okla.).
19. *People* v. *Conley*, 411 P. 2d 911 (1966, Calif.).
20. *People* v. *Rodriguez*, 186 Cal. App. 2d 433 (1960, Calif.).
21. *State* v. *Hintz*, 102 P. 2d 639 (1940, Idaho).
22. *State* v. *Frazier*, 98 S.W. 2d 707 (1936, Mo.).
23. California Penal Code, Section 192.3.
24. National Committee on Uniform Traffic Laws and Ordinances, *Traffic Laws Annotated—1972* (Charlottesville, Va.: The Michie Co., 1972), pp. 646–47; Uniform Traffic Code, Sections 11–903.
25. *People* v. *Rocha*, 3 Cal. 3d 893, 479 P. 2d 372 (1971).

# 14

# ROBBERY

## OBJECTIVES
*The objectives of this chapter are to detail the essential elements of the crime of robbery; to clarify the circumstances that spell out these elements; and to describe the assault factor that is inherent in the crime of robbery.*

## LEGAL TERMS
**Aggravating** factors. *One or more circumstances that make a crime more serious ("aggravating" the basic crime), i.e., use of a firearm in robbery. Where a crime is divided into degrees, an aggravating factor usually moves the crime into the degree warranting the most severe or additional penalty.*
**Asportation.** *Carrying away; removal of goods, things; the*
taker gains possession of the goods or things.
**Animus furandi.** *Intent to take the property of another feloniously; to steal.*
**In pari delicto.** *Equally culpable; in equal fault.*
**Things in action.** *The right to recover money or other personal property by judicial proceedings.*
**Hereditaments.** *A term meaning real property and other things that can be directly inherited.*
**Tenement.** *House or dwelling; property held by a tenant.*
**Metes and bounds.** *Limits; boundaries.*
**Ex vi termini.** *From the meaning of the word.*
**Syllabus.** *The headnote of a reported case.*

## QUESTIONS FOR STUDY
1. *What are the common elements of the crime of robbery?*
2. *What are common aggravating factors in robbery?*
3. *Is robbery an offense against ownership or possession of property?*

4. *What is the rationale for the "person or presence of another" element of robbery? For the "force or fear" element?*
5. *What are the similarities and differences between the crimes of robbery and extortion?*
6. *Define a deadly weapon.*
7. *What are the prosecution problems in robbery cases?*

**S**tatutes and case law throughout the United States show that there are common elements for the crime of robbery: (1) a felonious taking (taking with intent to steal) (2) of personal property of another (3) from his person or presence (4) by force or fear. (See Figure 12.)

There are state laws which add the words *in the possession of another* and *against his will*. It would seem that "against the will" of the victim is implied in the force and fear element; and the element of a felonious taking includes property "in the possession of another."[1]

The aggravating factors for all principals in robbery cases, whether they are present at the scene or not, are the following: the person accused of a robbery is aided by one or more other principals at the crime scene, and the accused or another principal at the crime scene is (1) armed with a deadly/dangerous weapon, or (2) has inflicted serious bodily injury upon a person (victim, witness). (See Figure 12.)

Robbery in essence is a larceny compounded by the elements of assault and which put the victim in fear. At common law it was described as the felonious and forcible taking from the person of another either goods or money to any value by putting him in fear.

Despite the fact that robbery can be defined as larceny from the person by violence and/or intimidation, robbery is generally viewed as an offense against the person. The offense against the property aspect of robbery is no more than theft. The use of force and intimidation threatens the physical safety of robbery victims and this makes robbery a potential physical-injury crime, unlike the other crimes against property.

Larceny and assault are crimes included within the total crime of robbery. A charge and conviction of robbery precludes an additional prosecution and conviction of either larceny or assault based upon the same transaction.[2] The larceny portion of robbery is the felonious taking (taking with intent to steal) of the personal property of another. The assault is the force and fear element of robbery.

## FELONIOUS TAKING AND ASPORTATION

It is the nature of robbery that a robber not only takes personal property with intent to steal but also carries it away.

James Van Wagner drove into Balboa Park with his girlfriend in the early evening (9:00–9:30 P. M.). They parked in a side street. Two men, Quinn and Alverson, approached the car and Alverson pointed a pistol at Van Wagner and ordered him out of the car. Alverson told Van Wagner to throw his wallet on the ground, which he did. Van Wagner then told the defendant there was no money in the wallet. Upon order of the defendant, Van Wagner picked up the wallet and showed the two men there was no money there. One of the two men then asked if Van Wagner's girlfriend had any money. He said she didn't and Van Wagner was instructed to get back into his car and get out of there. Quinn and Alverson were convicted of armed robbery. Quinn appealed on the grounds that neither he nor his crime partner took or carried away any personal property of their victim or the victim's girlfriend. The appellate court *affirmed* the conviction, and in its opinion* observed:

> The appellant's first contention is that the evidence is insufficient to sustain the verdicts in that it fails to show a taking and asportation of property which is sufficient to constitute the crime of robbery. Reliance is placed on the reference to manual possession in *People* v. *Beal*, 3 Cal. App. 2d 251 [39 P. 2d 504] and *People* v. *Clark*, 70 Cal. App. 2d 132 [160 P. 2d 553]. In the first of these cases it was said: "The crime of robbery is complete when the robbers without lawful authority and by means of force and fear obtain possession of the personal property of another in the presence of its lawful custodian and reduce it to their manual possession." That language was applicable to the facts in those cases but it was not intended to establish a fixed rule of law that the crime of robbery could not be complete unless the property in question was actually taken into the hands of the robber. Section 211 of the Penal Code defines robbery as follows: "Robbery is the felonious taking of personal property in the possession of another, from his person or immediate presence, and against his will, accomplished by means of force or fear." This requires the taking of personal property which is in the possession of another from his person or immediate presence but does not require that this be done by the use of the hands of the person doing the taking. Where there is an intent to so take the property while some asportation is required it is well settled that the distance it is taken may be very small. A very slight removal is sufficient. It would be a strained and unreasonable construction of the language of the statute to interpret it as necessarily requiring the taking of the stolen property into the hands of the one committing the robbery. The property taken might be a horse or a cow forcibly taken from the immediate presence and possession of the

*Extracts only; footnotes and citations are deleted.

| State | FELONIOUS TAKING | OF PERSONAL PROPERTY | IN THE POSSESSION OF ANOTHER | FROM HIS PERSON OR PRESENCE | AGAINST HIS WILL | BY FORCE OR FEAR | ARMED WITH WEAPON | CAUSES BODILY INJURY | AIDED BY ANOTHER PRINCIPAL |
|---|---|---|---|---|---|---|---|---|---|
| Alabama* | X | X | X |  | X |  |  |  |  |
| Alaska | X |  | X |  | X |  |  |  |  |
| Arizona | X | X | X | X | X |  |  |  |  |
| Arkansas | X |  | X |  | X |  |  |  |  |
| California | X | X | X | X | X | X |  |  |  |
| Colorado | X |  | X |  | X | X | X | X |  |
| Connecticut | X | X | X | X | X | X | X | X |  |
| Delaware | X | X | X | X | X | X | X |  |  |
| Florida | X |  | X |  | X |  |  |  |  |
| Georgia | X | X | X |  | X | X |  |  |  |
| Hawaii | X | X | X | X | X | X | X |  |  |
| Idaho | X | X | X | X | X | X |  |  |  |
| Illinois | X |  | X |  | X |  |  |  |  |
| Indiana | X |  | X |  | X |  |  |  |  |
| Iowa | X |  | X |  | X | X | X |  |  |
| Kansas | X | X | X |  | X | X | X | X |  |
| Kentucky | X |  | X |  | X | X | X | X |  |

| State | | | | | | | | |
|---|---|---|---|---|---|---|---|---|
| Maryland* | X | X | X | | X | X | | |
| Massachusetts | X | X | | | X | X | X | |
| Michigan | X | X | | | X | X | X | |
| Minnesota | X | X | X | | X | X | | |
| Mississippi | X | X | X | X | X | X | | |
| Missouri | X | X | X | X | X | X | | |
| Montana | X | X | X | X | X | | | |
| Nebraska | X | X | X | X | X | | | |
| Nevada | X | X | X | X | X | X | | |
| New Hampshire | X | X | X | | X | X | X | |
| New Jersey | X | X | X | | X | | | |
| New Mexico | X | X | X | | X | X | | |
| New York | X | X | X | | X | X | X | |
| North Carolina* | X | X | X | X | X | X | | |
| North Dakota | X | X | X | | X | X | X | |
| Ohio | X | X | X | | X | X | X | |
| Oklahoma | X | X | X | X | X | X | X | X |
| Oregon | X | X | X | | X | X | X | X |
| Pennsylvania | X | X | X | | X | | X | |
| Rhode Island* | X | X | X | X | X | X | | |
| South Carolina* | X | X | X | X | X | X | | |
| South Dakota | X | X | X | X | X | | | X |
| Tennessee | X | X | X | | X | | | |
| Texas | X | X | X | | X | X | X | |
| Utah | X | X | X | X | X | | | |
| Vermont | X | X | X | | X | X | X | |
| Virginia* | X | X | X | X | X | | | |
| Washington | X | X | X | X | X | X | | |
| West Virginia | X | X | X | | X | X | X | |
| Wisconsin | X | X | X | | X | X | | |
| Wyoming | X | X | X | | X | | | |

*Common law definition; not defined in statute.

**Figure 12. THE OFFENSE OF ROBBERY BY STATES; ESSENTIAL ELEMENTS AND AGGRAVATING FACTORS.**

victim. It would be possible to feloniously take such property from the possession and immediate presence of the victim, but it would be obviously impossible to take such property into the hands. *A taking of possession away from the victim and into the control of the taker is sufficient. In the instant case, there was admittedly an intentional removal of this wallet from the possession of its owner, accomplished by fear of a gun in the hands of one of the appellants, and a removal of the property for some six feet. That the property was thereafter returned when it was found to contain no money is not a material factor. There is nothing in the statute that requires any more in the way of a taking or asportation than here appears and the evidence is sufficient in the respect complained of.* [Emphasis added.][3]

Control by the accused rather than distance moved is the important issue to show asportation.

The taking itself must be with the intent to steal from another (a felonious taking). It is no robbery where the property taken belongs to the accused and he is in fact recovering or repossessing that property. In such cases the defense is the lack of criminal intent. In *People* v. *Rosen* the defendant claimed at trial he was only retaking money lost in gambling. The appellate court ruled* that this defense was a question of fact for the trial jury:

Section 20 of the Penal Code provides that in every crime or public offense there must exist a union or joint operation of act and intent. This requirement of union of intent and act has led to the uniform rule in robbery cases that there can exist no felonious intent when the owner takes his own specific property from the possession of another, even though the taking is under such circumstances as would constitute robbery if the possessor were the owner thereof. While there appears to be a conflict of authority on the question whether felonious intent is present when the defendant seeks the recaption of money lost by him at an illegal game the weight of authority supports the conclusion that the intent to steal is lacking in such a case, for the law recognizes no title or right to possession in the winner. It is the law in this state that certain games of chance, such as lotteries, are illegal; that the winner gains no title to the property at stake nor any right to possession thereof; and that the participants have no standing in a court of law or equity. In jurisdictions where such is the state of the law the weight of authority appears to favor the view that the recaption by force or fear of money lost at illegal games is not robbery, although the act may be punishable as an unlawful assault or trespass.

*Extracts only; footnotes and citations deleted.

The courts recognize that in such a case, whatever other element of crime may be present, there cannot exist an intent to steal or take feloniously the property of another, which is an essential element of the crime of robbery.

In *People* v. *Hughes* [39 Pac. 492] it was said: "In all criminal cases the question of intent is an important one. If this element is lacking, the general rule is that no offense has been committed. This rule is not only humane, but a contrary one would be opposed to all the principles which underlie human conduct as respects the bearing of individuals towards each other, and also as regards their position towards the state. And so the law is that, when evil intent is lacking, the act or omission, which otherwise would constitute an offense, is robbed of its criminality. The rule governing this class of cases seems to be well settled and thoroughly defined. In a note in 70 Am. Dec. 188 (*State* v. *McCune*), where a number of authorities are collected, this proposition is laid down: 'When the prisoner takes the property under a *bona fide* impression that the property belongs to him, he commits no robbery, for there is no *animus furandi'.* . . . The defendant in all cases is entitled to have the law governing his case given to the jury for their guidance, and in this case the question of honest belief and *bona fide* intention should have been submitted to and passed upon by the jury under proper instructions."

It has been suggested that the decisions which hold that felonious intent is lacking when the accused retakes money lost at illegal gambling, are based on statutory law which gives a right of action to the loser to recover the money lost. That view, however, does not necessarily form the exclusive basis upon which a charge of robbery has failed. A further basis appears to be that, where the winner obtains no valid title or right to possession of the money won, the loser cannot have a felonious intent in taking it. The view which seems to be consistent with the declared policy in this state is that the complaining witness, being in a sense *in pari delicto* with the accused, should not be heard in a court of justice on a charge of robbery against one whose only purpose was to retake money lost at an illegal game. This view neither condones nor invites the commission of crime, inasmuch as the accused must pay the penalty for the violation of any applicable penal law.

It has also been held that in resisting the charge of robbery by a showing that the intention was the recaption of money lost at an illegal game, it is not incumbent upon the defendant to prove that the money reclaimed was the identical money won from him. However, *the accused must intend in good faith to retake his own property. The question of intent is one for the jury which may find, if the facts justify it, that the defendant's*

*expressed intent was a mere pretext resorted to as a cover for an intent to steal*. [Emphasis added.][4]

The intent is vital. It is immaterial that the money taken was not identical to the money lost. The remoteness of times between the loss and retaking only goes to the question of whether the defendant acted in good faith.

It is unnecessary to prove the value of the thing taken, for it is sufficient if it had merely nominal value. The value of the property taken is not an element of the crime of robbery.[5]

## PERSONAL PROPERTY: OWNERSHIP/POSSESSION

One of the elements of the crime of robbery is the taking of property which belongs to someone other than the thief.[6] The property taken must be personal property. *Personal property* includes: money, goods, chattels, things in action, evidences of a debt, and movable property with some intrinsic value. It is different from *real property* which includes: lands, tenements, and hereditaments.[7]

Robbery is an offense against possession rather than ownership of property. The victim of the crime need not be the owner, but he or she must have lawful possession of the property taken.

## PERSON OR PRESENCE

This element is a necessary prerequisite of the force or fear element. Robbery is not only a crime against property, but also a crime against the person. Thus the requirement of the taking from the person or the immediate presence of the victim is essential to the crime.

*From the person* means from the victim's body or clothes he or she is wearing.

*From the immediate presence* means within sight or within the hearing of the victim, and in some instances even when the victim is completely removed from the place of the taking. In a 1934 case two men induced a clerk in a hotel to show them a room therein. The clerk was seized, gagged, placed on a bed, and his feet were tied to one of the bedposts. The two assailants then went to the hotel desk, where they took the contents of the cash register and fled. The two men were *convicted* of robbery, but appealed, contending that at the time the money was taken from the cash register the clerk was not at the hotel desk where the cash register was located, but rather was in a room in another part of the hotel, and the property was neither taken from the person of the clerk, nor from his immediate presence. The appellate court *affirmed* the trial court's action, noting numerous cases in support of their decision:*

*Extracts only; footnotes and citations are deleted.

What significance is to be attached to the word "presence" has been the subject of inquiry by the courts of many different jurisdictions. Some indication regarding the indefiniteness, or what may be termed the flexibility, of the word is contained in the opinion in the case of *Nock* v. *Nock's Ex'rs.*, 10 Grat. (51 Va.) 106, 117, where, in part, it was said:

"The meaning of the word 'presence' depends upon the circumstances of each particular case. It is a word of which every man has something like a just idea, but which no man can accurately define. In fact, it implies an area which has no metes and bounds, but it is contracted or enlarged according as the attestation (of a will) occurs, as it certainly may, in a small chamber, or a spacious hall, a public street, or an open field. The four walls of a room, whatever may be its size, so completely enclose its area, and exclude all improper interference from without, that whatever may be done within them may generally be said to be done in the presence of all who may be therein. Where it [presence] exists, sight is unnecessary. Though a thing cannot be done in the sight, it may be done in the presence, of a blind man. Proximity and consciousness may create a presence. A room, *ex vi termini*, denotes such proximity as is required to constitute presence; but there may be such proximity as well without as within a room. And wherever that proximity exists, and presence is created, it has the same effect as if the transaction occurred in the same room, and sight becomes unnecessary."

In the case of *Carlton* v. *State*, 58 So. 486, it was ruled that: "Where a person fires a pistol in a village, behind a cold drink stand within 100 yards of an officer's residence, it may fairly be said that the pistol was fired in the 'presence' of the officer. . . ."

In the case of *State* v. *Blackwelder*, 109 S.E. 644, it was held that (syllabus): "Where one heard hinge of his garage door creak, and, on going out, found the door open, he was warranted in arresting one in the vicinity for an attempt to steal a car therein, and that without a warrant; the crime being committed in his 'presence.' "

And in each of the following cases it was ruled that within hearing distance of a person is within his presence: *Miles* v. *State*, 236 P. 907; *State* v. *Koil*, 136 S.E. 510; *State* v. *Lutz*, 101 S.E. 434; *Simmons* v. *Commonwealth*, 262 S.W. 972.

And even where the person affected could neither hear nor see the commission of the acts in question, if by his sense of smell he became aware of the commission of such act, it was held that it was committed in his presence. (*State* v. *District Court*, 231 P. 1107.)

Referring to the case of *Clements* v. *State*, 11 S.E. 505, the following is a copy of the syllabus thereof:

"While B. was in his smoke-house, about 15 paces from his house, defendant came up and said that, if B. put his head out, he would 'shoot it off.' While B. was thus detained, co-defendant entered the house, and carried off valuables belonging to B., who did not know for what purpose he was being detained until defendant had left. *Held* a sufficient taking in the presence of B. to constitute robbery."

In *State* v. *Calhoun*, 34 N.W. 194, the following instruction given by the trial court (and approved by the Supreme Court) sufficiently sets forth the facts and the law applicable thereto:

"It is not necessary, in order to constitute a stealing and carrying away 'in the immediate presence of said Nellie Baldwin,' that it should have been done (if done) in her immediate view, or where she could see it done. And if you find from the evidence, beyond a reasonable doubt, that the defendant made a violent assault upon said Nellie Baldwin, by choking her and causing her to fall upon the floor of one of the rooms or apartments of her house, and then tied her hands and feet for the purpose and with the intention of stealing some money or property in the house; and you further so find that she, through fear or personal violence, told defendant where her money or watch was in an adjoining room or rooms; and you further so find that thereupon defendant passes through a door or doors into such room or rooms, and did there, within hearing of said Nellie Baldwin, take and carry away from said room or rooms the property described in the indictment, or some part thereof; and you further so find that such property was under her immediate control, and that such taking, if any, was against the will of the said Nellie Baldwin, and was without any right, or claim of right, of defendant in said property, and with the intent to permanently deprive her thereof—then and in such case there would be a sufficient stealing and taking from the *'immediate presence'* of the said Nellie Baldwin within the meaning of the law."

In *State* v. *Kennedy*, 55 S.W. 293, the facts were that the defendants therein had forcibly entered an express car on a railway train and by violence had ejected therefrom the express agent thereof, and thereafter, after having divided the train, had taken the engine and the express car about one-quarter of a mile away from the remainder of the train, at which point the defendants blew open and rifled the safe contained within the express car. It was held that although the express agent was not physically present at the time the safe was thus robbed of its contents, nevertheless he was constructively present at such time.

The facts in the case of *State* v. *Williams*, 183 S.W. 308, were similar to those in the instant case. It appears that the night operator and agent for a railroad company went from the ticket

office around into the ladies' waiting room, there being no door connecting the two, and while therein was shot by someone on the outside of the waiting room. Shortly thereafter, he heard someone endeavoring to open the cash drawer in the ticket office. If an attempt was made to open this drawer without knowing the combination, a bell would ring. Later, it was found that the cash drawer, which had contained about $11, had been broken open and the money taken therefrom. In connection with the case on appeal, the defendant complained of an instruction which defined the words "in the presence of," as used in the statute, and by which instruction the jury was informed that if it found that the defendant committed an assault upon the agent and then took the money in question from the ticket office while the agent was in a different room, the money was then and there in the immediate charge of said agent within the meaning of the statute, and that the same was taken in his presence. It was held that the instruction was not erroneous.

If [. . . ] it is properly held [that the victim] may be constructively present and consequently that the requirements of the statute in that regard may be complied with, we are constrained to rule that, in view of the elasticity of the word "immediate," the facts of the instant case bring it within the meaning and intent of our statute, and consequently that, although the clerk of the hotel was not actually physically present in the office thereof at the time when the money in the cash drawer was taken therefrom by defendant, nevertheless, considering the other facts hereinbefore set forth, the clerk was constructively "immediately" present.

At any rate, especially in view of the fact that the clerk could hear the operations of the robbers, if, as other facts of the case indicate, because of the felonious acts of defendant the clerk was prevented from being physically present at the scene of the robbery at the time of its actual completion, when otherwise the clerk would have been there, defendant should not be heard to raise the question as to whether the clerk was or was not "immediately" present.

[In this case,] [a]t least as early as the time *when the clerk was induced to leave the hotel office for the purpose of "showing" the room to defendant and his companion the crime of robbery was commenced; it was an overt act connected with the commission of the offense, at which time the clerk was "immediately" present. The trick or device by which the physical presence of the clerk was detached from the property under his protection and control should not avail defendant in his claim that the property was not taken from the "immediate presence" of the victim.* [Emphasis added.][8]

In all of the examples given in the foregoing opinion one thing remains constant; there must be some action by the accused against the person of the victim. There must be an assault, battery or such threat as to excite the fear of the victim, thus satisfying the elements which indicate this is not only a crime against property but also a crime against the person.

# FORCE OR FEAR

To constitute the crime of robbery there must be violence or intimidation of such character that the injured party is put in fear. The threat must be of such a nature as in reason and common experience is likely to induce a person to part with his property against his will, and temporarily to suspend his power of exercising his will.[9] Violence or intimidation must precede or be contemporaneous with the taking of property in order to constitute robbery, and the fear constituting an element of robbery is fear of present personal peril from violence offered or impending.

The difference between theft from the person of another and robbery lies in the force or intimidation used in robbery, and the absence of such force or intimidation in a mere theft.[10]

Where no force is used to engender fear, there must be such conduct on the part of the wrongdoer as to be reasonably calculated to put the victim in fear and cause him to part with his property for that reason.[11]

When the circumstances and conditions surrounding the robbery lead to a reasonable belief in the victim's mind that he may suffer injury unless he does comply with the robber's request, the "fear" required in robbery is present. The force or fear must be of such a nature as in reason and common experience is likely to induce a person to part with his property against his will, and to put him, as it were, under the temporary suspension of the power of exercising his will through the influence of the terror impressed.[12]

The difference between the crime of robbery and the crime of extortion is consent. Robbery is without the consent of the victim and against his will, which is overborne by the use of force or intimidation. On the other hand, extortion is the obtaining of property of another *with his consent*, when the delivery of the property was induced by fear, from threats made to accomplish that purpose. The threat necessary for extortion may be to do unlawful injury to the person or property of the victim; to accuse the victim or his family of a crime; to impute a crime, deformity or disgrace to the victim or his family; or to expose a secret affecting the victim or his family.[13]

# DEGREES OF ROBBERY

Robbery is generally divided into degrees to express the legislative intent that robberies involving weapons are more serious than those which are accomplished without a deadly weapon.

First-degree robbery may be accomplished by the use of a dangerous or deadly weapon such as a gun, dagger, dirk, blackjack, or other weapon or instrument that, from the manner of its use, or its capability of use, is likely to produce death or cause great bodily harm. There is no need to actually use the weapon or assault the victim with the weapon; it is only necessary that the robber be armed with such a weapon at the time of the offense. Unloaded guns, and in some cases even toy guns, may be resolved by the jury to be deadly weapons. The essential fact that a jury must decide is whether the instrument was a dangerous or deadly weapon and that the defendant was armed with such object at the time of the commission of the offense.

Second-degree robbery is a robbery accomplished by physical force (no weapon) and/or fear induced by threat of force or of a nonexistent weapon (hand in pocket). Even a purse snatch may constitute robbery of the second degree because of the necessary force used to wrest the purse from the woman's arm.

# PROSECUTION PROBLEMS AND COMMON DEFENSES

A basic problem in prosecuting robbers is establishing the essential element of force and fear. In states which require the additional element that the victim must give up his goods and money *against his or her will*, there is a special emphasis on the force and fear element. This is not unexpected because it is this element of force and fear that distinguishes robbery from theft (larceny).

No matter what threats are made, if there is no actual force and the victim-witness does not testify he or she handed over the property because of fear, there is no robbery. The crime in that instance would be a larceny at the most.

Since robbery is a face-to-face confrontation between victim and robber, the victim is expected to testify as an identification witness. Identification is always a major issue in the prosecution; and the testimony of supporting witnesses on the issue of identification is important, though not essential, to the prosecution's case.

If the defendant admits the act done (taking), a common defense is to deny criminal intent and/or the use of force or fear.

When the defendant denies the act done, a claim of mistaken

identification may be made. This is often supplemented by an alibi defense: that is, a claim of being elsewhere at the time of the crime. The alibi defense may be supported by other witnesses or be raised by the defendant's testimony alone.

## NOTES

1. *Mason* v. *Commonwealth*, 105 S.E. 2d 149 (1958, Va.).
2. Jeopardy clause, Fifth Amendment to the United States Constitution; *See also* California Penal Code, Section 654.
3. *People* v. *Quinn*, 176 P. 2d 404 (1947, Calif.).
4. *People* v. *Rosen*, 11 Cal. 2d 147 (1938).
5. *State* v. *Rowan,* 146 P. 374 (1915, Wash.).
6. *State* v. *Bowden*, 162 A. 2d 911 (1960, N.J.).
7. California Penal Code, Section 7.12.
8. *People* v. *Lavender*, 31 P. 2d 439 (1934, Calif.).
9. *Steward* v. *People*, 79 N.E. 636 (1906, Ill.).
10. *People* v. *Tolentino*, 216 N.E. 2d 191 (1966, Ill.).
11. *State* v. *Stephens*, 186 P. 2d 346 (1947, Ariz.).
12. *People* v. *Bodkin*, 136 N.E. 494 (1922, Ill.).
13. *People* v. *Dioguardi*, 188 N.Y.S. 2d 84 (1959, N.Y.). *See* California Penal Code, Sections 518–519.

# 15

# KIDNAPPING

## OBJECTIVES
*Chapter Fifteen develops the evolution of kidnapping as a crime; the similarities and differences between state and federal laws; and the circumstances of robbery and rape cases that spell out kidnapping.*

## LEGAL TERMS
Custody. *Care and possession, keeping and watching a person or thing; immediate charge and control.*

Ransom. *The money or other valuable consideration demanded and/or paid for the release of a person or persons from captivity. Also, the sum paid or agreed to be paid for the release of captured property.*

## QUESTIONS FOR STUDY
1. *What were the essential elements of common-law kidnapping?*
2. *List and describe the broad elements of state kidnapping statutes.*
3. *What circumstances related to the "movement" of the victim in robbery and rape cases constitute the crime of kidnapping?*
4. *What was the rationale for the federal law on kidnapping?*
5. *What are the essential elements of the federal law on kidnapping?*
6. *How does "child stealing" differ from kidnapping?*
7. *What are the common defenses to kidnapping?*

**K**idnapping at common law meant to forcibly abduct a person and to carry him or her from one country into another country. If the word kidnap has technical meaning it is derived from the common law, and it must be interpreted in that

light. At common law, kidnapping was composed of the elements of (1) taking and carrying away a person by unlawful force or by fraud and against his will, and (2) asportation of the seized person into another country.[1] The crime has been described as false imprisonment combined with asportation.

## STATE KIDNAPPING STATUTES

From its common-law beginning, the crime of kidnapping has undergone marked statutory changes. Statutes lessened the degree of asportation necessary for its commission and increased the punishment from a misdemeanor at common law to a felony and a capital offense. The only asportation necessary in many statutes is a "secret detention." (It is only the element of "secret" which distinguishes such statutes from those defining the crime of false imprisonment, which requires unlawful seizing of another with the intent merely to keep or detain him against his will.) These statutes substituted *secret detention* for the original *asportation*.

The state laws in this area were revised after the Congress enacted its legislation against interstate kidnapping. Except for the interstate element (transportation across state lines), the state statutes are similar to the federal legislation.

The broad elements of state kidnapping statutes include:
1. Seizing of another without his or her consent.
2. Transportation (asportation).
3. Unlawful confinement.

Some asportation or movement of the victim from one place to another is essential to distinguish kidnapping from lesser crimes. In a Michigan case an inmate (Adams) of the state prison and other inmates seized the chief guard at knifepoint. They forced him and other hostages, including one inmate (Hubbard) to go to the fifth floor of the prison hospital. For several hours they discussed their grievances with prison officials, then surrendered peacefully. The only hostage harmed was Hubbard, who was beaten severely and released during negotiations to show that they meant business. Adams was charged and *convicted* of kidnapping as defined by the Michigan statute. The text of the Michigan kidnapping statute involved (M.C.L.A. Sec. 750.349; M.S.A. Sec. 28.581) reads as follows:

> Any person who wilfully, maliciously and without lawful authority shall forcibly or secretly confine or imprison any other person within this state against his will, or shall forcibly carry or send such person out of this state, or shall forcibly seize or confine, or shall inveigle or kidnap any other person with intent to extort money or other valuable thing thereby or with intent either to cause such person to be secretly confined or imprisoned in this state against his will, or in any way held to service against

his will, shall be guilty of a felony, punishable by imprisonment in the state prison for life or for any term of years.

Adams appealed his conviction, arguing that the *movement* of hostages was less than that required in kidnapping. The appellate court *reversed* Adams's conviction. Selected exerpts from its opinion examine this element of *movement*:

At common law, kidnapping was a misdemeanor with well defined elements; first, the forcible abduction of a person from his own country, and second, sending him to another country. This was considered more than false imprisonment, since kidnapping included all the elements of false imprisonment with the additional element of asportation of the victim outside his own country and beyond the protection of its laws.

Statutory law, in modifying common-law kidnapping, has abolished the requirement that a national or regional boundary be breached. However, with the abolition of the breached boundary requirement, a lack of precision was created in the law as to the degree of asportation required to transform a lesser crime into kidnapping.

Torn between the common-law rule that a most significant asportation was required, and the obvious legislative intention to broaden the scope of the offense, the courts, virtually without exception, began by endorsing the idea that any movement, however slight, was sufficient to constitute the asportation element of kidnapping.

Representative of this formulation were the opinions of the California Supreme Court in *People* v. *Chessman*, 238 P. 2d 1001 (1951) and *People* v. *Wein*, 326 P. 2d 457 (1958). In *Chessman*, the defendant forced his victim to move 22 feet to his automobile, where he sexually assaulted her. The Court held that, "It is the fact, not the distance, of forcible removal which constitutes kidnapping in this state." In *Wein*, the Court applied the *Chessman* standard to uphold the kidnapping confession of a defendant who forced his victims to move from room to room in their own homes during a series of robberies and rapes.

However, after a time representative courts perceived that unrestrained recognition of any movement at all as adequate to support kidnapping was letting the pendulum swing to absurd and unconscionable results.

In 1969, the California Supreme Court overruled its prior constructions in the *Chessman-Wein* line of cases. *People* v. *Daniels*, 459 P. 2d 225 (1969), clearly repudiates the doctrine that any movement at all of the victim is sufficient to constitute the asportation element of kidnapping. There the victims had been forced to move about in their apartments during the commission

of crimes of robbery and rape. The Court declared: "We hold that the intent of the Legislature was to exclude from the statute's reach not only 'stand-still' robberies, but also those in which the movements of the victim are merely incidental to the commission of the robbery and do not substantially increase the risk of harm over and above that necessarily present in the crime of robbery itself."

And in *People* v. *Timmons*, 482 P. 2d 648 (1971), the Court elaborated on the *Daniels* standard by finding that forcing a robbery victim to drive five city blocks in order to facilitate the robbery, did not constitute kidnapping. The Court stated: "The true test in each case is not merely mileage but whether the movements of the victims 'substantially increase the risk of harm' beyond that inherent in the crime of robbery itself."

To summarize the twofold California test, the type of asportation necessary to buttress a kidnapping conviction is that:

1. The movement element must not be merely incidental to the commission of another underlying lesser crime.

2. The movement must substantially increase the risk of harm beyond that inherent in the underlying lesser crime.

The New York Court of Appeals, in *People* v. *Miles*, 245 N.E. 2d 688 (1969, N.Y.), established three rules to prevent the gross distortion of lesser crimes into kidnapping:

1. The movement element must not be merely incidental to the commission of another underlying lesser crime.

2. The movement of a more complicated nature may sustain a kidnapping charge.

3. Statutory kidnapping continues to include traditional or conventional kidnapping abductions designed to effect extortions or accomplish murder.

The first or "merely incidental" rule is common to New York and California, namely if the movement is merely incidental to the commission of another underlying lesser crime, it will not sustain kidnapping. We feel that this is the critical and significant criterion and regard the other two criteria illustrative and not controlling.

As we describe the kidnapping possibility, it is useful to bear in mind the New York Court of Appeals' definition of "traditional" or "conventional" kidnapping focusing on extortion, murder or taking hostage. Did the charged confinement here relate more to confinement for the sake of confinement or for the sake of assault or more to the idea of extortion, murder or taking hostage? A jury would not easily find murder in the picture, but might find that extortion or taking hostage was clearly in the picture more so than assault or confinement for confinement. The scenario opens with the defendant complaining about griev-

ances and ends with his discussing them with the warden, the press, and others. Grievances might be found by a jury to be the reason for the charged confinement and actual movement.

If these questions were answered affirmatively on the facts by the jurors under proper instructions, the underlying crime might be a kidnapping. *It would be the function of the jury to weigh the evidence presented to it in the light of the court's charge in order to determine whether the real crime herein involved was a minor one and the movement incidental thereto, or whether the real crime did indeed involve the taking of a hostage in order to extort something of value and that the movement was an asportation incidental to committing a kidnapping.* [Emphasis added.]²

Additional punishment is imposed where the simple kidnapping or unlawful seizure and secret detention or asportation is aggravated by the purpose of extortion of ransom, and/or harm inflicted upon the victim. Ransom is a price, money, or other consideration paid or demanded for the release of the victim. The additional punishment has often been death for this form of kidnapping.

## FEDERAL KIDNAPPING STATUTE

The federal statute on kidnapping was a response to a vicious series of kidnappings for ransom in the years following the repeal of the Eighteenth Amendment (Prohibition). Rival gangs struggled for new sources of income to replace the former profits from making and selling beer and whiskey, seized other members of the underworld, and held them until five- and six-figure ransoms were paid. In many of these "snatches" (as they were termed at the time by news media), victims were seized in one state and held in another. These seizures were followed by similar kidnappings by others of members of rich and wealthy families, and ransom demands went up.

The kidnapping for ransom and brutal murder of the child of Charles Lindbergh, contemporary hero because of his solo trans-Atlantic flight, pinpointed the need for a federal statute. The child was seized in New Jersey, but most of the ransom negotiations were conducted in other states. Since there was no effective kidnap law, Bruno Hauptmann was tried and convicted for first-degree murder, the murder being committed during a burglary. After this notorious case, Congress enacted suitable legislation which was originally known as the "Lindbergh Law." (The ensuing state kidnapping statutes were nicknamed "little Lindbergh laws.") The Federal Bureau of Investigation (FBI) was authorized by the new law to enforce its provision against interstate kidnapping.

The present provisions of federal legislation on interstate kidnapping are:

## TRANSPORTATION

(a) Whoever knowingly transports in interstate or foreign commerce, any person who has been unlawfully seized, confined, inveigled, decoyed, kidnaped, abducted, or carried away and held for ransom or reward or otherwise, except, in the case of a minor, by a parent thereof, shall be punished (1) by death if the kidnapped person has not been liberated unharmed, and if the verdict of the jury shall so recommend, or (2) by imprisonment for any term of years or for life, if the death penalty is not imposed.

(b) The failure to release the victim within twenty-four hours, after he shall have been unlawfully seized, confined, inveigled, decoyed, kidnaped, abducted, or carried away shall create a rebuttable presumption that such person has been transported in interstate or foreign commerce.

(c) If two or more persons conspire to violate this section and one or more of such persons do any overt act to effect the object of the conspiracy, each shall be punishable as provided in subsection (a). (Title 18, U.S. Code, Section 1201.)

## RANSOM MONEY

Whoever receives, possesses, or disposes of any money or other property, or any portion thereof, which has at any time been delivered as ransom or reward in connection with a violation of Section 1201 of this title, knowing the same to be money or property which has been at any time delivered as such ransom or reward, shall be fined not more than $10,000 or imprisoned not more than ten years, or both. (Title 18, U.S. Code, Section 1202.)

The legislation expresses the intention of Congress to prevent transportation in interstate or foreign commerce of a person who is being unlawfully restrained in order that that person's captor might secure some benefit to himself.[3]

The object of these sections prohibiting kidnapping is to secure the citizens' personal liberty and to secure to them the assistance of law enforcement agencies necessary to release them from unlawful restraint.[4]

Under the statute barring interstate kidnapping, a major essential element is the transportation of the victim across state boundaries as the following decisions show:

## 1.

In prosecution for kidnapping, government need not prove as an element of the offense that the defendant had specific knowledge of the exact location of the state line at the time he crossed it with the victim in the automobile with him, but it was enough affirmatively to show that he knowingly set in motion the interstate trip, that he intentionally went to the place of his own

selection and that in doing so he crossed the state line with the kidnapped victim in his custody.[5]

And, in an earlier decision:

## 2.

A defendant intentionally transporting a kidnapped person to a designated place which is across a state line is guilty of the offense of transporting a kidnapped person from one state to another, whether or not defendant had knowledge at any time of having crossed a state line, even if defendant mistakenly crossed state line while intending not to do so.[6]

The aggravation factor in the statute is the harm to the victim. The legislation does not require harm to the victim as an essential element of the crime of kidnapping; the harm factor relates only to the degree of punishment.[7]

## CHILD STEALING

Federal law exempts from its kidnapping statute parents seizing and carrying away their minor children. This view is shared by most jurisdictions. However, child-stealing statutes have been passed in the states either as part of the kidnapping sections or separate from kidnapping.

The child-stealing offense provides a penalty for one who leads, takes, entices, or detains a child under a specified age with intent to conceal the child from its parent or other person having lawful care or control. The specified age may vary from under the age of twelve to any minor child.

The particular jurisdiction determines whether a parent is liable for the taking of his or her child from the other parent under this statute. Usually the issue is *legal* custody. The taking parent may not be prosecuted if he or she has custody, where no court order of custody has been made, or where there is only an agreement between the parents as to custody.

## PROSECUTION PROBLEMS AND COMMON DEFENSES

When the victim is alive and a witness at the trial of his or her kidnapper(s), the problem of identification—of linking the defendant to the crime—is minimal. When the victim is not alive at the time of the trial, other identification evidence must be developed by the prosecutor through circumstantial evidence.

The common defense is a general denial, sometimes supplemented by an alibi; the defense normally attacks the substance of identification evidence.

There may be a claim of consent by the victim, and if there

was a consent there is no crime. If the victim is a child, the consent by the child may be no defense since the child is incapable of giving legal consent. Consent of the parent of a child, however, can be a bar to conviction.

Ignorance or mistake of fact may be a defense raised where there is a reasonable belief of a set of facts which, if true, would not constitute a crime.

## NOTES

1. *Bumm* v. *Colvin*, 312 P. 2d 827 (1957, Kan.).
2. *People* v. *Adams*, 205 N.W. 2d 415 (1973, Mich.).
3. *Gooch* v. *United States*, 297 U.S. 124 (1936).
4. *State* v. *Brown*, 312 P. 2d 832 (1957, Kan.).
5. *Eidson* v. *United States*, 272 F. 2d 684 (1959).
6. *United States* v. *Powell*, 24 F. Supp. 160 (1938).
7. *United States* v. *McGrady*, 191 F. 2d 829 (1951).

# 16

# ARSON

## OBJECTIVES

Chapter objectives are to show the development of the concept of the crime of arson from its origin as a crime against the habitation to its contemporary role as a crime against most buildings and burnable property; and to detail the essential elements of arson and the factors "aggravating" this crime.

## LEGAL TERM

Curtilage. *The space, usually enclosed, around a dwelling house.*

## QUESTIONS FOR STUDY

1. What is the link between arson as fire-setting and damage to property by explosives?
2. What are the common elements of arson?
3. What circumstances constitute "a burning"?
4. What are the "aggravating factors" in arson?
5. Develop the theme that the only intent required in arson is the intent to burn.
6. Specifically, what property may be the subject of arson?
7. What is the major problem in the prosecution of arson cases?

In most jurisdictions a person is guilty of arson when he or she starts a fire or causes an explosion with intent to damage the property of another (without consent of such other) or with intent to defraud an insurer. Arson has always been identified with fire-setting. The inclusion of bombs and other destructive devices is a natural growth from arson-as-firesetting: (1) explosions usually result in fires, and (2) bombs and other destructive devices are a means of damaging property similar to fire-setting.

At common law, arson was an offense against the home (habitation). It was defined as the malicious and willful burning of the dwelling (house or outhouse) of another, and extended to structures within the curtilage of the dwelling.

Federal and state statutes defining arson include the following elements: (1) A burning (2) with intent to burn (willful, intentional, malicious) (3) the dwelling house, structure, or other burnable property, real or personal, including fields and crops, (4) of self or another.[1] (See Figure 13.)

Statutes may include as the offense of aggravated arson, any arson in which there is:

1. The use of explosives.
2. The presence of persons, or persons being placed in danger at the place burned. (See Figure 13.)

Aggravation of arson exists when the explosives are used for the purpose of injury or structural damage, or when at the time of the fire or explosion a person other than the arsonist is within or upon the structure damaged. Inherent in this present or placed-in-danger element of aggravated arson is the fact that actual physical injury can result from the fire or explosion.

## THE BURNING

The burning must constitute an actual burning within the meaning of the word *burning* at common law. It is a cardinal principle of the law of arson that some part of the building must actually be burned or consumed in order for the offense to be complete.[2]

The cases which consider the issue of whether there was or was not a burning use some basic concepts:

> The offense is completed by burning, however slight, of any part of the house; and the house is burned when it is charred; that is when any of the wood is reduced to coal, and its identity changed, but not if it was merely scorched or smoked. There need be no blaze, and it is immaterial how soon the fire be extinguished or whether it had to be put out or went out itself.[3]

## CRIMINAL AGENCY (INTENT)

Arson is not a crime involving any additional specific intent than the act done. The intent to burn is the only intent required.

When related to arson, the word *malice* denotes nothing more than deliberate and intentional firing of a building, or other structure, as contrasted with the accidental or unintentional ignition of it: in short, fire of incendiary origin.[4]

*Malicious* as used in defining arson does not have literal meaning: such malice need not be expressed, but may be implied, and need not take the form of malevolence or ill will, but is sufficient

if one deliberately and without justification or excuse sets out to burn the dwelling house of another.[5] It is a wish to vex or annoy or injure, the intent to do a wrongful act.

When the burning of insured property by the owner or his agent is concerned, the necessary intent is to defraud the insurer.

Criminal agency—that is, an unlawful intentional burning—is the most difficult element to prove. It must be shown that a human being set the fire with an intent to do so. In many cases the fire consumes the evidence of how the fire started, and in order to introduce a defendant's own admissions the prosecutor must produce some *prima facie* evidence of the *corpus delicti* (burning, criminal agency, property). There is evidence which can *prima facie* show the criminal agency: smell of kerosene, piles of matches, or different points of origin. It is not necessary for the *corpus delicti*, or for a conviction, to show a specific intent to destroy. Circumstantial evidence of the *corpus delicti* is sufficient for conviction.

These are the areas of a reviewing court's observations in a 1916 case:

> The very nature of the crime of arson is such that it becomes necessary in many cases to rely upon circumstantial evidence to establish the guilt of the accused. The locked rooms, nonaccessible, under a reasonable reading of the evidence, except to the defendant and his wife; the presence in unusual places in the rooms of quantities of gasoline, a most active agent in promoting a conflagration; the occurrence of the conflagration under the circumstances shown; the differences in the furnishings of the rooms immediately after and several days prior and subsequent to the fire; the absence of defendant and his wife at the time of the fire; and the presence of a $2,000 insurance policy on defendant's property—constituted a chain of circumstances of sufficient strength to authorize the trial court in submitting the issue of defendant's guilt to the jury.
>
> Proof of intent, regardless of the origin of the crime, always devolves upon the state, and may be shown by inferences from all the facts and circumstances in the case. If, therefore, the jury believed, as they said in their verdict, that defendant willfully and feloniously set fire to the goods as charged in the information under the circumstances detailed in evidence, then the inevitable conclusion from this finding is that he intended the natural consequences of his act, viz., to burn the goods with intent to defraud the insurance company.[6]

At common law the offense of arson required the burning to be unlawfully started by a human being (defendant). Statutes have included the circumstance of an accidental beginning and a subse-

| State | BURNING | WILFUL/INTENTIONAL | MALICIOUS | DWELLING HOUSE | OTHER STRUCTURE | PERSONAL PROPERTY | INSURED PROPERTY | OF SELF | OF ANOTHER | EXPLOSION | PERSON PRESENT OR ENDANGERED |
|---|---|---|---|---|---|---|---|---|---|---|---|
| Alabama | X | X | X | X | X | X | X | X | | | |
| Alaska | X | X | X | X | X | X | X | X | | | |
| Arizona | X | X | X | X | X | X | X | X | | | |
| Arkansas | X | X | X | X | X | X | X | X | | | |
| California | X | X | X | X | X | X | X | X | | | |
| Colorado | X | | X | X | X | X | | X | | | |
| Connecticut | X | | X | X | X | | | | X | X | |
| Delaware | X | | X | X | X | X | X | | X | X | |
| Florida | X | X | X | X | X | X | X | X | X | X | |
| Georgia | X | | X | X | X | | | | | X | |
| Hawaii | X | X | X | X | X | X | X | X | | | |
| Idaho | X | X | X | X | X | X | X | X | | X | |
| Illinois | X | | X | X | X | X | | | X | | |
| Indiana | X | X | X | X | X | X | X | X | | | |
| Iowa | X | X | X | X | X | X | X | X | | X | |
| Kansas | X | | X | X | X | X | | X | | X | |
| Kentucky | X | | | X | X | X | X | X | | X | |
| Louisiana | X | X | | X | X | X | X | X | | X | |

| State | 1 | 2 | 3 | 4 | 5 | 6 | 7 | 8 | 9 |
|---|---|---|---|---|---|---|---|---|---|
| Maine | X | X | X |  | X | X | X |  |  |
| Maryland | X | X | X | X | X | X | X |  |  |
| Massachusetts | X | X | X | X | X | X | X |  |  |
| Michigan | X | X | X | X | X | X | X |  |  |
| Minnesota | X | X |  | X | X | X | X | X | X |
| Mississippi | X | X | X | X | X | X | X |  |  |
| Missouri | X | X |  | X | X | X | X |  |  |
| Montana | X |  | X | X | X |  |  | X | X |
| Nebraska | X | X | X | X | X | X | X | X |  |
| Nevada | X | X | X | X | X | X | X |  |  |
| New Hampshire | X |  | X | X | X | X | X | X | X |
| New Jersey | X | X | X | X | X | X | X |  |  |
| New Mexico | X | X | X | X | X | X | X | X | X |
| New York | X | X | X | X | X | X | X | X | X |
| North Carolina | X | X |  | X | X |  |  |  |  |
| North Dakota | X | X |  | X | X |  |  | X | X |
| Ohio | X |  | X | X | X |  |  |  |  |
| Oklahoma | X | X | X | X | X | X |  |  |  |
| Oregon | X | X | X |  | X | X | X | X |  |
| Pennsylvania | X | X | X | X | X | X | X | X | X |
| Rhode Island | X | X | X | X | X | X | X |  |  |
| South Carolina | X | X | X | X | X | X | X |  |  |
| South Dakota | X | X | X | X | X | X | X |  |  |
| Tennessee | X | X | X | X | X | X | X |  |  |
| Texas | X | X |  | X | X |  | X | X | X |
| Utah | X | X |  | X | X |  | X | X | X |
| Vermont | X | X | X | X | X | X | X |  |  |
| Virginia | X | X | X | X | X | X | X |  |  |
| Washington | X | X |  | X | X | X |  |  | X |
| West Virginia | X | X | X | X | X | X | X |  |  |
| Wisconsin | X | X | X | X | X | X | X |  |  |
| Wyoming | X | X | X | X | X | X | X |  |  |

**Figure 13. ARSON BY STATES; ESSENTIAL ELEMENTS AND AGGRAVATING FACTORS.**

quent formulation of intent to allow the property to burn with the capability to put out the fire.[7]

# THE PROPERTY

Arson was originally directed at the dwelling, rather than at other structures or insured property. A dwelling house is a building in which any part has been usually occupied at night by a person lodging therein and any structure joined or immediately connected to such building.

Arson was an offense against the security of the habitation. The modern definition of the crime of arson has expanded it to include the burning of most structures, personal property, and crops and fields.

A general definition of *property* as used in relation to the crime of arson is real or personal property capable of being damaged.

*Structures* may also be used in arson statutes to distinguish structure from non-structure arson. In this relationship, a structure means any building, tent, or vehicle, and can be extended to include bridges and tunnels as well as power plants. Jurisdictions vary the extent of punishment depending upon the nature of the property burned and the danger to persons involved.

Under the common law and statutes which followed it, the owner of property could not be indicted for its burning. The common law required the burning to be of the property of another. Even a security interest was not protected.

A dwelling in Kansas was owned and in the possession of the defendant. The dwelling was mortgaged to a savings and loan company. The defendant was tried and *convicted* of the crime of arson as a result of setting fire to this dwelling. He appealed on the grounds that his dwelling was not the property of another as required by the Kansas statute on arson. The appellate court *reversed* this homeowner's conviction despite the fact that the dwelling was mortgaged. Selected excerpts from its opinion state:

> The state argues that as a mortgagee possesses an "estate" or "interest" in the mortgaged property, therefore the words "property of another person" in the arson statute embrace and include the house here in question, that is—it was the property of the mortgagee mentioned in count one within the meaning of the statute, and cites *Bodwell* v. *Heaton*, 18 P. 901, in support thereof.
>
> Stated in simple terms, the question amounts to this:
>
> *A* owns a dwelling house upon which *B* holds a mortgage. *A* willfully burns the house. Is *A* guilty of the offense of burning the "property of another person"—that is to say, is the house the property of *B* within the meaning of the statute?

The question is new in this state, and strangely enough, apparently has not been answered by the courts of other jurisdictions. Counsel for neither side in this appeal has cited any authority touching the precise point and advise us that after diligent search none is to be found. Our own limited independent research also has proved fruitless.

Conceding, for the sake of argument, that in one sense of the word a mortgagee has an "interest" in the mortgaged property, we are not here concerned with civil rights and liabilities growing out of the relationship, such as for acts of waste committed by the mortgagor, and the like. Our question is whether mortgaged real property is "the property of another person" (the mortgagee) within the meaning of the statute.

We think the answer is to be found in the principles and rules applicable to criminal prosecutions generally, a primary one being that criminal statutes are to be given a strict construction.

The legislature has enacted at least six arson statutes, but in none of them has it seen fit to say that the burning by a mortgagor of the mortgaged real property is a burning of "the property of another," or that for purposes of the law of arson mortgaged real property is to be regarded as the property of the mortgagee. We are not dealing with any question of public policy—that is a legislative function, and whether the alleged offense charged should be included within the ban of the statute is a matter for the legislature to decide.

*In our opinion the dwelling house here involved was not the "property" of the mortgagee [Goodland Savings and Loan Association] within the meaning of the statute, and therefore the information does not allege a public offense.* [Emphasis added.][8]

Under the statutes of many jurisdictions (see Figure 13), an unlawful burning is prosecutable, despite ownership by one of the principals, as the crime of arson. Originally an offense against the security of habitation, it was a crime against lawful possession rather than ownership. An owner who burned his building which was possessed and occupied by a tenant could be charged and convicted of arson.[9]

Thus the property or structure *of another* means any property or structure (as defined) which any person other than the defendant owns or possesses.

## PROSECUTION PROBLEMS AND COMMON DEFENSES

The major problem of prosecution in arson cases is the criminal-agency element. The prosecutor must prove a defendant "wanted" the fire or explosion (intent) and had the *opportunity* to and did start

the fire (presence at scene) or caused another to commit the actual arson.

In rational arson cases, the arsonist benefits from the crime: revenge, jealousy, fraud. In irrational arson cases, the so-called benefit may be a desire to see flames, smoke, and fire engines, or the experience of a sexual release.

In arson cases in which a timing device is used to ignite a fire or explode a bomb or other destructive device, the "opportunity" factor of presence at the crime scene can be extended to several hours or more before the actual event of the explosion and/or fire.

The most common defense is a claim that the fire resulted from accident, misfortune, or natural causes; or, if by a criminal agency, the defendant was not that agent.

## NOTES
1. California Penal Code, Section 447 *et seq.*
2. *Washington* v. *State*, 276 So. 2d 587 (1973, Ala.).
3. *Kehoe* v. *Commonwealth*, 149 S.W. 818 (1912, Ky.).
4. *People* v. *Andrews*, 234 Cal. App. 2d 69 (1965).
5. *Commonwealth* v. *Lamothe*, 179 N.E. 2d 245 (1961, Mass.).
6. *State* v. *Santino*, 186 S.W. 976 (1916, Mo.).
7. *Commonwealth* v. *Cali*, 141 N.E. 510 (1923, Mass.).
8. *State* v. *Crosby*, 324 P. 2d 197 (1958, Kan.).
9. *Daniels* v. *Commonwealth*, 1 S.E. 2d 333 (1939, Va.).

# 17

# BURGLARY

## OBJECTIVES

*Chapter Seventeen shows the transition from the common-law crime of breaking and entering to the contemporary crime of burglary; shows that the primary objective of burglars is theft; and defines the* essential elements and "aggravating" factors of burglary.

## LEGAL TERMS

Ubi supra. *Where mentioned above.*

Gravamen. *The material part of a grievance or charge.*

## QUESTIONS FOR STUDY

1. *What is the basic criminal objective of burglary?*
2. *What is the rationale for modifying common-law breaking and entering into its present statutory form?*
3. *What are the essential elements of burglary?*
4. *What are the "aggravating" factors in burglary?*
5. *What is the difference between "breaking" and "entering" in burglary?*
6. *Define the structures that may be the subject of burglary.*
7. *What is the prosecution's major problem in burglary cases?*

**B**urglary at one time was viewed as a crime against the habitation, an invasion of the home. The common-law definition of burglary was simply the breaking and entering of a dwelling house of another at night with intent to commit a felony therein. It was viewed as a crime against people: a nocturnal criminal intrusion of a home when its occupants were sleeping.

During the evening hours on the first day of March, 1932, the baby of Charles Lindbergh was taken from the Lindbergh home in

New Jersey. The baby was put to bed about 8:00 P.M. and discovered missing at about 10:00 P.M. A ransom letter was found on the window sill, which lead to subsequent negotiations. After the negotiations a ransom was paid. The child was not returned and his body was found in a shallow grave several miles away on the twelfth of May. Bruno Richard Hauptmann was arrested and charged with murder, and *convicted* after a jury trial. The prosecution theory of first-degree murder was the killing of the child during the perpetration of a burglary. On appeal the defendant Hauptmann claimed that there was no burglary.

The appellate court *affirmed* Hauptmann's conviction. Its opinion links burglary and larceny as the grounds for Hauptmann's felony-murder conviction:

> A burglar, says Blackstone (4 Blk. 229) following Coke, is "he that by night breaketh and entereth into a mansion house, with intent to commit a felony." In 1 Russ. Crimes 785, burglary is defined as "a breaking and entering the mansion house of another in the night, with intent to commit some felony within the same, whether such felonious intent be executed or not." In *State v. Wilson*, 1 N.J. Law (Coxe) 439, 1 Am. Dec. 216, Chief Justice Kinsey, charging a jury, defined burglary as "the breaking and entering into the mansion house of another with the intent to commit some felony therein, and that in the night time."
>
> *There was proof [in the present case] to meet all these conditions: A breaking and entering, and into a mansion house; in the nighttime; and with intent to commit a felony.* [Emphasis added.] Only the last merits any particular discussion. The intent is to be gathered from what was done, viz., the stealing of the child and its clothing, as charged by the trial judge. Kidnapping was no felony at common law; but larceny was a felony, whether grand or petit. It is suggested that there was no proof of value of the clothing, and hence that proof of larceny was incomplete; but we see no merit in this. The matter of value was material in trying an indictment for larceny (and perhaps also in framing such indictment) because of the greater punishment in cases of grand larceny; but, as Blackstone says, *ubi supra*, grand and petit larceny are "offences which are considerably distinguished in their punishment, but not otherwise," and in treating of burglary the distinction is not even alluded to.[1]

Concerning the issue of whether or not there was an intent to steal, the court explained in the following selected extracts:

> The evidence tended to show that the child, when stolen, wore the sleeping garment; that there was no such garment on the body when it was found; that defendant had this garment in

his possession; that he so told Dr. Condon* at the outset of negotiations for ransom, and agreed to send it to him as evidence that Condon was dealing with "the right party"; that he wrote Condon, saying that the ransom would be $70,000 and that ("we") would send the sleeping suit, though it would cost $3 to obtain another one; that the ransom must be paid before seeing the baby, and eight hours after payment Condon would be notified where to find the baby. The sleeping suit came by mail, and then Condon put a reply advertisement in a New York paper, accepting the proposition conditionally.

The claim now made is that, in view of the surrender of the sleeping suit, there was no larceny; relying on the rule declared in such cases as *State* v. *South*, 28 N.J. Law, 28, 75 Am. Dec. 250, that an intent to deprive the owner permanently of his property must be an element in the taking of that property. So, in a class of cases which may be loosely described as borrowing without leave and with intent to return after temporary use, the courts seem to hold that larceny is not committed. But the intent to return should be unconditional; and, where there is an element of coercion or of reward, as a condition of return, larceny is inferable.

In the present case the evidence pointed to use of the sleeping suit to further the purposes of defendant and assist him in extorting many thousand dollars from the rightful owner. True, it was surrendered without payment; but, on the other hand, it was an initial and probably essential step in the intended extortion of money, and it seems preposterous to suppose that it would ever have been surrendered except as a result of the first conversation between Condon and the holder of the suit, and as a guaranty that there was no mistake as to the "right party." It was well within the province of the jury to infer that, if Condon had refused to go on with the preliminaries, the sleeping suit would never have been delivered. In that situation, the larceny was established.[2]

Because a burglar's criminal objective is primarily theft, burglary is now classed as a crime against property, and it is no longer confined to the nighttime nor to a dwelling. Burglary is now a day or night crime, and commercial premises and most other structures can be the subject of burglary.

A survey of the details of state statutes indicate the new dimensions of burglary:

1. The common-law breaking-and-entering has been modified to include:
   a. Breaking (no entry).

*Represented the Lindberghs.

b. Entering (no breaking).

c. Entering or remaining.

2. Nighttime has been modified to night or day.

3. Burglary now includes, in addition to a dwelling house, any buildings and certain vehicles and vessels.

4. The necessary criminal intent now has a wide range:

a. Intent to commit a felony.

b. Intent to commit a felony or theft.

c. Intent to commit any crime.

5. Burglary is aggravated when:

a. Perpetrator is armed.

b. Perpetrator assaults someone or threatens.

c. Perpetrator is armed with explosives.

d. Building is occupied at the time of the burglary.

e. There is a forcible bursting and entry.

f. Perpetrator uses false keys or picks.

g. Perpetrator is aided by accomplice. (See Figure 14.)

## BREAKING

The breaking aspect of burglary need not be forcible; the mere opening of a closed door, which need not be locked, was sufficient to constitute a breaking.[3]

An appellate court in North Carolina made these observations about the "breaking" element of burglary:

> In order to constitute a breaking in this case, either the window blind must have been fastened or else the door to the dining-room and cook-room opening to the outside must have been fastened. To constitute a fastening in either instance it is not necessary that the inmates of the house should have resorted to locks and bolts. If held in their position (having been shut by the witness, Denby James), by their own weight and in that position relied on by the inmates as a security against intrusion, it is sufficient. It would not be sufficient breaking if the blinds, or door were ajar however slightly, and the prisoner simply increased the size of the opening and through it entered. The jury must be fully satisfied from the evidence in the case that either the window blind or the dining-room door was so shut, fastened and relied upon as a security against intrusion at the time of the entry into the house; for burglary cannot be committed by the entering through an open door or window.
>
> The charge of the court as to what would be a sufficient "breaking" is fully sustained by the precedents. If a door is firmly closed, it is not necessary that it should be bolted or barred. *State v. Boon*, 35 N.C. 244; and cases cited. Take the case of raising a window not fastened; or where the prisoner, by raising or pulling

down the sash, kept in its place merely by pulley-weight; or by pushing open a closed door, not latched; or closed but not locked or firmly closed, though there was no fastening of any kind on the door; or where the glass of a window had been cut, but every portion of the glass remained in its place until the prisoner pushed it in and so entered; or where a window was on hinges, with nails behind it as wedges, but which nevertheless, would open by pushing, and was so opened by the prisoner; in all of which cases the "breaking" was held to be sufficient. If the entrance was either by pulling open the blinds which had been firmly closed, whether fastened by the catch or not, or through the door which had been bolted, the above decisions apply."[4]

The breaking, while no longer required as an essential element, is relevant on the issue of license or privilege to enter or remain on the premises entered.

## ENTRY

The majority of the states do not require a breaking for the crime of burglary. One who enters a room or building with intent to commit a felony is guilty of burglary, even though permission to enter has been extended to him personally or as a member of the public.[5]

Entry is a basic element of the modern statutory definition of burglary. As one decision explains: "The gravamen of burglary is the act of entry."[6] The word *enter* does not mean the intruder must place his entire body inside the premises. The insertion of any part of the body or of any instrument or weapon held in the hand is sufficient entry.[7]

The crime of burglary is complete when the evidence shows the defendant entered the building, with the intent to commit the crime, whether the intended theft (or crime) was committed or not.

Entry into one's own home even with a felonious intent is not the entry required for burglary. The entry must be an invasion of a possessory right in a building and must be committed by a person who has no right to be there.[8]

Many states use, in addition to or in conjunction with the element of entry, the term *remains* or *remains unlawfully*. As used in this context the meaning is that a person can enter a premises lawfully with "license or privilege," but if he or she remains on the premises after the termination of such license or privilege such conduct constitutes the entry element of burglary.[9]

As an example of one having permission or license to enter the premises and yet being convicted of burglary, a California court held that a shoplifting in a grocery store during business hours was a burglary.[10] The proof was sufficient to show the intent to steal at the time of entry into the open store.

Comparison of state burglary statutes — Essential Elements and Aggravating Factors

| State | BREAKING | ENTERING | ENTERS OR REMAINS | DWELLING HOUSE | ANY STRUCTURE/VEHICLE/VESSEL | NIGHTTIME | DAY OR NIGHT | WITH INTENT TO COMMIT FELONY | WITH INTENT TO COMMIT FELONY OR THEFT | WITH INTENT TO COMMIT ANY CRIME | ARMED WITH WEAPON | ASSAULTS OR THREATENS SOMEONE | ARMED WITH EXPLOSIVES | BUILDING OCCUPIED | FORCIBLY BURSTING & ENTERING | USE OF KEYS OR PICKS | AIDED BY ACCOMPLICE |
|---|---|---|---|---|---|---|---|---|---|---|---|---|---|---|---|---|---|
| Alabama | X | X | X | X | X | X | | | | | X | | | | | | |
| Alaska | X | X | X | X | X | | | | | | X | | | | | | |
| Arizona | X | X | X | X | X | X | | X | X | X | | X | | | | | |
| Arkansas | X | | X | X | X | X | X | | | | | | | | | | |
| California | | X | | X | X | X | X | X | X | X | X | | | | | | |
| Colorado | | | X | X | | | | X | X | X | | X | | | | | |
| Connecticut | X | X | X | X | | | | X | X | X | | X | | | | | |
| Delaware | X | X | X | X | | | | X | X | X | | X | | | | | |
| Florida | X | X | X | X | | | | X | X | | X | X | | | | | |
| Georgia | X | | X | | | X | | | | | | | | | | | |
| Hawaii | X | X | X | | X | X | | | X | | | | | | | | |
| Idaho | | | | | | | X | X | X | | | X | | | | | |
| Illinois | X | X | | | | X | X | | | | | | | | | | |
| Indiana | X | X | X | X | X | X | | X | X | X | | X | | | | | |
| Iowa | X | X | X | X | X | | | X | X | X | | X | X | | | | X |
| Kansas | X | | X | X | | X | | | | | X | | | | | | |

| | | | | | | | | | | | | | | | | | | |
|---|---|---|---|---|---|---|---|---|---|---|---|---|---|---|---|---|---|---|
| Maine | X | X | | X | X | X | | | X | | | X | X | X | X | | | |
| Maryland | X | | | X | X | X | X | | X | | | | | X | | | | |
| Massachusetts | X | X | | X | X | X | X | X | | | | X | X | X | | | | |
| Michigan | | X | | | X | X | X | | X | | | | | X | | | | |
| Minnesota | | | X | | X | | | | | X | | X | X | X | X | | | |
| Mississippi | X | X | | X | X | | X | | | | | X | | X | X | | | |
| Missouri | X | X | | X | X | | | | X | | | X | | X | X | X | X | |
| Montana | | X | | | X | X | | | X | | | | | X | | | | |
| Nebraska | X | X | | | X | | | | X | | | X | X | X | | | | |
| Nevada | | X | | | X | | X | | X | | | | | X | | | | |
| New Hampshire | | X | | X | X | X | | | | X | | X | X | X | | | | |
| New Jersey | | X | | | X | | | X | | | | | | X | | | | |
| New Mexico | | X | | | X | | | | X | | | X | X | | | | | |
| New York | | | X | X | X | X | | | | X | | X | X | | | | | |
| North Carolina | X | X | | X | X | X | | X | X | | | | | X | X | | | |
| North Dakota | X | X | | | X | | | | | X | | | | | | | | |
| Ohio | X | X | | | X | | | | X | | | X | X | X | X | | | |
| Oklahoma | X | X | | X | X | X | | | X | | | X | | | | X | X | X |
| Oregon | | | X | X | X | | | | | X | | X | X | | | | | |
| Pennsylvania | | X | | | X | | | | | X | | | | | | | | |
| Rhode Island | X | X | | X | | X | | X | | | | | | | | | | |
| South Carolina | X | X | | X | | X | | X | | | | | | | | | | |
| South Dakota | X | X | | X | | X | X | | | X | | X | | | | X | X | X |
| Tennessee | X | X | | X | X | X | | X | | | | X | | X | | | | |
| Texas | | X | | | X | | | | X | | | X | X | X | X | | | |
| Utah | | X | | | X | X | X | | X | | | | | X | | | | |
| Vermont | X | X | | | X | X | | X | | | | | | | X | | | |
| Virginia | | X | | X | X | X | | X | X | | | | | | | | | |
| Washington | | X | | X | | X | | | | X | | X | X | | | | | X |
| West Virginia | X | X | | X | X | X | X | | X | | | | | | | | | |
| Wisconsin | | X | | | X | | | X | | | | X | X | X | | | | |
| Wyoming | | X | | | X | | | | X | | | X | X | X | | | | |

**Figure 14. THE OFFENSE OF BURGLARY BY STATES; ESSENTIAL ELEMENTS AND AGGRAVATING FACTORS.**

## TIME OF DAY

The common-law requirement of nighttime meant the period between sunset and sunrise. Burglary may now be committed at any time of the day or night in the majority of the states. There is still some emphasis, however, on the concept of burglary as a crime against the habitation. Twenty-seven states do consider a burglary committed at night to be an aggravated form of the crime. (See Figure 14.)

## DWELLING HOUSE, BUILDING, STRUCTURES

The basic building in burglary cases has long been a dwelling house. State statutes usually define a dwelling house as follows: every house or edifice, any part of which has usually been occupied by any person lodging therein at night, and any structure joined to and immediately connected with such a house or edifice. However, the majority of the states have now replaced the dwelling-house requirement with the terms *building* or *structure*. Most of these states define a building as a structure which may be entered and utilized by persons for business, public use, lodging or storage of goods, or more simply as a structure with four walls and a roof. Many states now include vehicles and vessels within the concept of structures which can be burglarized, particularly the so-called residential vehicles: trailers and campers.

A Colorado appellate court, confronted with the question of whether a telephone booth was a *structure* within the scope of Colorado's burglary statute, stated:

> Rather than limiting the definition of a building to a structure with walls and a roof, which would include the telephone booth in question, we believe it is the legislative intent that a building is a structure which has a capacity to contain, and is designed for the habitation of man, or animals, or the shelter of property.[11]

A definition of this nature would exclude such enclosures as a cemetery vault.[12] The definition would seem to include showrooms, offices, banks, bath houses, bunkhouses, cabins, cabin cruisers, closets, garages, hotels, inns, motel rooms, and natural rock caves used to contain powder and equipped with a door.

## INTENT NECESSARY IN BURGLARY

The common-law requirement was that the burglar have a felonious intent. All states now require a criminal intent in some form; specific intent is an essential element of burglary. About half of the states require the culpable state of mind in burglary to be the intent

to commit a felony or theft, which may be petty theft (a misdemeanor). A lesser number of states specify that proof of an intent to commit any crime is sufficient intent for a conviction in burglary prosecutions.

It is necessary that the intent be formed prior to or at the very moment of entry.

Inherent in the criminal intent aspect of burglary is that the intended crime be "therein," within the premises entered.

## PROSECUTION PROBLEMS AND COMMON DEFENSES

A major problem in burglary prosecutions is proving "opportunity," that the accused was at the crime scene. A successful prosecution often depends upon the care exercised by police in their case preparation. It is not often that witnesses can be found who will identify a defendant as a person observed at or near the crime scene at or about the time of the crime, but police often find and develop physical evidence that will circumstantially link the defendant with the crime scene.

Tracing the proceeds of a burglary from the sale or other disposal of the stolen property may link a defendant with its taking.

When a burglar operates with a crime partner, the prosecutor may enter into a plea bargain with one defendant for testimony against a co-defendant. Such testimony would need supporting evidence.

The most common defense in burglary cases is a complete denial of guilt. This need not be accompanied by an alibi defense as the proof that the defendant was at the crime scene is often weak and inconclusive.

When the stolen property has been traced to the defendant as seller or disposer of it, the usual defense is that it was bought from, or exchanged with, a person unknown to the defendant. This defense requires the prosecution to produce contrary evidence if it is to overcome any reasonable doubt in the minds of the triers of fact.

If the defendant was arrested prior to the commission of the necessary felony or theft, his intent is a major issue. Intent becomes the issue in most contested burglary charges which involve shoplifting from a store and apprehension in or around the store.

## NOTES

1. *State* v. *Hauptmann*, 180 A. 809 (1935, N.J.).
2. *State* v. *Hauptmann*, 180 A. 809 (1935, N.J.).
3. *State* v. *Perry*, 145 N.W. 56 (1914, Iowa).
4. *State* v. *McAfee*, 100 S.E. 2d 249 (1957, N.C.).
5. *People* v. *Talbot*, 414 P. 2d 633 (1966, Calif.).
6. *People* v. *Failla*, 414 P. 2d 39 (1966, Calif.).

7. *Evans* v. *State*, 90 S.E. 743 (1916, Ga.).
8. *People* v. *Gauze*, 15 Cal. 3d 709 (1975).
9. *People* v. *Licata*, 268 N.E. 2d 787 (1971, N.Y.).
10. *People* v. *Barry*, 29 P. 1026 (1892, Calif.).
11. *Sanchez* v. *People*, 349 P. 2d 561 (1960, Colo.).
12. *People* v. *Richards*, 15 N.E. 371 (1888, N.Y.).

# 18

# THEFT CRIMES

## OBJECTIVES

The primary objective of this chapter is to detail the broad scope of theft crimes from the crime of petty larceny to the felony of grand larceny, and from larceny as the trespassory taking and carrying away of another's property to larceny by false pretense in which the thief gains ownership of the property involved. Secondary objectives are to reveal the essential elements of the different kinds of theft and to describe the basic mens rea or criminal intent in thefts.

## LEGAL TERM

Conversion. An unauthorized assumption of ownership of the property of another which deprives the true owner of his or her property for an indefinite period or permanently.

## QUESTIONS FOR STUDY

1. What is the scope of theft crimes?
2. What is the distinction (breaking point) between petty and grand larceny in most states?
3. Describe theft by trick or device. List the essential elements.
4. Describe theft by false pretense. List the essential elements.
5. Describe embezzlement. List the essential elements.
6. What property may be the subject of theft crimes?
7. What criminal intent is necessary in the various theft crimes?
8. What are the possible defenses to prosecution for theft crimes?
9. What is the difference between "larceny" generally and embezzlement? Between "larceny" generally and larceny by false pretense?

**T**heft is the unlawful taking or stealing of property or articles without the use of force or violence. It can include crimes such as shoplifting, pocket-picking, purse snatching, thefts from autos, thefts of autos, bicycle thefts, embezzlement, con games and other frauds, forgery, and worthless checks.

While many jurisdictions define the theft of various items of property as a felony (bovine animals, firearms, etc.), the usual distinction between larceny as a felony as opposed to larceny as a misdemeanor is the value of the property stolen. The property that is the subject of larceny must have some basic value that can be expressed in dollars: its worth.

The classic distinction between grand larceny or petty larceny has been a "breaking point" in the value of the property stolen. At one time most jurisdictions used $50 as the line marking the difference between grand and petty theft. In post-WWII years the inflationary spiral has affected these statutory provisions. The breaking point of almost half the states is $100, and many states set this breaking point at $200. A few states have specified larger amounts, and others continue to offer legislation consistent with the inflationary nature of the economy. (See Figure 15.)

## DEFINITIONS

Terms with a common meaning associated with larceny are:

1. *Property*: Anything of value.
2. *Property of another*: Property in which any person other than the defendant(s) has a possessory or ownership interest.
3. *Deprive*: To withhold the property of another.
4. *Services*: Transportation; hotel/motel accommodations; public utility use.

New terms used in crime-victimization studies offer some clarification on the scope of common forms of larceny:

1. *Household larceny*: Theft of property or cash from the home, involving neither forcible nor unlawful entry, or from its immediate vicinity.
2. *Personal larceny without contact*: Theft without direct contact between victim and offender of property or cash from any place other than the victim's home or its immediate vicinity.
3. *Personal larceny with contact*: Theft of purse, wallet, or cash by stealth directly from the person of the victim, but without force or the threat of force; and sometimes includes what is commonly termed purse snatching.[1]

## LARCENY

At common law, larceny was defined as a trespassory taking and carrying away of personal property belonging to another with an in-

| | | | |
|---|---|---|---|
| Alabama | 25 | Montana | 150 |
| Alaska | 100 | Nebraska | 100 |
| Arizona | 50 | Nevada | 100 |
| Arkansas | 35 | New Hampshire | 100 |
| California | 200 | New Jersey | 500 |
| Colorado | 100 | New Mexico | 100 |
| Connecticut | 50 | New York | 250 |
| Delaware | 100 | North Carolina | — |
| Florida | 100 | North Dakota | 100 |
| Georgia | 100 | Ohio | 150 |
| Hawaii | 200 | Oklahoma | 20 |
| Idaho | 150 | Oregon | 200 |
| Illinois | 150 | Pennsylvania | 2000 |
| Indiana | 100 | Rhode Island | 500 |
| Iowa | 20 | South Carolina | 20 |
| Kansas | 50 | South Dakota | 50 |
| Kentucky | 100 | Tennessee | 100 |
| Louisiana | 100 | Texas | 200 |
| Maine | 500 | Utah | 250 |
| Maryland | 100 | Vermont | 100 |
| Massachusetts | 100 | Virginia | 100 |
| Michigan | 100 | Washington | 200 |
| Minnesota | 100 | West Virginia | 50 |
| Mississippi | 100 | Wisconsin | 100 |
| Missouri | 50 | Wyoming | 100 |

**Note:** Anything below the amount specified is a misdemeanor: anything of value of the amount shown or higher is a felony.

## Figure 15. GRAND VS. PETTY LARCENY BY "BREAKING POINTS": VALUE OF PROPERTY STOLEN.

tent to deprive the owner of such property permanently.[2] The formation of the crime of larceny in more ancient times was a process of limitation since the early penalty for larceny was death. The courts tended to distinguish and limit the application of larceny and formed other theft crimes as separate and distinct (embezzlement, false pretense, trick or device). Thus the new or different theft crimes were not subject to the punishment of death.

Many modern statutes include all or most of the theft crimes under one definition, and as one crime: a taking possession and carrying away or conversion of property by stealth, trespass, fraud, or trick with intent to deprive the owner permanently of his property. One code states:

### THEFT DEFINED:

(a) Every person who shall feloniously steal, take, carry, lead, or drive away the personal property of another, or who shall fraudulently appropriate property which has been entrusted to him, or who shall knowingly and designedly, by any false or fraudulent representation or pretense, defraud any other person of money, labor or real or personal property, or who causes or

procures others to report falsely of his wealth or mercantile character and by thus imposing upon any person, obtains credit and thereby fraudulently gets or obtains the labor or service of another, is guilty of theft. In determining the value of the property obtained, for the purposes of this section, the reasonable and fair market value shall be the test, and in determining the value of services received the contract price shall be the test. If there be no contract price, the reasonable and going wage for the service rendered shall govern. For the purposes of this section, any false or fraudulent representation or pretense made shall be treated as continuing, so as to cover any money, property or service received as a result thereof, and the complaint, information or indictment may charge that the crime was committed on any date during the particular period in question. The hiring of any additional employee or employees without advising each of them of every labor claim due and unpaid and every judgment that the employer has been unable to meet shall be *prima facie* evidence of intent to defraud.

(b) Except as provided in Section 10855 of the Vehicle Code, intent to commit theft by fraud is presumed if one who has leased or rented the personal property of another pursuant to a written contract fails to return the personal property to its owner within 20 days after the owner has made written demand by certified or registered mail following the expiration of the lease or rental agreement for return of the property so leased or rented, or if one presents to the owner identification which bears a false or fictitious name or address for the purpose of obtaining the lease or rental agreement.

(c) The presumptions created by subdivision (b) are presumptions affecting the burden of producing evidence.

(d) Within 30 days after the lease or rental agreement has expired, the owner shall make written demand for return of the property so leased or rented. Notice addressed and mailed to the lessee or renter at the address given at the time of the making of the lease or rental agreement and to any other known address shall constitute proper demand. Where the owner fails to make such written demand the presumption created by subdivision (b) shall not apply.[3]

The difference between common-law and statutory larceny (theft) is the manner of taking and the property subject to theft.

## THE TAKING (LARCENY)

The common-law definition of larceny always involved a trespass. The definition of *trespass* in the crime of larceny is a transgression which causes harm to property. There must be some wrongful force in the taking; a taking against the will of the possessor or owner.

Much of the development of the definitions of larceny and theft crimes involved the distinctions made between larceny, embezzlement, trick or device, or fraud (false pretenses).

The crime of larceny involved a defendant who took possession of the property unlawfully; embezzlement was distinguished by the fact that possession was lawfully in the defendant but he later unlawfully converted that property to his own purposes. The law has seen a difference in the terms *possession* and *custody*. Larceny is a crime against a lawful possession while mere custody is delivery of property by the owner to another for some limited, temporary, or special purpose. The taking of such property to one's own use is larceny. Possession is a lawful dominion over the property, with some substantial powers and duties respecting the property. The reason for the early distinction between custody and possession was that a person who had lawful possession could not commit larceny since larceny required a trespassory taking. However, a person who held property as a mere custodian could "take and carry away" property and satisfy the trespass requirement of larceny. With the development of the crime of embezzlement the distinction could determine the crime charged.[4]

## TRICK OR DEVICE

Obtaining possession of money or other property by means of a fraudulent trick or device is larceny. The fraud involved is deemed to replace or substitute for the usual requirement of trespass. Fraud to gain *possession* is a larceny; fraud to gain *title* (ownership) is the crime of false pretenses. The issue is whether the victim intends to give over only possession of the property, or whether he intends to pass title to the property.

In a 1959 case, the complaining witness, Alice, met defendant in March while both were working at a hotel. In July she started seeing him socially. After about two weeks defendant proposed marriage. The same night after saying that since they were going to get married, everything that was his was hers, he asked her for money to go to Washington on a business deal. She gave him $300. A few days later at his request she gave him $500 more for the same trip. On August 12, she loaned him $900 in order for him to obtain a license for a bar and a lease at Bush Street and Grant Avenue. August 16, she loaned him $450 for fixtures and supplies. September 3, she loaned him $325 for a license from the Board of Equalization. September 10, she loaned him an additional $300 for the bar. These loans were to be repaid after the first of the year. When Alice informed defendant that was all the money she had, he began to admire her ring, which had cost her $290 in 1940. He told her that he could get some money for it. He promised to return the ring in a week, saying that he intended to use the money from pawning it for

the bar. Stating that it was necessary in order for him to be able to pawn the ring, he produced from his pocket a paper which he asked her to sign. It stated: "This is to inform anyone concerned that I have authorized J. Lafka to make a loan on this ring, and to use said monies for himself as he sees fit." Alice stated, "It isn't saying that you are using it for the bar." He again reassured her that it was for the bar, that he would return the ring in a week, and that he had to word the paper that way in order to pawn the ring. Alice then signed the note and gave him the ring. Alice took a trip to Portland and was met by Lafka upon her return. Thereafter he no longer visited her or talked of marriage. She called him and inquired about the ring. Toward the end of October, Alice consulted the district attorney as Lafka refused to keep his promise of returning the ring. Alice testified that she would not have loaned defendant the money if it was not to be used for the purposes defendant described. Lafka did not testify at his larceny trial. He was *convicted*. On appeal Lafka argued that the facts in this case did not warrant his larceny conviction. The appellate court *affirmed* Lafka's conviction, ruling that the evidence at trial supported the trial verdict:

It is clear that defendant used the device of pretending that he was "negotiating" for a license and a lease to deprive Alice permanently and wholly of her property, and without any intention of using it for the purposes promised. The department (license) had no record of any application or "negotiations" of any sort by defendant. Moreover, the department's supervising agent testified that the department would not accept an application for a liquor license without a particular premise being specified. As to a lease, defendant called Paul Kwan who owned a store at Bush and Grant Avenue. He testified that defendant had expressed interest in renting the store for a bar but did not go so far as to discuss a lease. Kwan could not remember, however, the month in which defendant came to see him. The jury could very well have believed that it was in November or December, after Alice began to stir up trouble for defendant, that he saw in Kwan an attempt to supply proof of defendant's good faith.

Considering defendant's failure to testify, the fact that as soon as Alice's money was gone defendant's romantic interest in her also waned, the fact that defendant did not discuss a lease with Kwan, and all the other circumstances, there was sufficient evidence to amply demonstrate the defendant had no intention of using the money and ring for the purposes specified nor of repaying the money or returning the ring, and therefore extracted the money and ring by trick and device.

"Larceny amounting to grand theft can be committed by trick and device and usually results when the victim of a fraud

intends not to pass complete title to his property, but that it shall be applied to a special purpose while the recipient intends to appropriate it to his own use."

It is well settled that a loan of money induced by a fraudulent representation that it will be used for a specific purpose accompanied by an intent to steal amounts to larceny by trick and device.

*The elements of theft by trick or device, (1) the taking, (2) asportation (3) of the property of another (4) with a fraudulent intent, are satisfied here.* [Emphasis added.] Clearly there was a "taking" and "asportation." The fraud vitiated the transaction and the owner is deemed still to retain a constructive possession of the property. The owner does not part with title to the alleged thief where, as here, she delivered it to appellant [Lafka] to be applied by the latter to a particular purpose and the recipient, having obtained possession with the preconceived intention to appropriate the money to his own use, subsequently did convert it to his own use instead of applying it to the purpose contemplated by the owner. Under the facts here present there was in contemplation of the law of larceny a "taking."[5]

Where property is taken with the consent of the possessor or owner the crime of larceny has not been committed. The essence of the larcenous taking is that it be against the will of the owner or person in legal possession.

If the defendant and an employee conspire to steal from the employer and the employee tells his employer, who then tells the employee to take the property and give it to the defendant to catch him in the act; then there will be no larceny by the employee or the defendant since there was a taking with consent of the owner.

However, if a policeman, in order to catch thieves, feigns drunkenness and helplessness to catch the drunk roller in the act, there will be larceny and no consent. A defendant seeing a seemingly helpless officer took three dollars from the officer's pocket. The officer offered no resistance and intended the thief to take his money in order to catch and prosecute him. The reviewing court noted:

It is, no doubt, true, as a general proposition, that larceny is not committed when the property is taken with the consent of its owner; but it is difficult in some instances to determine whether certain acts constitute, in law, such "consent"; and, under the authorities, we do not think that there is such consent where there is mere passive submission on the part of the owner of the goods taken, and no indication that he wishes them taken, and no knowledge by the taker that the owner wishes them taken, and no mutual understanding between the two, and no

active measures of inducement employed for the purpose of leading into temptation, and no preconcert whatever between the thief and the owner.

From the authorities, and upon principle, we are of opinion that the conduct of the victim-witness Slanker, as detailed by him in his testimony, did not amount to consent in law, and affords no reason why the act of appellant in taking the money (if he did take it in the manner sworn to by Slanker) was not larceny. If there had been preconcert of action between Slanker and appellant, a different question would have been presented.[6]

## CAPTION AND ASPORTATION

Caption is the laying hold of, seizing, or grasping of property with intent to steal; asportation is the gaining of control of property and moving it while under the control of the thief.

The distance of movement is not important. The importance is the fact of the movement, no matter how slight. Even the movement made by a pickpocket in moving the victim's wallet from the depths of his pocket to the pocket opening is sufficient to satisfy the element of asportation.[7]

Theft from a store requires a carrying away which is movement past the place where payment can be expected by the store owner. Any movement from the store's control is sufficient and store employees usually wait until the thief is past the check-out stations or outside the store before effecting an arrest.

An imputed trespass may exist where the actual carrying away is accomplished by another at the direction of the defendant (an agency theory).

The law appears to be settled that where, with the intent to steal, the thief employs or sets in motion any agency, either animate or inanimate, with the design of effecting a transfer of the possession of the property of another to him in order that he may feloniously convert and steal it, the larceny will be completed, if, in pursuance of such agency, the goods come into the hands of the thief and he feloniously converts them to his own use. In such a case a conviction may be had upon a common-law indictment charging a felonious taking and carrying away of such goods.[8]

Larceny is a continuing offense. Every new caption and asportation is an offense against the owner. This is so even if the property is unlawfully taken and carried away by one from another who himself previously stole the property.[9]

## THE PROPERTY

At common law the property subject to larceny had to meet the definition of *personal property*. If it was property attached to realty (real property) it could not be the subject of larceny. The term *per-*

sonal property includes chattels, money, things in action, and all written instruments (as distinguished from the rights to which they relate)—everything, except real property, which may be the subject of ownership. It should have corporeal existence, physical presence, quantity, or quality which is detectible or measurable. A right only existing in law is not the subject of larceny. Thus rights, services, and realty are not the subjects of larceny, yet the unlawful appropriation of electricity or gas is larceny.[10]

Though a right may not be the subject of larceny, the piece of paper on which it is written (no matter what the intrinsic value) is the subject of larceny.

The modern doctrine is that anything which may be converted is the subject of theft whether realty (real property) or personal property.[11]

Larceny is an offense against lawful possession. If a person had lawful possession and converted goods completely to his own use depriving the owner of his interest, the offense would not be larceny. It would be embezzlement.

In common-law jurisdictions the husband could not commit larceny by converting the money of his wife to his own use. By common-law rule the ownership of the wife's property was vested in the husband. By modern statute, which allows the spouses their separate property, each spouse must observe the difference between "mine and thine" or be subject to prosecution for a theft.

In partnership arrangements one partner could not commit larceny of the partnership funds. Until divided, each partner has an undivided possessory or ownership interest in all the partnership's property.

An owner may in some circumstances steal his own property. A defendant pledged his automobile to an attorney for advanced fees and services rendered. He then took the car from the attorney's possession without the attorney's knowledge or consent. The general rule is that a person cannot commit larceny by taking possession of his own property. However, if he transfers a special interest or ownership to another, a subsequent retaking with intent to deprive the other of his interest can be larceny.[12]

## INTENT TO STEAL (MENS REA)

At one time the offense of larceny required an intent to deprive the owner permanently of his property. An intent to deprive the owner temporarily of his property was not larceny even though it might be some other offense such as trespass. Contemporary statutes have made it a crime to take property even when the intent is only to temporarily deprive the owner of his property.[13]

The intent to steal is a question of fact to be decided by the jury based upon the evidence presented.

In a Maryland case, one Sheffield took a car without consent and by stealth, and drove it through several states. After a few days he began driving back in the general direction of the place where he took the car. Sheffield claimed at trial that he intended to return the car to a place near the place from which he took it. He was arrested while he was still out of the state of the taking. He was convicted of auto theft. On appeal Sheffield argued his defense of intent to return the car. The appellate court *affirmed* Sheffield's conviction. Its opinion stated:

There can be no doubt that the original taking by the defendant in this case deprived the owner of important property rights and benefits. The right to the possession and use of property, especially an automobile, is a very important property right. In this case on the facts when the defendant took the property he clearly intended to drive it through three States for several hundred miles and necessarily thereby depriving the owner for several days of the use and possession of her own property. Not only was the original taking within the ordinary acceptation of theft but the continued use of it by the defendant deprived the owner for several days of her rights and benefits of ownership.

The original taking having clearly been unlawful and by trespass, we are not dealing with a case where the original taking was not by trespass but obtained by false pretenses or embezzlement. In the latter case the technical requirement of the common-law larceny would not be gratified although such a taking was later made a statutory offense both in England and in many of the States of the United States. And now it has clearly been decided by the Supreme Court that the word "stolen" as used in the statute would apply to any kind of felonious taking which constitutes a deprivation of the rights and benefits of ownership.

*When an automobile is taken without right of colorable authority and by stealth and to be used by the taker for his own use and benefit for an indefinite period of time, I think there is properly a presumption, or at least sufficient evidence, for an inference of fact that it is being taken to deprive the owner of the rights and benefits of his property; and the mere statement of a defendant who has so feloniously taken a motor car that he intended to abandon it somewhere in the same city (one of several thousand inhabitants) is not sufficient to destroy the inference unless well supported by collateral facts.* [Emphasis added.][14]

The taking of another's property in good faith by inadvertence or by mistake does not constitute larceny. If the person taking the property mistakenly believes he had the legal right to hold the property of another until damages caused by the owner were paid, there is no trespass, no intent to steal, and thus no larceny.[15]

An honest mistake of law is a defense since it negates the intent to unlawfully deprive the owner of his property. However, there may be larceny even though there is no desire by the defendant of personal gain. There may be a question of asportation in such matters as killing an animal or destroying the property of another. Most state laws have a malicious mischief statute to include those unlawful acts which deprive the owner of his property but which do not meet the requirements of larceny or statutory theft.

Lost or mislaid property raises special problems. The law considers title and constructive possession to remain in the owner of lost property. Therefore when the finder takes possession with the intent to appropriate the property to his own use without an attempt to find the owner, a larceny may be charged. The intent to steal must be present at the time the finder takes possession. Particular statutes often deal directly with this situation:

> One who finds lost property under circumstances which give him knowledge of or means of inquiry as to the true owner and who appropriates such property to his own use, or to the use of another person not entitled thereto, without first making reasonable and just efforts to find the owner and to restore the property to him, is guilty of theft.[16]

## EMBEZZLEMENT

Embezzlement is a theft without a taking by trespass, trick, device, or fraud. The property and the intent elements are the same as needed in larceny and the property must be converted to the thief's purposes. Important terms in the crime of embezzlement include the following:

*Lawful possession*: The defendant must be in lawful possession of the property by some trust, bailment, or agency. The banker receiving money for deposit and the innkeeper receiving valuable property to keep in his safe during the owner's stay at the hotel are examples of the lawful possession necessary for this crime.

*Conversion*: The defendant must appropriate the entrusted property of another to his own use. Such conversion includes the usual element of carrying away seen in the larceny elements.

*The intent to steal*: The intent to steal must be formed after the lawful possession is acquired.

The crime of embezzlement was created to cover the instance of a wrongful conversion of another's property which did not have the concurrence of unlawful taking and intent necessary for larceny.[17]

## FALSE PRETENSES

A further complication arose in the development of the theft laws in those instances where the thief, by his fraudulent representa-

tions, was voluntarily given title to property by the owner. Larceny required the release of possession only by trespass or fraud. There was no passing of ownership from the owner to the thief. The essence of the crime of theft by false pretenses is that title (ownership) is intended to pass and does vest in the thief. Therefore the thief does not take and carry away the "property of another." Relevant terms include the following:

*Taking title*: It is the intent of the victim to pass ownership to the thief. The interest passed must be more than mere possession though it may be less than outright ownership; beneficial ownership or a security interest may be sufficient title.

*False pretense*: The pretense must be of a past or existing fact or situation. Mere promises or statements of intention or opinions about the future, even if false, will not be sufficient to satisfy this element. However, a promise made without intention to perform is a misrepresentation of a state of mind, and thus a misrepresentation of existing fact, and is a false pretense. The essence of the offense of obtaining property by false pretenses is (as it has always been) the fraudulent intent of the defendant. This intent must be proved by the prosecution; a showing of non-performance of a promise or falsity of a representation will not suffice.[18]

A finding of false pretenses does not require personal benefit from the fraudulent acquisition. The false pretense (or promise) must have materially and substantially influenced the owner to part with his money or property. The victim must be deceived. However, the false pretense need not be the only inducing cause.[19] If the conviction rests primarily on the testimony of a single witness that the false pretense was made, the making of the pretense must be corroborated.[20]

## PROSECUTION PROBLEMS AND COMMON DEFENSES

The major prosecution problems relate to establishing each of the essential elements of the crime of theft as charged. (See Figure 16.) Each of the various types of theft has its own problems. In jurisdictions which adhere to the common-law distinctions the question of which theft crime to charge can be difficult. The utmost care and evaluation is necessary to determine the crime violated.

Denial of any criminal involvement is a common defense to simple theft. The absence of a trespassory act of taking and carrying away; the lack of intent; and mistake of fact or law are equally common defenses to theft.

Possible defenses to larceny by false pretense include claims that the representations were not known to be false at the time, that they were based on a future rather than a present/past fact, or that the victim was not deceived by the lies. Not infrequently, a defense

**Figure 16. MAJOR ELEMENTS OF THEFT CRIMES.**

| | TAKING | | ASPORTATION | | INTENT | |
|---|---|---|---|---|---|---|
| | Method | Interest Taken | Victim's Interest | | What Intent | When Formed |
| **Larceny** | TRESPASS FRAUD TRICK OR DEVICE | POSSESSION | POSSESSION OR TITLE | CARRYING AWAY | PERMANENTLY DEPRIVE | AT TIME OF TAKING |
| **Embezzlement** | LAWFUL (BAILMENT) (TRUST) (AGENT) | POSSESSION | POSSESSION OR TITLE | CONVERSION TO OWN USE | PERMANENTLY DEPRIVE | AFTER TAKING LAWFUL POSSESSION |
| **False Pretenses** | FALSE PRETENSES (PAST OR PRESENT FACT) (FALSE PROMISE) | TITLE (OWNERSHIP INTEREST) | TITLE (OWNERSHIP) | CONVERSION TO OWN USE | PERMANENTLY DEPRIVE | AT TIME OF MAKING FALSE PRETENSES |

may claim the victim was negligent in not checking out the representations; the victim's gullibility contributed to the crime. If false promises are included within the crime of false pretenses the defense of economic failure rather than initial fraudulent intent is available.

# NOTES

1. U.S. Department of Justice, Law Enforcement Assistance Administration, National Criminal Justice Information and Statistics Service, *Criminal Victimization in the United States—1973 Advance Report* prepared for the National Crime Panel (Washington, D.C.: Government Printing Office, 1975), pp. 43–44.
2. *State* v. *Voiers*, 61 S.E. 2d 521 (1950, W. Va.).
3. California Penal Code, Section 484.
4. *Commonwealth* v. *Ryan*, 30 N.E. 364 (1892, Mass.).
5. *People* v. *Lafka*, 344 P. 2d 619 (1959, Calif.).
6. *People* v. *Hanselman*, 18 P. 425 (1888, Calif.).
7. *State* v. *Chambers*, 22 W.Va. 779 (1883).
8. *State* v. *Laborde*, 11 So. 2d 404 (1942, La.).
9. *Dunlavey* v. *Commonwealth*, 35 S.E. 2d 763 (1945, Va.).
10. *People* v. *Ashworth*, 222 N.Y. Supp. 24 (1927).
11. *Model Penal Code*, 1962 draft (Philadelphia: American Law Institute), Section 223.2.
12. *State* v. *Hubbard*, 266 P. 939 (1928, Kan.).
13. California Vehicle Code, Section 10851.
14. *United States* v. *Sheffield*, 161 F. Supp. 387 (1958, Md.).
15. *State* v. *Sawyer*, 110 A. 461 (1920, Conn.).
16. California Penal Code, Section 485.
17. *People* v. *Riggins*, 148 N.E. 2d 450 (1958, Ill.).
18. *People* v. *Ashley*, 267 P. 2d 271 (1954, Calif.).
19. *People* v. *Ashley*, 267 P. 2d 271 (1954, Calif.).
20. California Penal Code, Section 1110.

# 19

# RAPE

## OBJECTIVES

This chapter depicts rape as the major sex crime against women; details the similarities and differences between "statutory" rape and forcible rape; describes the essential elements and "aggravating" factors of the crime of rape; and discusses prosecution and defense problems in rape cases.

## LEGAL TERMS

Carnal knowledge. *Sexual intercourse; a man having sexual connection with a woman.*
Dildo. *A device resembling a penis.*

## QUESTIONS FOR STUDY

1. What uniformity is there among state statutes concerning forcible rape?
2. How does statutory rape differ from forcible rape?
3. What are the "aggravating" factors in rape cases?
4. What are the means used to overcome the will of the female victim in rape cases?
5. What sex act is necessary in rape cases?
6. Develop the meaning of "without consent" and "against the will" in rape cases.
7. Is criminal intent necessary in the crime of statutory rape? Explain.
8. Develop the theme that consent is a valid defense to an accusation of forcible rape.

A male person is guilty of rape when he has sexual intercourse with a female person not his spouse

by compelling her to submit to the act by the use of force or threat of force (forcible rape); or if he knows she is unable to consent or refuse due to a physical or mental condition.

At common law *rape* was termed the carnal knowledge of a woman with force and without her consent.[1]

Building on this common-law base, legislatures have extended the concept of forcible rape to cases in which the act is accomplished through fraud or the administration of drugs or liquor. There has also been a legislative extension to cases involving children: *statutory rape* is the carnal knowledge of a female below a specified age with or without her consent.

State statutes uniformly describe forcible rape as sexual intercourse without consent of the female victim.

There are states which add the almost unnecessary provision that the rape victim cannot be the wife of the perpetrator. (See Figure 17.)

There is also a remarkable uniformity in the inclusion of "statutory rape" in these statutes; almost all jurisdictions recognize as rape the carnal knowledge of a child despite any claim that the child consented to the act.

The means used to overcome the will of the female victim is always a major issue in the rape prosecution:
1. Force or threat of the use of force.
2. The administering of drugs (or liquor).
3. Impersonation of the husband.
4. Incapacity of the victim to consent (physical or mental condition; age).[2] (See Figure 17.)

Rape is aggravated and additionally punished when the rapist:
1. Is armed with a dangerous weapon.
2. Kidnaps the victim.
3. Inflicts bodily injury (other than the injury of penetration).
4. Is in a position of familial, custodial, or official authority over victim (custody or control). (See Figure 17.)

The emergence of these new forms of aggravated rape is evidence of a legislative concern as to the adequacy of penalties for the crime of rape and for rape combined with other crimes.

## SEXUAL INTERCOURSE (CARNAL KNOWLEDGE)

Any sexual penetration of the female victim by the male perpetrator, however slight, is sufficient to complete the crime of rape.

The guilt of rape consists in the outrage to the person and feelings of the female victim. Thus the fact of sexual penetration is the issue, not the degree or extent of penetration.[3]

It is generally conceded that a woman is incapable of committing the act of rape since the sexual intercourse must be by means of the male sexual organ penetrating the female sexual organ.

The penetration of any other object, whether fingers or dildo, may be the crime of assault, battery or other statutory offense, but it is not rape. Nonetheless a woman may be convicted of rape:

> It is generally held that a woman may be convicted as a principal in the crime of rape, although incapable herself of committing the deed, if she aids, abets, and assists the actual perpetrator in the commission of the crime. . . . Since this is true, it follows that in a joint act of two or more persons, committing rape, one may furnish one of the elements and the other another, whereby each is guilty as a principal. In the case at bar, the respondent used the necessary force, while another performed the act of sexual intercourse, all being against the will and without the consent of the woman.[4] Earlier in the same case, it was held: "It is immaterial that the aider and abettor is disqualified from being the principal actor by reason of age, sex, condition or class."

While a husband cannot commit the crime of rape of his wife, he may be a principal to another's act of rape if he procured or assisted in the act done.

In 1921 a husband forced his wife to engage in prostitution. He remained in the near vicinity while various men had intercourse with his wife. The husband was charged and convicted of rape. Although it is well settled that a man can be a principal to the rape of his wife by aiding and abetting its perpetration by another man, the court in this case saw a distinction. Here the men who had sexual intercourse with his wife were not themselves guilty of rape since they thought she was a consenting prostitute. Therefore the harm against the defendant's wife was committed by the husband alone "although done through the instrumentality of an innocent third person."[5]

Legislatures may take care of this problem by statute:

> Every person who, within this state, takes any female person against her will and without her consent, or with her consent procured by fraudulent inducement or misrepresentation, for the purpose of prostitution, is punishable by imprisonment in the state prison not exceeding five years, and a fine not exceeding one thousand dollars.
>
> Every person who sells any female person or receives any money or other valuable thing for or on account of his placing in custody, for immoral purposes, any female person, whether with or without her consent, is guilty of a felony.
>
> Every man who, by force, intimidation, threats, persuasion, promises, or any other means, places or leaves, or procures any other person or persons to place or leave, his wife in a house of prostitution, or connives at or consents to, or permits the placing

| | SEXUAL INTERCOURSE PENETRATION | WITHOUT CONSENT | NOT WIFE | FORCIBLY OR THREATENS | ADMINISTERING DRUGS | IMPERSONATING HUSBAND | INCAPABLE OF CONSENT | ARMED WITH DANGEROUS WEAPON | KIDNAPPING | BODILY INJURY | PHYSICAL FORCE | CUSTODY OR CONTROL OVER VICTIM | AIDED BY CONFEDERATE |
|---|---|---|---|---|---|---|---|---|---|---|---|---|---|
| Alabama | X | X | X | X | X | | | | | | | | |
| Alaska | X | X | X | | | | | | | | | | |
| Arizona | X | X | X | X | X | | X | | | | | | |
| Arkansas | X | X | X | | X | | | | | | | | |
| California | X | X | X | X | X | | | | | | | | |
| Colorado | X | X | X | X | X | | | X | X | | | | |
| Connecticut | X | X | | | X | | | | | | | | |
| Delaware | X | X | | | | | | | X | | | | |
| Florida | X | X | X | X | X | | X | | X | | X | | |
| Georgia | X | X | X | | | | | | | | | | |
| Hawaii | X | X | X | | X | | | | X | | | | |
| Idaho | X | X | X | X | X | | | | | | | | |
| Illinois | X | X | X | X | X | | | | | | | | |
| Indiana | X | X | | X | X | | | | | | | | |
| Iowa | X | X | X | | | | | | | | | | |
| Kansas | X | X | X | X | X | | | | | | | | |
| Kentucky | X | X | X | | X | | | | X | | | | |
| Louisiana | X | X | X | X | X | | | | | | | | |

| State | 1 | 2 | 3 | 4 | 5 | 6 | 7 | 8 | 9 | 10 | 11 | 12 | 13 |
|---|---|---|---|---|---|---|---|---|---|---|---|---|---|
| Maine | X | X | | | | | | | | | | | |
| Maryland | X | | X | | | | | | X | | | | |
| Massachusetts | X | | X | | | | | | | | | | |
| Michigan | X | | X | | | | | | X | | X | | X |
| Minnesota | X | X | X | X | X | | | | X | | | | |
| Mississippi | X | | | X | | | | | | | | | |
| Missouri | X | X | X | | | | | | | | | | |
| Montana | X | X | X | X | X | | | | | | | | |
| Nebraska | X | | X | | | | | | | | | | |
| Nevada | X | X | | | | | X | | | | | | |
| New Hampshire | X | X | X | | | | | | X | | | | |
| New Jersey | X | X | X | | | | | | | | | | |
| New Mexico | X | X | X | X | | | | | X | | | | |
| New York | X | X | | | | | | | X | | | | |
| North Carolina | X | | X | X | | | | X | | | | | |
| North Dakota | X | X | X | X | | | X | | X | | | | |
| Ohio | X | X | X | | | | | | | | | | |
| Oklahoma | X | X | X | | | | | | X | | | | |
| Oregon | X | | X | | | | | | X | | | | |
| Pennsylvania | X | X | X | | | | | | X | | | | |
| Rhode Island | X | X | | | | | | | | | | | |
| South Carolina | X | | X | | | | | | | | | | |
| South Dakota | X | | X | X | | | | X | | | | | |
| Tennessee | X | | X | X | | | | | | | | | |
| Texas | X | X | X | X | | | | | X | | | | |
| Utah | X | X | X | | | | | | | | | | |
| Vermont | X | | X | | | | | | | | | | |
| Virginia | X | | | | | | | | X | | | | |
| Washington | X | X | X | X | | | | | X | | | | |
| West Virginia | X | X | | | | | | | | | | | |
| Wisconsin | X | X | X | X | | | | | X | | | | |
| Wyoming | X | | | | | | | | | | | | |

**Figure 17. RAPE; ESSENTIAL ELEMENTS AND AGGRAVATING FACTORS.**

or leaving of his wife in a house of prostitution, or allows her to remain therein, is guilty of a felony and punishable by imprisonment in the state prison for not less than three nor more than ten years; and in all prosecutions under this section a wife is a competent witness against her husband.[6]

## WITHOUT CONSENT: AGAINST THE WILL

An additional necessary element of rape is that the sexual intercourse be without the consent or against the will of the female victim.[7] This element requires some resistance by the victim which needs force to overcome.

A consent induced by fear of bodily injury or personal violence is no consent; and it is against the victim's will if a man uses an array of physical force to overcome the victim's mind so she dare not resist.

Consent after penetration is no defense to forcible rape, but consent at any time before the act of penetration is complete relieves the offense of its felonious character. Lack of consent, resistance, and force are the trilogy of rape. Each is a necessary outgrowth of the other.

A conviction of rape may be reversed on the ground that the element of force was lacking, if consent (of one capable of consent) was procured by fraud. The essence of the crime of forcible rape is not the fact of intercourse but the injury and outrage to the feelings of the woman by the forceful penetration of her person. It is a crime radically different from assault and battery although the latter offense is incidental to it.[8]

Without specific statutory provision, consent obtained by artful seduction or false promise of love or marriage will not substitute for the force needed to overcome the will to resist. For instance, statute law in California provides:

Every person who, under promise of marriage, seduces and has sexual intercourse with an unmarried female of previous chaste character, is punishable by imprisonment in the state prison for not more than five years, or by a fine of not more than five thousand dollars, or by both such fine and imprisonment. The intermarriage of the parties subsequent to the commission of the offense is a bar to a prosecution for a violation of the last section; provided such marriage take place prior to the finding of an indictment or the filing of an information charging such offense.[9]

## FORCE AND OTHER MEANS USED IN RAPE

Force is an essential element of the crime of rape and, to justify a conviction, the evidence must warrant a conclusion either that the victim resisted and her resistance was overcome by force, or that

she was prevented from resisting by threats to her safety. Persuasion, not accompanied by threat expressed or implied, or by actual force, is not rape. Special statutes involving fornication, bigamy, and adultery may include these situations. However, the thrust of legislation is now to decriminalize completely sexual acts between consenting adults.

Legislation in California, effective in 1976, illustrates this thrust by removing criminal sanctions from adulterous cohabitation, and from sodomy and oral copulation except when either are committed with a minor, or by force, violence, duress, menace, or threat of great bodily harm; or where the participants are confined in a state prison. The legislation also makes a sexual assault on an animal a misdemeanor.[10]

The law does not provide any specific formula for resistance by a prosecutrix to rape by force and violence. The resistance required of the prosecutrix depends upon the circumstances of the case, such as the relative strength of the parties, the uselessness of resistance, the degree of force manifested, and other factors.[11]

The common law recognized that there were conditions which presumed a lack of consent and sufficient force was only that necessary for the act. In an 1870 Massachusetts case a Mr. Burke and a Mr. Green had carnal intercourse with a Mrs. Caton while she was utterly senseless and incapable of consenting because of intoxication. They appealed their rape conviction. The appellate court *affirmed* their conviction, denying the claim of consent under these circumstances. Its opinion stated:

> Decisions have established the rule in England that unlawful and forcible connection with a woman in a state of unconsciousness at the time, whether that state has been produced by the act of the prisoner or not, is presumed to be without her consent, and is rape. If it were otherwise, any woman in a state of utter stupefaction, whether caused by drunkenness, sudden disease, the blow of a third person, or drugs which she had been persuaded to take, even by the defendant himself, would be unprotected from personal dishonor. The law is not open to such a reproach.[12]

In addition, mental disease or defect has been deemed a condition in which a person is incapable of consent and a sexual act with such a female under such circumstances has been deemed rape. A man who, knowing of a woman's insanity, takes advantage of her helpless condition to gratify his own lustful desires is guilty of felonious rape though he uses no more force than that involved in the carnal act, and though the woman offers no resistance to the consummation of his purpose. The term "present physical or mental condition" (victim's) includes any insanity and other unsoundness

of mind, as well as intoxication or physical unconsciousness which so incapacitates a victim she is unable to consent or to refuse to consent to the act.

However, the mere fact that a woman is weak-minded does not prevent her from giving a valid consent to the act of sexual intercourse. A woman with a lesser degree of intelligence than is required to make a contract may consent to sexual intercourse so that the act is not the crime of rape.[13] The disability must be such that the woman is incapable of understanding the act, its motive, and the possible consequences.[14] The issue of consent surfaces in the statutory law to cover the various situations where social conscience dictates a consent cannot be given or where force is not necessary to the sexual act in order to commit a public offense:

A person who perpetrates an act of sexual intercourse with a female not his wife, against her will or without her consent; or,

1. When through idiocy, imbecility or any unsoundness of mind, either temporary or permanent, she is incapable of giving consent, or, by reason of mental or physical weakness, or immaturity, or any bodily ailment, she does not offer resistance; or,

2. When her resistance is forcibly overcome; or,

3. When her resistance is prevented by fear of immediate and great bodily harm, which she has reasonable cause to believe will be inflicted upon her; or,

4. When her resistance is prevented by stupor, or weakness of mind, produced by an intoxicating, or narcotic, or anaesthetic agent; or, when she is known by the defendant to be in such a state of stupor or weakness of mind from any cause; or,

5. When she is, at the time, unconscious of the nature of the act, and this is known to the defendant; or when she is in the custody of the law, or of any officer thereof, or in any place of lawful detention, temporary or permanent,

Is guilty of rape in the first degree and punishable by imprisonment for not more than twenty years or by imprisonment for an indeterminate term, the minimum of which shall be one day and the maximum of which shall be the duration of his natural life.[15]

The admissible evidence as to the issue of consent has also been the object of attack. This attack was spearheaded by women's groups across the nation and has culminated in legislative changes of the rules of evidence. The general law has long allowed the introduction of evidence about the reputation of the prosecutrix in a rape case, as well as evidence of specific incidents of sexual conduct, as evidence tending to show consent rather than resistance overcome by force. As of 1974, California has generally prohibited such evidence in its Evidence Code:

I.    (a) Notwithstanding any other provision of this Code to the contrary, and except as provided in this subdivision, in any prosecution under Section 261 (rape), or 264.1 of the Penal Code, or for assault with intent to commit, attempt to commit, or conspiracy to commit a crime defined in any such section, opinion evidence, reputation evidence, and evidence of specific instances of the complaining witness' sexual conduct, or any of such evidence, is not admissable by the defendant in order to prove consent by the complaining witness.

(b) Paragraph (a) of this subdivision shall not be applicable to evidence of the complaining witness' sexual conduct with the defendant.

(c) If the prosecutor introduces evidence, including testimony of a witness, or the complaining witness as a witness gives testimony and such evidence or testimony relates to the complaining witness' sexual conduct, the defendant may cross-examine the witness who gives such testimony and offer relevant evidence limited specifically to the rebuttal of such evidence introduced by the prosecutor or given by the complaining witness.

(d) Nothing in this subdivision shall be construed to make inadmissible any evidence offered to attack the credibility of the complaining witness as provided in Section 782.

(e) As used in this Section, "complaining witness" means the alleged victim of the crime charged, the prosecution of which is subject to this subdivision.[16]

II.    (a) In any prosecution under Section 261 (rape), or 264.1 of the Penal Code, or for assault with intent to commit, attempt to commit, or conspiracy to commit any crime defined in any such Section, if evidence of sexual conduct of the complaining witness is offered to attack the credibility of the complaining witness under Section 780, the following procedure shall be followed:

(1) A written motion shall be made by the defendant to the court and prosecutor stating that the defense has an offer of proof of the relevancy of evidence of the sexual conduct of the complaining witness proposed to be presented and its relevancy in attacking the credibility of the complaining witness.

(2) The written motion shall be accompanied by an affidavit in which the offer of proof shall be stated.

(3) If the court finds that the offer of proof is sufficient, the court shall order a hearing out of the presence of the jury, if any, and at such hearing allow the questioning of the complaining witness regarding the offer of proof made by the defendant.

(4) At the conclusion of the hearing, if the court finds that evidence proposed to be offered by the defendant regarding the sexual conduct of the complaining witness is relevant pursuant to Section 780, and is not inadmissible pursuant to Section 352

of this Code, the court may make an order stating what evidence may be introduced by the defendant, and the nature of the questions to be permitted. The defendant may then offer evidence pursuant to the order of the court.

(b) As used in this Section, "complaining witness" means the alleged victim of the crime charged, the prosecution of which is subject to this section.[17]

## STATUTORY RAPE:
## VICTIM BELOW AGE OF CONSENT

Children have long been specially protected in the codes and laws of the various states. The differences between statutes are basically differences in the age span to be protected.

Neither force nor violence is essential to the commission of the crime of rape upon a female under the statutory age of consent and it is immaterial that the act of sexual intercourse was with her full consent. Where the female is under the age of consent, it need not be alleged or proved that the intercourse was had forcibly or against her will.

There are other definitions of offenses which prohibit lesser or different sexual acts with a child of less than the stated statutory age. The feeling or touching of the sexual organs of the child by the adult or the prompted feeling or touching of the sexual organs of the adult by the child can be found prohibited in general child-molesting sections and may be punished as a felony or misdemeanor, or both, at the discretion of the court or jury.

The culpable mental state in rape is the intent to compel the victim to submit to the act of sexual intercourse whatever the means used (force, drugs, impersonation, etc.) to achieve the act of intercourse. However, the crime of rape is a general intent crime and does not require the allegation of a specific intent to commit a crime.[18] The law has inferred a criminal intent from the act itself.[19]

The safety in knowing the woman has consented is not available to the perpetrator of statutory rape: lack of knowledge of age, misrepresentation of age, lack of chastity, or even prostitution does not give the man a legal right to sexual intercourse with a child under the specified age.

The man is promiscuous at his peril to know the age or other disability to consent of the woman.[20] However, courts have taken a second look at the problem of knowledge and intent in the crime of rape, particularly in statutory rape.

In a California case, the defendant (Hernandez) engaged in a voluntary act of sexual intercourse with a girl who was seventeen years and nine months of age and not his wife. The California Penal

Code defined as rape sexual intercourse with a female under the age of eighteen years. Hernandez was convicted of statutory rape. On appeal, Hernandez argued that the trial judge refused him the opportunity to present evidence going to his good faith and reasonable belief that the girl was eighteen years of age or more. The appellate court *reversed* Hernandez's conviction, ruling such evidence might have negated the criminal intent necessary. Its opinion observed:

The issue raised by the rejected offer of proof in the instant case goes to the culpability of the young man who acts *without* knowledge that an essential factual element exists and has, on the other hand, a positive, reasonable belief that it does not exist.

Statutory rape has long furnished a fertile battleground upon which to argue that the lack of knowledgeable conduct is a proper defense. The law in this state now rests, as it did in 1896, with this court's decision in *People* v. *Ratz*, 115 Cal. 132 [46 P. 915]: "The claim here made is not a new one. It has frequently been pressed upon the attention of courts, but in no case, so far as our examination goes, has it met with favor. The object and purpose of the law are too plain to need comment, the crime too infamous to bear discussion. The protection of society, of the family, and of the infant, demand that one who has carnal intercourse under such circumstances shall do so in peril of the fact, and he will not be heard against the evidence to urge his belief that the victim of his outrage had passed the period which would make his act a crime." The age of consent at the time of the *Ratz* decision was 14 years, and it is noteworthy that the purpose of the rule, as there announced, was to afford protection to young females therein described as "infants."

The rationale of the *Ratz* decision, rather than purporting to eliminate intent as an element of the crime, holds that the wrongdoer must assume the risk; that, subjectively, when the act is committed, he consciously intends to proceed regardless of the age of the female and the consequences of his act, and that the circumstances involving the female, whether she be a day or a decade less than the statutory age, are irrelevant. There can be no dispute that a criminal intent exists when the perpetrator proceeds with utter disregard of, or in the lack of grounds for, a belief that the female has reached the age of consent. But if he participates in a mutual act of sexual intercourse, believing his partner to be beyond the age of consent, with reasonable grounds for such belief, where is his criminal intent? In such circumstances he has not consciously taken any risk. Instead he has subjectively eliminated the risk by satisfying himself on reasonable evidence that the crime cannot be committed. If it occurs that he has been misled, we cannot realistically conclude that for such reason

alone the intent with which he undertook the act suddenly becomes more heinous.

While the specific contentions herein made have been dealt with and rejected both within and without this state, the courts have uniformly failed to satisfactorily explain the nature of the criminal intent present in the mind of one who in good faith believes he has obtained a lawful consent before engaging in the prohibited act. As in the *Ratz* case the courts often justify convictions on policy reasons which, in effect, eliminate the element of intent. The Legislature, of course, by making intent an element of the crime, has established the prevailing policy from which it alone can properly advise us to depart.

We are persuaded that the reluctance to accord to a charge of statutory rape the defense of a lack of criminal intent has no greater justification than in the case of other statutory crimes, where the Legislature has made identical provision with respect to intent.

Our departure from the views expressed in *Ratz* is in no manner indicative of a withdrawal from the sound policy that it is in the public interest to protect the sexually naive female from exploitation. No responsible person would hesitate to condemn as untenable a claimed good faith belief in the age of consent of an "infant" female whose obviously tender years preclude the existence of reasonable grounds for that belief. However, the prosecutrix in the instant case was but three months short of 18 years of age and there is nothing in the record to indicate that the purposes of the law as stated in *Ratz* can be better served by foreclosing the defense of a lack of intent. This is not to say that the granting of consent by even a sexually sophisticated girl known to be less than the statutory age is a defense. *We hold only that, in the absence of a legislative direction otherwise, a charge of statutory rape is defensible wherein a criminal intent is lacking.* [Emphasis added.][21]

# PROSECUTION PROBLEMS AND COMMON DEFENSES

Since rape is a seldom-witnessed crime, the major problem of prosecuting rapists is to secure the supporting evidence necessary to depict the victim as a truthful witness to the circumstances of the act of rape.

Collaterally, the prosecution must affirmatively overcome any defense showing of consent by the victim. Evidence of the victim's resistance and attempts at flight, unless faced by an overwhelming amount of force or its immediate threat, are helpful to the prosecution; evidence that the victim had been drinking or partying with the rapist prior to the rape are not helpful.

In statutory rape cases, a problem may develop in proving the age of a girl victim. The law may allow jurors in statutory rape cases to scan the *apparent* age of the girl victim and the reasonable belief of the defendant.

The most common defense against an accusation of rape is that the victim consented to the sexual intercourse. It can be a devastating defense despite a good prosecution case if there is an inexplicable lack of resistance or attempt to escape, a failure to promptly report the attack, or friendly interactions with the accused rapist prior to the attack.

When involvement is denied, the common defense is mistaken identity, sometimes accompanied by an alibi defense. The claim of being elsewhere at the time of the rape supports the defense of mistaken identification.

A claim of impotency is not uncommon, particularly when older men are accused of rape, but unless the defense can develop effective medical testimony in support of this claim, it is difficult to prove impotency of a nature barring the penetration necessary to the sexual intercourse element of rape. Allied to impotency is the claim of no penetration which may gain credence by a lack of medical evidence of sexual penetration.

# NOTES

1. *Askew* v. *State*, 118 So. 2d 219 (1960, Fla.).
2. New York Penal Code, Section 2010.
3. California Penal Code, Section 263.
4. *State* v. *Flaherty*, 146 A. 7 (1929, Maine).
5. *Myers* v. *State*, 197 P. 884 (1921, Okla.).
6. California Penal Code, Section 266 (a), (f), and (g).
7. *State* v. *Raymond*, 124 P. 495 (1912, Wash.).
8. *Commonwealth* v. *Goldenberg*, 155 N.E. 2d 187 (1959, Mass.).
9. California Penal Code, Sections 268–269.
10. California Penal Code, Sections 286, 286.5, 288(a).
11. *People* v. *Burnette*, 102 P. 2d 799 (1940, Calif.).
12. *Commonwealth* v. *Burke*, 105 Mass. 376 (1870).
13. *McQuirk* v. *State*, 4 So. 775 (1925, Ala.).
14. *State* v. *Jewett*, 192 A. 7 (1937, Vt.).
15. New York Penal Code, Section 2010.
16. California Evidence Code, Section 1103.
17. California Evidence Code, Section 782.
18. *People* v. *Gold*, 232 N.E. 2d 702 (1967, Ill.).
19. *Askew* v. *State*, 118 So. 2d 219 (1960, Fla.).
20. *State* v. *Duncan*, 266 P. 400 (1928, Mont.).
21. *People* v. *Hernandez*, 393 P. 2d 673 (1964, Calif.).

# 20

# ATTEMPT TO COMMIT CRIME AND SOLICITATION

## OBJECTIVES

The objectives of the concluding chapter of this text are to reveal as a crime in all its details the attempt to commit any of the crimes detailed in prior chapters; to develop the "substantial step" doctrine in attempts to commit crime; and to discuss voluntary abandonment as a defense in attempt cases. In addition, a lesser objective is to reveal solicitation as a crime aligned with but different from an attempt to commit a crime and to show the "once removed" factor in solicitation.

## LEGAL TERM

Battery. *Unlawful beating; physical violence.*

## QUESTIONS FOR STUDY

1. *What are the similarities and differences between the crime of attempt and the crime of solicitation?*

2. *What is the "substantial step" doctrine in attempts?*

3. *Develop the theme, pro or con, that there can be no such crime as attempted assault.*

4. *What circumstances justify a defense of abandonment in attempt cases?*

5. *What is the "once removed" factor in solicitation cases?*

6. *How is the* corpus delicti *developed to sustain an accusation of an attempt to commit a crime? An accusation of solicitation to commit a crime?*

**A**n attempt to commit a crime consists of two basic elements: (1) intent to commit a crime, and (2) performance of some act toward the commission of that crime. Inherently, in any attempt, there is a failure to consummate the crime involved. The crime of solicitation is unaccompanied by an act moving directly toward the commission of a crime. Solicitation may be limited by statute to particular crimes,[1] or may be applicable to any *malum in se* or infamous offense.

## ATTEMPT TO COMMIT CRIME

It is the well-settled rule that there cannot be a conviction for an attempt to commit a crime unless the attempt, if completed, would have constituted a crime.[2]

In a New Jersey case a public prosecutor (Weleck) was accused of attempted extortion. It was alleged that under color of his office he demanded money that was not allowed him by law. Weleck was *convicted*. On appeal he argued that the facts did not spell out a crime and that the indictment was defective. The appellate court *affirmed* Weleck's conviction of attempted extortion, rejecting his dual argument in these words:

> The defendant attacks the indictment on the grounds that a mere solicitation or demand is not an attempt and that there is no allegation of any overt acts constituting an attempt. The attack is without merit. The overt acts necessary to constitute an attempt must be viewed in the light of the intended crime. As previously indicated, if the defendant had actually taken money under the circumstances alleged he would have committed extortion. The next step short of actually taking money is to demand it. The demand is the overt act constituting the attempt. If a demand were not here sufficient, then it would be impossible to allege and prove the crime of attempted extortion for we can imagine no other act which would suffice.
>
> The defendant's final contention is that the indictment fails to allege an intent to commit the crime of extortion. We recognize that to be guilty of an attempt to commit a crime a defendant must have intended to commit the crime itself. The only question here is whether the indictment sufficiently alleges the requisite intent. While the word "intent" does not appear in the indictment, it is alleged that the defendant did "attempt to extort." These words we believe are equivalent to an allegation that the defendant acted "with intent to extort."[3]

Intent alone, not coupled with some overt act toward putting the intent into effect, is not a crime. In determining what constitutes an overt act toward accomplishment of a crime each case depends largely on its own particular facts and the inferences that

might reasonably be drawn from them. It is sufficient that the act go far enough toward accomplishment of the crime to amount to the *commencement of its consummation*. While the efficiency of a particular act depends on the facts of the particular case, the act must always amount to more than mere preparation, and move directly toward the commission of the crime. In any event, the act need not be the last proximate step leading to the consummation of the offense. While the term *overt act* should be given a liberal construction, there is a wide difference between the preparation for the commission of an offense and the commission of the offense itself, or even the attempt to commit it. The preparation consists in devising, arranging, or accumulating the means or measures necessary for the commission of the crime; the attempt or overt act is the direct movement toward the commission after the preparations are made.[4]

An overt act may not only show intent, but may also consummate the attempt to commit a crime if the act is apparently done to produce the result intended. In a Virginia case, D.E. Preddy, a sixty-seven-year-old grandfather, was convicted of the attempted rape of a ten-year-old girl. At Preddy's trial, the following testimony* was developed:

## 1. Victim's Mother:

Zelda Dean testified that she was the mother of Joyce Jackson [the child victim], and that on the 22nd day of July she was cleaning her room and found, secreted behind a mirror on the dresser, a pair of silk pants belonging to Joyce which had some blood upon them; that she questioned Joyce who then told her "about it."

## 2. Arresting Officer:

J.H. Freed, the town sergeant of Gordonsville, testified as follows:

Q. Mr. Freed, Mr. Preddy here is charged with attempted rape on Joyce Jackson. Did you investigate the case, Mr. Freed?
A. I did.
Q. What facts did you find in your investigation?
A. The girl's mother came to me on Saturday afternoon, July 22nd, and told me that she was afraid something had happened to her daughter but she wouldn't tell her anything, and asked me what I thought she had better do. I told her the main thing was to try to find out from the child if anything really had happened. She went back and talked to her and came to me again and told me the girl had told her something and she wanted me to come up there. She said the girl would tell me what had happened, so I went up there and she told me what had taken place and I told

*Selected extracts only.

the girl's mother I thought she should take her to the doctor and have her examined. I took her to the doctor and had her examined and brought her back home and told her mother what the doctor had told me and . . . got the warrant and I arrested Mr. Preddy that afternoon.

Q. Did you have any conversation with Mr. Preddy in reference to the case?

A. He didn't express himself in any shape or form.

Q. Did you ask him if he did what he is charged with?

A. No, I did not.

Q. Did you ask him anything?

A. I just read the warrant to him and he was shaving at the time and he asked me if he could finish shaving and I told him he could. After he finished shaving I brought him in.

Q. When you read the warrant to him did he deny the charge in the warrant?

A. He did not deny it.

Q. That was on July 22nd she was taken to the doctor?

A. Yes, sir.

## 3. Examining Physician:

Dr. W.C. Mason testified as follows:

The patient was brought to me by the town sergeant around 2:30 in the afternoon, the 22nd day of July, for examination, and told me her mother thought she had been raped—gave a history of bleeding at the vagina for several days—said this happened around ten days ago, the rape. On examination I found the *labia majora* and *labia minora* swollen and slightly bluish. On separating the *labia majora* I found the hymen to be torn, and the edges of the torn hymen to be red, not as yet healed. The mucous membrane of the hymen was red. There was no bleeding from the vagina at this time although there was a slight whitish discharge. Diagnosis: bruised condition of the vagina; lower part of the *labia majora* and *labia minora* bruised, and a torn hymen, from some cause external to the body.

## 4. The Victim:

Joyce Jackson testified that at the time of the trial she was eleven years of age; that she was a fifth-grade pupil in the public school of Gordonsville, Virginia, her home town; that on the day of the alleged crime she met the accused, with whom she was acquainted, on the street; that he engaged her in conversation and told her he had some candy for [her]; that after this conversation she went to her home and finding her mother was out working, asked of her grandmother permission to go to the home of the accused; that when she arrived at the home she found the accused there; that he met [her] in the hall and they went into a room

and sat down; that he told her he had some comic books in the back room for her; that when [she] arrived in the back room accused threw her on a bed; that she tried to "holler" but on account of the dust which smothered her, she was unable to do so; that he pulled down her bloomers; that he kneeled on one of her arms and began to "bother her" with his hands; that she could not "holler" on account of the dust; that she could not tell if he put his hand "inside her," but that he hurt her when he "bothered" her; that her "panties" had something on them; that while she was on the bed and he was "bothering" her, her grandmother came to the back porch and accused got up, opened the door, and went to where her grandmother was on the back porch; that during the time he was "bothering" her he did not expose any part of his person; that she was scared and did not tell her grandmother what had happened; but that she told her mother sometime afterwards of her experience.[5]

On review of the *Preddy* case, the appellate court *affirmed* Preddy's conviction. Its opinion noted:

[I]ntent is the crucial question in cases of attempt to rape. But when it is shown by the evidence that the accused did any overt act showing intent, then the crime is consummated. This has been the rule of law in this Commonwealth since our decision in *Lufty* v. *Commonwealth*, 126 Va. 707, 713, 100 S.E. 829, 831. Over the objection of the accused, in that case, the trial court gave the following instruction: "The court instructs the jury that if you believe from the evidence beyond a reasonable doubt that Ethel Garrison is under 15 years of age, and if you further believe from the evidence beyond reasonable doubt that the accused, Moses Lufty, attempted by force to have intercourse with her, and that he did any overt act toward carrying out that purpose, such as taking hold of her, or throwing her down, then he would be guilty of attempted rape as charged in the indictment in this case."

In approving the instruction, Kelly, J., said: "It is claimed that this instruction ignored the defendant's view of the case. His view simply was that he was not guilty, and the instruction expressly recognized that view by imposing upon the commonwealth the burden of proving beyond a reasonable doubt that he did the things which were recited in the instruction, and the doing of which plainly rendered him guilty of attempted rape."[6]

## THE "SUBSTANTIAL-STEP" DOCTRINE IN ATTEMPTS

Case law has created a "substantial-step" doctrine in evaluating the behavior associated with attempts to commit a crime. Briefly, a per-

son is guilty of an attempt to commit a crime when, with intent to commit the crime, he or she engages in conduct which constitutes a substantial step toward the commission of the crime. When a substantial step is taken toward the commission of a crime, it is no defense to the charge of attempt to claim it was impossible to commit the crime.

A *substantial step* may be defined as conduct beyond that which occurs during the planning period, but not necessarily behavior amounting to the commencement of the consummation of the crime. For instance, using this doctrine, a criminal abortionist's liability for attempted criminal abortion does not begin with travel arrangements or when the abortionist furnishes an office for such purpose, but it does begin when he receives a pregnant woman in that office and directs her to undress and lie on the operating table.

The issue of whether the act done was a substantial step, as well as the issue of factual impossibility, was reviewed in *Gargan v. State*.* The defendant, Gargan, was charged with attempting to steal U.S. coins from a coin-operated washing machine owned by Imperial Vending Company, Inc., and located in the laundry room of the Hollywood Vista Apartments in Anchorage. (There was one other washing machine and two dryers in this room; all four units could be activated by the insertion of quarters.)

For several months prior to February 17, 1966, the corporation (which had coin-operated machines placed at numerous locations throughout the Anchorage area) had experienced pilferage of the contents of its washing machines' coin boxes. Early in the evening of February 17, John Ball, a major stockholder in Imperial Vending Company, secreted himself in a closet directly across the hall from the laundry room door of the Hollywood Vista Apartments. He stationed himself on a four-foot stepladder which enabled him to gain an unobstructed view of the laundry room from over the top of the closet's eight-foot wall. According to Ball, for the first few hours of his watch, the laundry room was occupied by families washing and drying clothes. Business then subsided until just before 10:00 P.M., when the witness observed Gargan going into the laundry room.

As part of the state's case at trial, Ball testified that appellant Gargan knelt on one knee, placed the key in the lock, and started turning it counterclockwise. As he was unscrewing the lock, he kept glancing back over his right shoulder looking at the door. On cross-examination Ball admitted that he did not see a key or an instrument in appellant's hand. He testified that he assumed it was a key that appellant had in his hand at the time in question.

Gargan was *convicted* of attempted theft. On appeal, Gargan claimed error because the prosecution failed to prove at trial that any coins were contained in the machine which appellant allegedly

*436 P. 2d 968 (1968, Alaska).

attempted to open (factual impossibility to commit the crime). The appellate court *affirmed* Gargan's conviction. Its opinion* noted:

We are of the opinion the portions of John Ball's testimony furnish a sufficient evidentiary basis for the jury's drawing the reasonable inference and conclusion that there was money in the coin box of the washing machine at the time in question. Alternatively, we are of the view that the lower court's ruling can be sustained even though the machine's coin box was in fact empty. In short, we adopt the "empty pocket doctrine." In *People* v. *Rollino*, 233 N.Y.S. 2d 580 (1962), 583, the court stated in part: "Examples of cases in which *attempt* convictions have been sustained on the theory that all that prevented the consummation of the completed crime was a 'factual impossibility' (as distinguished from a 'legal impossibility') are: (1) an attempt to steal from an empty receptacle or (2) an empty house."

*We are of the opinion that a factual impossibility which was not apparent to the actor at the time should not, as a matter of policy, insulate him from conviction for attempting the commission of the offense.* [Emphasis added.][7]

In some cases the substantial step is clear, but the link-up with a legal impossibility may threaten a successful prosecution. However, in *Faustina* v. *Superior Court*,[8] the reviewing court held that a receiver of stolen property could be convicted of attempted receiving despite the fact police had "recovered" the stolen goods from the thief and thus the goods were no longer stolen property, and that the criminality of an attempt was not destroyed by the impossibility caused by the fact that the police had recovered the goods and taken them from the place where the would-be receiver went to get them.

## ABANDONMENT OF ATTEMPT

Abandonment is a defense if the attempt to commit a crime is freely and voluntarily abandoned, and no outside cause prompted such abandonment.

If a design to commit a crime is followed by a direct movement toward the commission of a crime, manifested by acts which would end in the commission of the particular offense, abandonment because of the appearance of police does not constitute a free and voluntary abandonment.

John C. Von Hecht was convicted of the attempted grand theft of certain property of Firestone Stores. Von Hecht claimed abandonment. The defendant drove to a Firestone store (auto service center) and ordered a set of wire wheels for his car, presenting a credit

*Extracts only; footnotes and citations are deleted.

card in the name of one J. Ronan. Firestone personnel used the card to stamp an order form and promised the wheels would be installed by five o'clock. The defendant left the Firestone store. He was arrested upon his return as the credit card had been reported stolen. On appeal, Hecht argued his defense of abandonment. The appellate court *affirmed* his conviction. The court's opinion* stated:

We are satisfied that the testimony presented to the trial court a factual question as to whether appellant's failure to complete a crime was such a free and voluntary act constituting abandonment or whether his conduct was because of fear of discovery of his unlawful acts or the appearance of the police at the service station. If the latter was true then there was no abandonment, as that term is known to the law.

Appellant insists that the evidence is insufficient to establish an attempt to commit the crime charged; that it shows no more than preparation to do so, and an abandonment of the project before any appreciable fragment of the crime had been accomplished. In support of his claim, appellant asserts that "the undisputed fact is that before appellant came back to the Firestone store he consciously and intentionally placed out of his reach the one indispensable instrument essential to commencement of the consummation."

While it is true that appellant left in a telephone book [in a nearby cocktail lounge] the credit card which he had originally presented to the service station manager, it cannot be said to be "indisputable" that he did so to deprive himself of the opportunity to consummate his previously initiated plan. It could, in view of the facts and circumstances shown in this case, be reasonably inferred that appellant placed the card in the telephone book close by the store so that if, when he returned to the store he was apprehended by the police, he would be free of the incriminatory card which would have furnished evidence of his criminal activities; and that if, when he returned to the store, he needed the card to secure delivery of the wheels, he could excuse himself to go and get it, and then present it to get the delivery. Thus, it appears that the act of the appellant in putting the card in the telephone book did not necessarily indicate that he had abandoned his plan to secure the wheels, as it could reasonably be inferred that his act was done to get the evidence of his criminal activity out of his possession until such time as it might be needed for the consummation of the crime. Further, there is no showing that the appellant would have had to present the credit card in order to get delivery of the wheels after his return to the store. As he had already presented the card and the name and

*Extracts only; footnotes and citations are deleted.

number had been taken from it, it appears reasonable to infer that he would not have had to present it again, as the store had the pertinent information contained on it, and that he would have had only to sign for the receipt of the merchandise in order to get delivery.

It is true, as appellant insists, that preparation alone is not sufficient. The act must reach far enough towards the accomplishment of the desired result to amount to the commencement of the consummation of the particular offense unless frustrated by extraneous circumstances. And, once the design of a person to commit crime is clearly shown, slight acts in furtherance of the design will constitute an attempt.

In the instant case it could reasonably be inferred that when the appellant approached the store, perhaps because he saw the officers at the store and his car without the new wheels, he became apprehensive that his criminal act had been discovered and in an effort to rid himself of the evidence thereof, he went into the cocktail lounge and hid the card, and then returned to the station with the explanation that he intended to pay cash for the wheels. *This would not be a voluntary abandonment, but rather an abandonment because of the appearance of the police, which would not constitute a termination of the criminal act sufficient to save the appellant from criminal liability for his attempt.* [Emphasis added.][9]

## SOLICITATION TO COMMIT CRIME

A person is guilty of solicitation to commit a crime when, with intent that a crime be committed, he commands or requests another person to commit that crime. Solicitation relates only to cases in which a crime is planned and projected but never completed. The *corpus delicti* of this crime is the criminal intent of the solicitor and the act of solicitation.

While statutory law provisions as to solicitation vary with the jurisdiction, a considerable number of cases from an array of states indicate it is a crime (felony or misdemeanor) to solicit the commission of a crime.

In the crime of solicitation there is not that dangerous proximity to success common in attempts to commit a crime, and there is the "once-removed" factor: the solicitor is the person who tries to get *another person* to commit the crime.

One soliciting another person to commit a crime such as robbery or murder, which is actually committed, is punishable as a principal in such crime. In *People* v. *Harper,* the act of soliciting by one or the other of the defendants in this case and its merger with the crime itself upon its commission is described in a concurring opinion (Justice Carter):

The two defendants (Harper and Bolden) undoubtedly entered into an agreement to "roll" Bennett (the crime's victim) and rob him of his money. Harper says the plan to "roll" someone and get "a piece of money" was first suggested by Bolden. On the other hand, Bolden testified that he knew nothing about any plan to rob anyone until the morning of the crime, and that he was then told by Harper that he (Harper) had their victim ready and asked Bolden to go along; that the latter would have nothing to do and that there would be no "kick." Whether Harper or Bolden was the originator of the plan, it is evident from the admitted facts in this case that Harper, unknown to Bolden, made all arrangements for the robbery and had the victim ready for the fatal trip before he informed Bolden of his plan.

Whether Bolden seduced the ex-convict Harper into the commission of the crime with which they are charged, or whether Bolden was beguiled by Harper, an older man and hardened criminal, to go along, Bolden did become a party to the plan to rob and murder Bennett and he is responsible for every act that was committed by either of them in furtherance of that plan.[10]

## NOTES

1. California Penal Code, Section 653 f.
2. *State* v. *Weleck*, 91 A. 2d 751 (1952, N.J.).
3. *State* v. *Weleck*, 91 A. 2d 751 (1952, N.J.).
4. *State* v. *Quick*, 19 S.E. 101 (1942, S.C.).
5. *Preddy* v. *Commonwealth*, 36 S.E. 2d 549 (1946, Va.).
6. *Preddy* v. *Commonwealth*, 36 S.E. 2d 549 (1946, Va.).
7. *Gargan* v. *State*, 436 P. 2d 968 (1968, Alaska).
8. *Faustina* v. *Superior Court* In and For Los Angeles County, 345 P. 2d 543 (1959, Calif.). *See* contra *People* v. *Jaffe*, 78 N.E. 169 (1906, N.Y.), no *attempt* if the completed act would not be a crime (receiving stolen property case).
9. *People* v. *Von Hecht*, 283 P. 2d 764 (1955, Calif.).
10. *People* v. *Harper*, 156 P. 2d 249 (1946, Calif.).

# CASE INDEX

# INDEX

use of force or fear in, 210
*See also* Burglary; Larceny; Theft crimes
Roman law, 5–7, 42, 47
Roosevelt, Franklin D., 41


Sanction law, 14, 108
*Scienter,* 107
Self-defense. *See* Criminal responsibility, and self-defense
*Senchus Mor,* 7
Separation of powers, 40–41
Sex offenses, 170–171
*See also* Rape
*Shepard's Acts and Cases by Popular Names,* 28
*Shepard's Citations,* 31
sample page from, 32
Shepardize, 31
*Sine qua non,* 107, 121
Smith Act, 50
Sodomy, 53, 57–58, 170–171
Solicitation, 274
*Stare decisis,* 3, 10
Status crimes, 57, 59, 119
Statute law, 22–23
Statute of limitations, 154
*Supra,* 107
*Supreme Court Reporter,* 25, 28
*Syllabus,* 199, 207

*Tenement,* 199, 206
Theft, and theft crimes, 169, 239–251
*See also* Burglary; Larceny; Robbery
*Things in action,* 199
Thomistic theory of law, 16
*Tort,* 53–54, 128
*Tort-feasor,* 127, 134
*Treatise on the Laws and Customs of England* (de Glanville), 10


*Ubi supra,* 229–230
*Uniform Crime Reports,* 136
Uniform Vehicle Code, 194
United States Code, 22–23, 108
*United States Reports,* 23, 28, 31
sample page from, 26
*Utter,* 127, 129–130, 169


*Venue,* 139, 141–143
*Vicinage,* 139, 142
Victimless crimes, 54, 57
*Voir dire,* 139, 143


*West's Annotated California Codes,* 23
sample page from, 24
Writs, English system of, 10–11


*Year-Books,* 11